AF441696

The CRM handbook

- from group to multi-individual

The CRM handbook
- from group to multi-individual

PricewaterhouseCoopers
Tuborg Boulevard 1
DK-2900 Hellerup
Denmark
Telephone +45 3945 3945
Facsimile +45 3945 9987

If you need further information, please contact Per Østergaard Jacobsen

Layout: falcon - grafisk design
Print: Nørhaven A/S

ISBN: 87-987455-4-9

The CRM handbook

- from group to multi-individual

"It is not bad quality, when you
only understand half of the story"

Karen Blixen

PricewaterhouseCoopers

PricewaterhouseCoopers is the world's leading accounting and consulting firm. The company employs approximately 150,000 people in some 152 countries world-wide. Our Management Consulting practices comprise a full global-service with approximately 45,000 employees, focusing on holistic solutions from strategy to implementation. PricewaterhouseCoopers offers consulting services in three main areas:

- Strategic change management
- Process improvement
- Technological solutions

In addition, we have special focus on areas such as e-business, knowledge management and data warehousing.

In Scandinavia, PricewaterhouseCoopers has more than 1,000 management consultants - of these, some 80 work with CRM-related assignments. By working with CRM projects - both globally and regionally - we have acquired wide experience and extensive expertise, plus a good knowledge of many CRM systems.

PricewaterhouseCoopers carries out analyses of various CRM systems on an ongoing basis, participates in conferences, and writes articles and books on the subject.

For more information, see: *www.pwcglobal.com*

Foreword

This Customer Relationship Management (CRM) handbook - from group to multi-individual - is a PricewaterhouseCoopers contribution to making the implementation of a CRM strategy an enterprise success. Our experience demonstrates that many enterprises now realise the importance of Customer Relationship Management, yet still fail to implement CRM properly.

We see many enterprises invest a great deal of time and resources to find the right system. In fact, it is relatively easy to find the right system when you know where you are going. But to know where you want to go, it is important to know where you are at the moment. CRM is a strategy that focuses on creating relationships between the customer and the enterprise. By means of these relationships, value is created for both the customer and the enterprise.

It is our hope that this book will give enterprise decision-makers and project managers a useful tool for the implementation of CRM. We offer an overview of the CRM concept and an analysis of a number of leading system suppliers. In addition, we offer a method which the enterprise can use to evaluate these systems. Our method which examines the main functionalities which need to be considered in order to select those systems which appear most relevant for the enterprise.

PricewaterhouseCoopers met with all the suppliers presented in this book and each supplier's system was demonstrated. In addition, PricewaterhouseCoopers developed a customised questionnaire which all the suppliers answered. Thereafter, at least two consultants analysed the replies and evaluated them in relation to the agreed criteria. Finally, a system was prepared which is described in Chapter 8.

We would like to share the experience and knowledge we have gained in this area with other enterprises to facilitate successful, effective and profitable investments. Therefore, it is our sincere hope that this handbook will stimulate enterprise activities and be a source of inspiration in the complex process of implementing a CRM strategy.

Acknowledgements

Professional content:
Allan Kiby
Michael Rangstrup
Mike D. Andreasen
Tomas Rotovnik
Henrik Andersen

Supplier analyses:
Michael Rangstrup (Editor)
Allan Kiby
Mike D. Andreasen
Tomas Rotovnik
Peter Ulka
Nina B. Pedersen
Thomas Rasmussen
Thomas Hvalsø Hansen

Proofreading, design, layout, English adaptation, etc.:
Lise Bencke
Louise Krarup
Malene Hasløv
Tina Rossbach Kofod
Kitti Christiansen
Anna Falcon Møller
Barbara Berger
Jens Guttormsen
Peter Ernstved Rasmussen
Mark Rudings
Wassim Kawash
Karen Sigsgaard
Gitte Jørgensen

For inspiration & ideas, I would like to thank:
Professor Adrian Payne, Cranfield University, School of Management
Lecturer Moira Clark, Cranfield University, School of Management
Denis Collart, PricewaterhouseCoopers
Gavin Potter, PricewaterhouseCoopers
Jon O'Donnel, PricewaterhouseCoopers
Robert Notebom, PricewaterhouseCoopers
Henrik Andersen, PricewaterhouseCoopers
Stanley A. Brown, PricewaterhouseCoopers

A special thanks to:
- Lena, my wonderful wife, for her patience and support
- Henrik Andersen, who made it all possible
- Mike D. Andreasen, for such good teamwork
- Michael Rangstrup, for doing such a good job

Editor
Per Østergaard Jacobsen
July 1999

Contents

Executive Summary

Everyone is talking and reading about CRM. But talk alone is not enough! Inspiration and thoughts must be turned into action. This book provides a "tool-box" for getting started with CRM.

CRM can be compared to a journey. In *Chapter 1, Introduction to CRM*, we begin this exciting and challenging journey by defining the CRM concept. We look at the introduction of a CRM strategy, which is a prerequisite to initiating comprehensive changes in enterprise processes, systems, organisation, corporate culture and the competencies of the enterprise's employees. We also look at the ways in which the above mentioned are interconnected. And last, but not least, we consider general trends and developments in this fast-growing area.

In *Chapter 2, The CRM Strategy*, customer loyalty and customer value are discussed. We show how dialogue replaces traditional segmentation on the CRM journey as the enterprise approaches the final goal of Strategic Customer Relationship Management. We also examine ways to increase customer value via cross- and up-selling and the active use of segment-oriented campaigns.

In *Chapter 3, What drives Investments in CRM Software?*, the reasons why enterprises decide to acquire CRM systems are explored. We consider the scarcity of customers and the need for targeted, relevant communication to break through the "noise" barrier. In addition, knowledge-sharing across customers is discussed because it is a vital element in every CRM strategy - and a decisive factor behind the acquisition of a CRM system.

In *Chapter 4, The Challenges of Introducing CRM*, we consider how deeply CRM influences enterprise operations. We take a close look at the interaction between the CRM strategy and the enterprise's internal processes. Finally we discuss change management, which is required to make the enterprise customer-oriented.

When implementing CRM, there are many pitfalls. In *Chapter 5, The Practical Implementation of CRM*, we share our experience in this area. Why do things sometimes go wrong? Why are so many companies unable to achieve the performance breakthrough that matches their investments in technology?

In *Chapter 6, Beginning the CRM Journey,* we examine how to prepare properly for the journey so the experience will be positive. Many initiatives are off to a poor start because the initiators have not sold the idea to the enterprise. CRM is a strategic decision that management must champion - and it requires the support of the whole enterprise.

The market for CRM software is experiencing explosive growth. That is why in *Chapter 7, Guidelines for Choosing a Supplier,* we offer our guidelines for the selection process and examine areas which are important to focus on.

We also examine the relationship between supplier and user-enterprise. It is important to ensure that supplier and users agree on the key criteria for a CRM system.

In Chapter 8, Supplier Analysis, we examine the market for IT-based, integrated marketing, sales and service systems known as CRM systems. Our supplier analysis includes both global market leaders and the most important suppliers in the Nordic markets. The analysis presents the most important differences in the selected systems and classifies the systems' functionalities in relation to company-specific requirements.

Chapter 1

Introduction to CRM

"We all live under
the same sky - But we don't have
the same horizon"

Konrad Adenauer

One concept – many names

The discussion continues - and more and more words are added. The Danish language, for example, is experiencing a veritable explosion of foreign words which are fast becoming incorporated in our everyday language. Customer Relationship Management, or CRM, is one of them. In recent years, much has been said and written about CRM: This concept is thus known under many names. Concepts such as "holistic", the customer in the centre, one-to-one, dialogue marketing, and many more are used freely. But CRM is not just Customer Relationship Marketing. "The One to One Fieldbook" by Don Peppers and Martha Rogers, for example, is a book about marketing and probably one of the most widely read in the field, but the book you're sitting with in your hands right now goes further. For us, CRM is not just about marketing, it's about the whole enterprise and its vision. That is why our concept is called *Customer Relationship Management or CRM.*

CRM is about strategy and communication - and about integrating processes, systems, organisations, people and cultures. All around the world, countless discussions and conferences are being held on the subject - and the abbreviation CRM keeps on popping up, again and again. Thus there can be no doubt: CRM has come to stay. But at PricewaterhouseCoopers, we don't intend to just let it remain idle talk. We also want to help. That is why we have designed this book like a toolbox that contains the tools that are needed to create value.

For that is what it is all about. Creating value - for both the enterprise and the customer. The goal is to establish long-term relationships between the customer and the enterprise. CRM helps to create these relationships and to maintain them. In this way, values are optimised for both the enterprise and the customer. A definition of CRM could be as follows:

CRM is a business strategy - an attitude to employees and customers - that is supported by certain processes and systems. The goal is to build long-term relationships by understanding individual needs and preferences - and in this way add value to the enterprise and the customer.

The implementation of a CRM strategy therefore presupposes comprehensive changes in the enterprise's processes, systems, organisation as well as in the enterprise's corporate culture and in the competencies of its employees.

CRM replaces the grocer concept

CRM is about maximising the lifetime value of the customer - to gain the maximum future stream on the profit side, thus making CRM a central element in the creation of *Shareholder Value (I)*. In reality, however, CRM is a further development of the old grocery store concept. In a corner grocery store, the grocer gave his customers targeted and individual treatment. From behind his counter, the grocer could maintain an overview of the grocery store. By means of ledgers and memory, his wife managed his knowledge base so that both Jane and Peter received optimal service. In this way, the grocer created value for them both, and via their loyal behaviour, they were valuable to the grocer. But that is as far as the analogy goes.

The marketplace in the year 2000 is vaster and more complex, and both *the business-to-business (II)* and *business-to-consumer (III) markets* are often characterised by being global. And because of the size and complexity of these markets, today's marketplace requires a wide range of business processes and IT tools if a variety of cost efficient relationships are to be created.

When we look at today's CRM Grocer, s/he can offer the customer two things: An efficient store with low prices and individual customer service, the result being an increase in value for both the customer and the store.

In principle it is of less importance if we say *business-to-business market* or *business-to-consumer market*. When a CRM strategy is 100% implemented, the individual will be in focus in both cases. The requirements, however, to enterprise hardware and software will vary greatly depending on the size of the market. The same holds true for the number of customers, the amount of customer information, and the availability of this information in the enterprise.

CRM is a journey in time

The implementation of a CRM strategy is a long and demanding journey towards the goal where the enterprise and customer achieve the same value.

The goal is to enable the enterprise to capture the maximum lifetime value of the customer relationship. This is achieved through building individual customer relationships, which ensures satisfaction and loyalty to the enterprise.

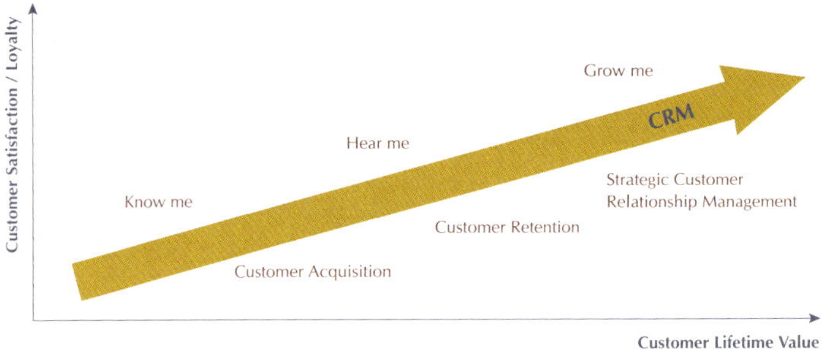

Fig. 1.1: The journey towards CRM

The CRM journey proceeds through several characteristic phases or stages as
described below:

A: Know me: *Focusing on the customer as an account*
At the beginning of the journey, the main question is to understand who the
customer is. A computer distributor, for example, who has selected
PricewaterhouseCoopers as a potential customer because of the CRM strategy,
will begin by trying to get an idea of where in the world PricewaterhouseCoopers
offices are located. At the same time, they will consider the business opportunities
their enterprise can expect from PricewaterhouseCoopers. In other words, there is
a clear focus on *Accounts and Leads (IV)*.

Volume and pricing agreements typically characterise and regulate the relationship between supplier and customer at this stage. When the supplier has
sufficient knowledge of PricewaterhouseCoopers and other high-priority customers, they will begin to increase volume through cross- and up-selling. These
sales will be based on knowledge about the individual customer being shared
and extended across the enterprise.

B: Hear me: *Focusing on retention (V)*
The first midway stop or station occurs when the enterprise realises that just
knowing PricewaterhouseCoopers and the other companies as accounts is not
sufficient. In order to keep PricewaterhouseCoopers, for example, as a customer, the supplier must create value, and that will require the supplier to have
an in-depth knowledge of the individual contact, buyer and decision-maker at
PricewaterhouseCoopers.

The enterprise must listen to PricewaterhouseCoopers in order to understand
how the enterprise functions. It must understand the conditions that influence
the individual decision-maker and PricewaterhouseCoopers's business as a

whole - as well as those conditions that are decisive for the individual and the success of the enterprise.

Contacts and activities are now in focus. The computer supplier will, by means of their knowledge of the individual customer organisation, be able to tailor activities towards the specific buyer and decision-maker at the customer enterprise. Customer satisfaction is achieved in this way and loyalty to the supplier increases. At the same time, the computer enterprise maximises the value of prioritised customers.

As this knowledge is accumulated, it will finally bring the enterprise to the last stop on the journey: *Strategic customer relationship management.*

C. Grow me: *Strategic customer relationship management*

The last stop on the journey is a veritable magic cauldron because the computer enterprise now provides individual service to its prioritised customers, not on the basis of what the enterprise believes about the customer's needs, but on the basis of real knowledge alone. The computer enterprise can now, based on its knowledge of the prioritised customers (*accounts, leads, contacts, and activities*), generate targeted cross- and up-selling partially based on knowledge-sharing internally in the organisation and partially based on knowledge-sharing internally in the customer organisation.

When the end station is characterised by a great deal of dynamic activity, it's because the enterprise is constantly increasing its knowledge base by means of the ongoing registration of relevant information about its customers. In this way, the basis for providing customers with advice regarding business development is constantly increasing - for the benefit of both parties.

The challenges of the journey

Only very few companies have implemented a CRM strategy in practice, even though many claim to have done so.

The model below gives an overview of what an enterprise can expect and how far it has progressed on the CRM journey. The model also explains why some CRM initiatives have not been successful. This usually happens when the enterprise jumps directly to the end goal on the IT front without keeping up on the business process side.

In the model, we have used sales, marketing and service efforts as reference points for determining how far the enterprise has progressed in the CRM journey. But keep in mind, CRM is not just about *marketing*, it's also about *management.* Sales, marketing and service efforts are just the tip of the iceberg and are used here only to give an idea of where the enterprise finds itself today.

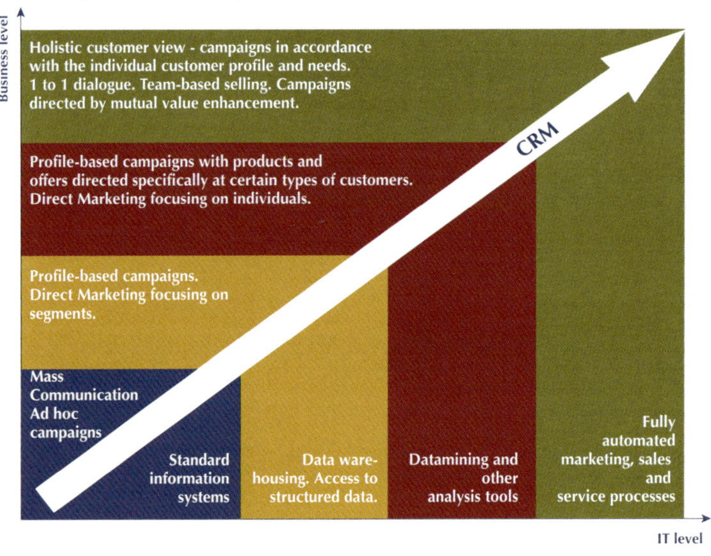

Figure 1.2: Comparison of business processes and IT in relation to CRM

The business level axis

The model shows the different stops on the road to full implementation of a CRM strategy. The first focus area is on ad hoc campaigns, mass communication, volume discount agreements, and identical treatment of all customers when customer information is not available. Here focus is typically directed towards turnover per salesperson and number of customers.

At the opposite end of the scale, there is full implementation of a CRM strategy with individual customer service and treatment depending on the potential and value of the customer for the enterprise. In this case, the enterprise has a good overview of customers and easy-to-access data concerning customers and their history. The enterprise creates a dialogue with customers and the focus is thus moved from turnover per salesperson and number of customers to developing relationships and measuring the lifetime value of customers.

IT axis

It is important to point out that business processes and IT must be integrated. During the first stage of the journey, the challenge as mentioned above is to understand who the customers are. The focus on the IT front is directed towards building up information about *accounts* and *leads*. Thus it is useless, for example, to send questionnaires to customers as long as it is not possible to use the answers and update the information about the customer in the enterprise's systems.

Later, when the enterprise has an overview of *accounts* and *leads*, the challenge on the IT front will be to accumulate more in-depth knowledge about the customer - knowledge of *contacts* and *activities*. In this connection, it will usually be relevant to set up a Data Warehouse (VI) to manage all the data that needs to be stored.

When the enterprise has this information at its disposal, it is ready to begin the last part of the journey to *strategic customer relationship management*. On the IT front, Data Mining (VII) tools come into focus. They form the basis for analyses of customers, extending across customers to ensure a relevant and value-creating dialogue with each individual customer.

If the two figures above are compared, it becomes clear that the CRM journey requires careful planning and that the route can be determined only from the business side. IT is simply a tool to ensure proper navigation during the journey. Another important aspect to remember is that the enterprise must typically stop along the way to acclimatise itself. In this way, the journey is naturally divided into a number of midway stations.

The new customer understanding: How fast and far should we go?

Most enterprises have realised the importance of a customer-oriented strategy. This was confirmed by a market study (VIII) carried out by PricewaterhouseCoopers in 1998 of 70 of the largest Nordic enterprises. The study also clearly demonstrated that numerous barriers are experienced in connection with the creation of a customer-oriented enterprise.

These barriers can be divided into two groups:

The first group is the depth of the information concerning the individual customer. The main barriers here are the lack of information systems to collect and process customer data, lack of opportunity to calculate earnings per individual customer, and imprecise customer segmentation.

The second group is the availability of information in the enterprise. Barriers here are lack of access to customer data, insufficient customer information across the enterprise, and lack of insight into the benefit of customer value analyses.

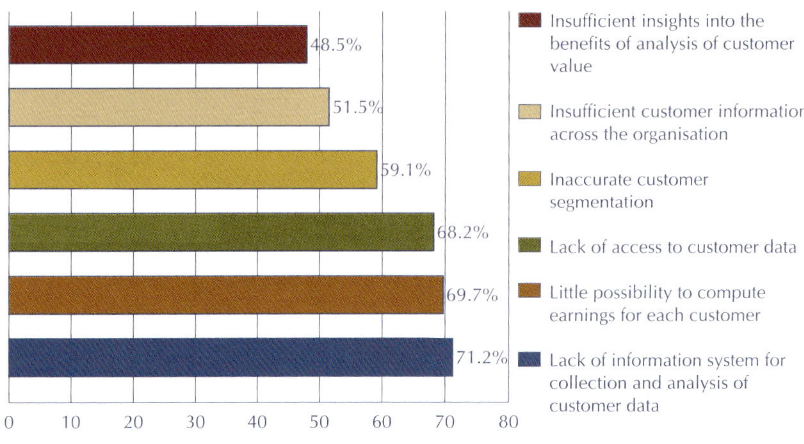

Figure 1.3: Barriers to measuring customer value, Scandinavian Market and Customer Management study 1998
Source: PricewaterhouseCoopers

In the same analysis (3) 96% of the enterprises admit that it is important to be able to measure customer value and customer loyalty to ensure the future com-

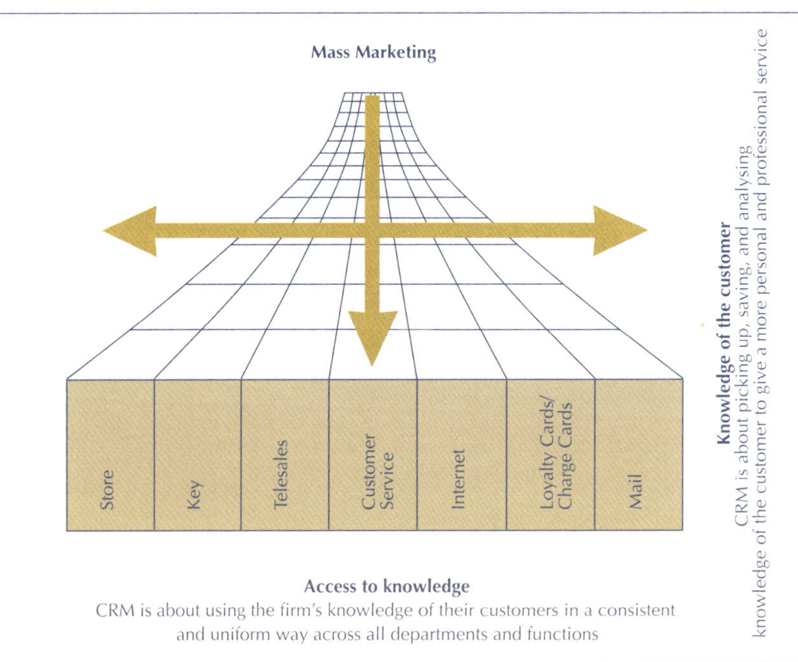

Figure 1.4: Depth/width model

petitiveness of the enterprise. In addition, 88% say that they have plans to make further improvements in these areas.

Planning the journey: Implementing a CRM strategy

Experience shows that the implemented systems are not utilised optimally, and that therefore potential *benefits* in connection with the utilisation of the systems are not achieved. The decision-making basis has been insufficient and as a result, the effect of the investment is lost.

In most cases, this happens because the enterprises have focused exclusively on the system when implementing CRM. Business processes, organisational structure, company culture and human resource aspects of the system implementation were not given a high enough priority. A CRM strategy must be not only widely formulated, it must be operational at all levels. Some 75% of the success can be attributed to the processes, the organisation, the people and the culture - and some 25% to the software.

The hard stuff is the easy stuff - The soft stuff is the hard stuff

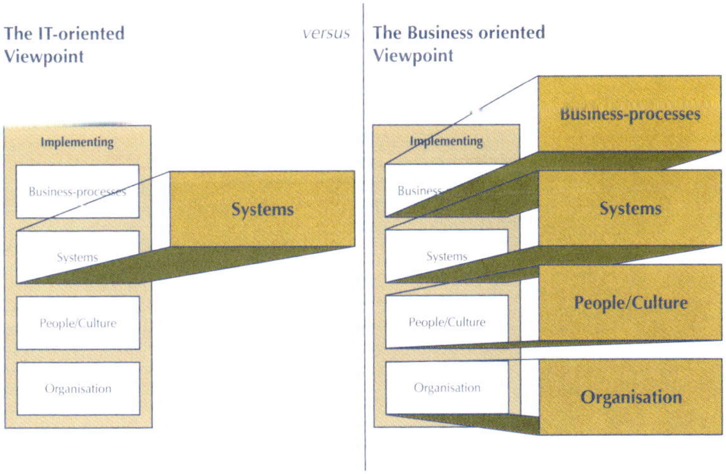

Figure 1.5: Success factors

The above is based on experience in implementing Sales Force Automation (IX), which is part of a complete CRM system. The analysis in figure 1.5 demonstrates that only 15% of implementations met expectations. 20% partially met expectations and as much as 65% did not live up to expectations at all.

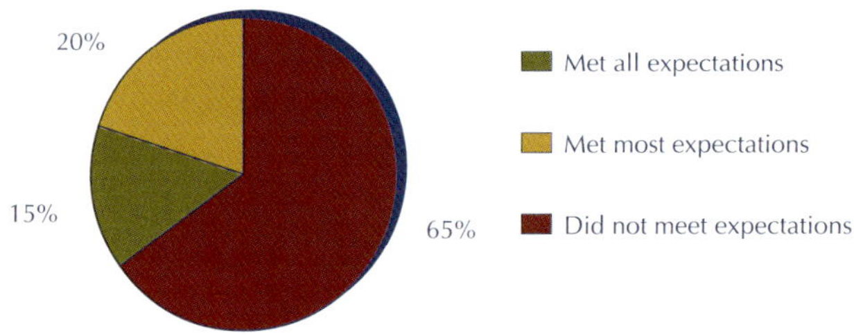

Figure 1.6: 65% of all Sales Force Automation (SFA) projects did not live up to customer expectations. SFA is an element of CRM implementation.
Source: Insight Technology Group, 1996

We look upon it as a challenge to improve the above statistics, which is one of the reasons for this book.

What is a CRM system?

As described in figure 1.2, implementation of a CRM strategy typically requires the support of IT tools. To determine the requirements, PricewaterhouseCoopers has developed the model shown in figure 1.7 that describes the CRM system in relation to other enterprise IT systems.

The basic functionality of a CRM system is covered by the front office module for marketing, sales and service. The technologies that support customer contact can be found under the customer touch points. The back office is the enterprise's ERP (X). Data warehousing and processing take place in the operating storage system and the data warehouse.

The boundaries between a CRM system and the technology used for the customer contact points are fast disappearing. Likewise, one often sees CRM systems that include data warehouse functionalities for marketing, sales and service.

The CRM system ensures that the enterprise has the opportunity to achieve an overview of its relations to the individual customer. The system can be made open to everyone who has direct contact with the customer. In this way when there is a potential lead, every employee who is connected to, or has relations with, a customer can contribute input or seek information for the sales person responsible.

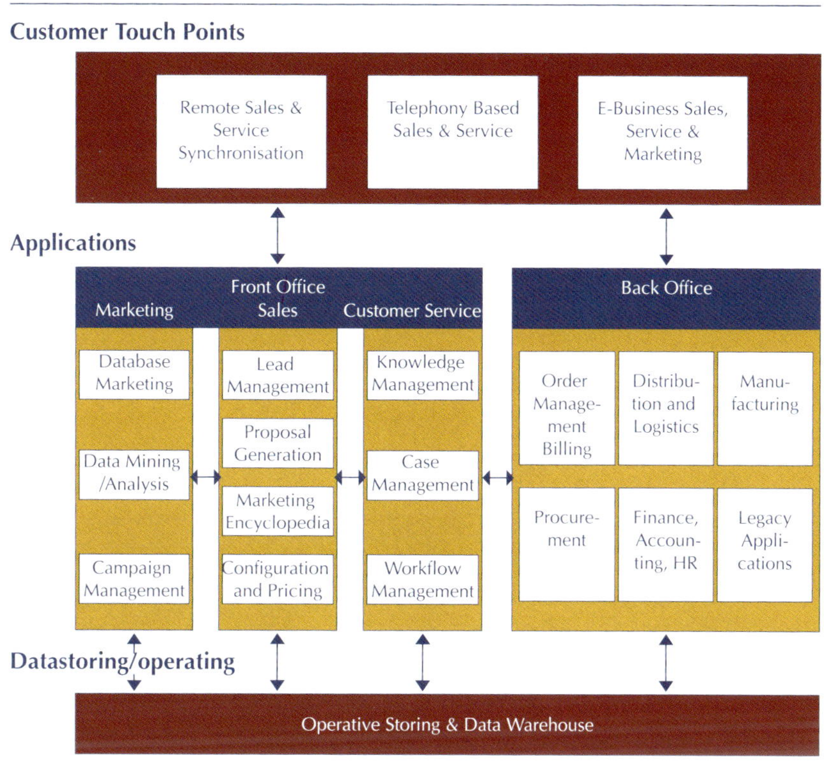

Figure 1.7: What is CRM software? The Market Intelligent Enterprise (sm)

It is also important to be able to easily create a good overview of the individual customer, selected segments, and all customers - regardless of whether the perspective is marketing, sales or customer service. And regardless of whether it is on a very detailed or general level. Customers should be treated individually and according to their value or potential to the enterprise.

The system also includes the ability to update information on-line, which is then available to everyone with access to the system. Naturally there can be several different levels of information that can be adjusted to the users according to their requirements. Or, put more simply, an overview can be created for each customer. All relevant information is shown on this overview, and it is possible to correct addresses, register complaints and see which campaigns the customer has received.

The software can cover all or just some of the areas in the model. Systems such as Sales Force Automation or the Call Centre module often stand alone. Still such tools are often called CRM software, which is a little misleading. The explanation is that the abbreviation *CRM* is becoming more and more popular and is sometimes used too loosely.

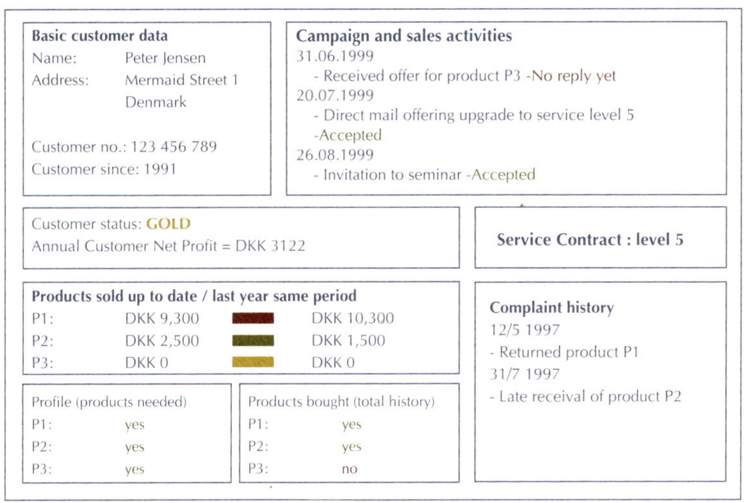

Figure 1.8: CRM software is about creating the "perfect" overview. Here is an example of a screen dump.

As mentioned earlier, CRM is not a new concept. Grocer Smith knew his customers personally and could therefore give them individual and personal service. The service matched each customer's needs and created loyalty. At that time, the grocer and his employees were able to maintain an overview of their marketplace. Today it is far more difficult to maintain an overview of all one's customers, but it is possible if one uses the right tools. Even in the global marketplace, it is possible to provide customers with individual and personal service. The only question is if the enterprise has the will to do so and access to the proper tools.

An overview of the CRM software market

As shown in figure 1.9, the market for CRM software is growing rapidly.

Updating CRM software is likewise in a phase of explosive growth and the number of suppliers in the market is large.

The above prognoses indicate that it is all about getting the CRM process started. Those enterprises that do not start this process risk losing competitive advantage in relation to their competitors when it comes to maintaining and developing profitable customers and attracting the right new customers. It is, however, important that the decision to implement CRM is not made too hastily. It must be done properly, and everyone in the enterprise must be ready for the process, otherwise the desired result will not be achieved.

In 2000 $3.5bn Licence Revenues
Drive $7bn in Services

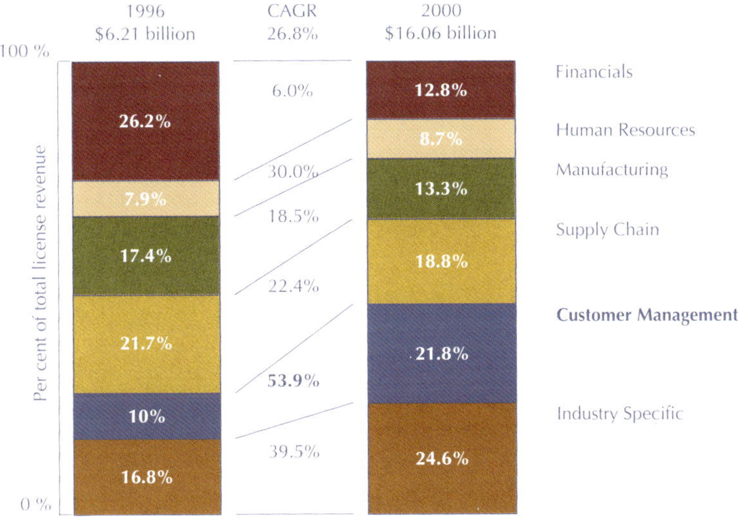

Figure 1.9: Developments in the market for software products 1996-2000
Source: Forrester Research 97

Each enterprise should select a system based on its own specific needs and
requirements. There is no standard system that will precisely suit every company. A certain amount of adjustment will probably be necessary to create the
optimal system. Business-wise, it is naturally important that a _cost/benefit_ analysis has been performed and that this is part of the decision-making process. It
must therefore be clear what the enterprise needs - and then the system must be
purchased that best matches these requirements.

Expected development of the CRM Software market world wide _______________

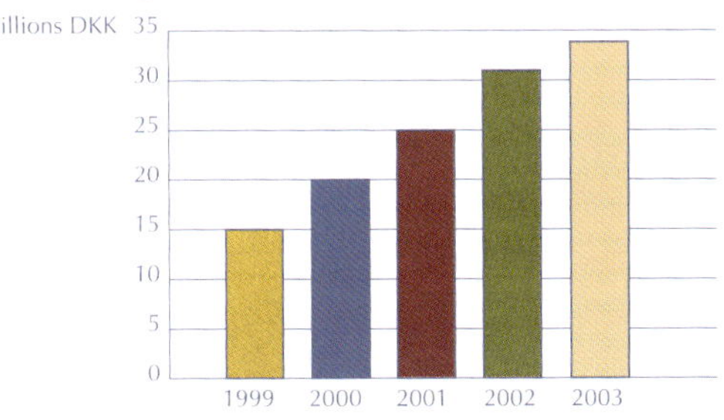

Figure 1.10: PricewaterhouseCoopers 1999

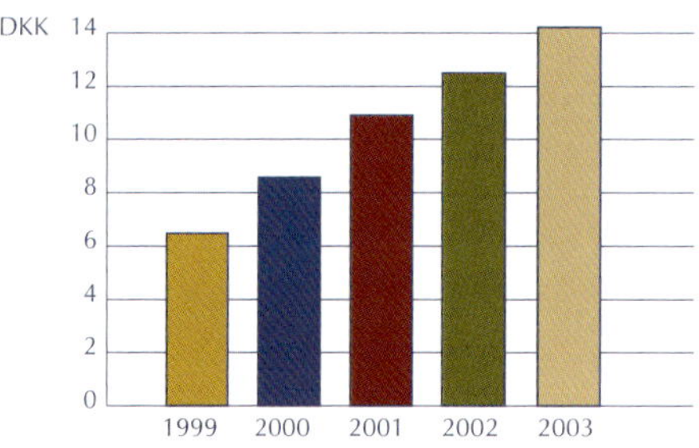

Figure 1.11: PricewaterhouseCoopers 1999

Who have we selected for this analysis?

It is naturally a challenge to attempt to create an overview of the suppliers in the marketplace. Consequently, we have chosen to focus on some of the large global suppliers as well as selected suppliers in the Nordic and European markets. In this book, we examine the following systems:

- Abalon
- Baan
- Caesar
- CDM
- Clarify
- Core Point
- Dialog Manager
- MultiMark
- Oracle Applications
- Prime Response
- SAP
- Siebel
- Software Innovation
- Vantive

In order to examine the individual systems, it is necessary to understand the reasons why enterprises consider investing in CRM software systems.

Questions for the reader:

- What does the enterprise know about its customers?
- How often is this information updated?
- Is this information easily available or is it necessary to perform special operations to retrieve it?
- How does the enterprise use this information?
- Who has access to this information?
- Does the enterprise have several different systems that are not integrated?
- How are these systems updated?
- How many overviews must one look at in order to answer a customer inquiry?
- Do employees ever ask the customer for information that is not going to be used anyway?
- How many segments does the enterprise have and how are they defined?
- Is knowledge and information about the customer updated?
- Where does the enterprise stand in the CRM process?

Notes:

I   Shareholder Value:
To create more value for the company's shareholders.

II   Business to Business:
The concept is used about companies that sell to other industrial customers.

III Business to Consumer:
The concept is used about companies that sell directly to consumers.

IV   The four main elements in the sales function of the CRM system are typically:
1) Accounts - customers
2) Leads - sales opportunities
3) Contacts - contact people inside the customer organisation
4) Activities - activities directed towards customers

V   Retention
Keeping customers.

VI   Data warehousing:
Data warehousing is a structured collection of data from different systems. The data is integrated in a logical business model and is saved in a way that is easy to understand for non-technical decision-makers. The system delivers data to decision-makers across the organisation.

VII Data mining:
Data mining is an advanced, partially automated statistical method for studying and modelling the interaction/interconnectedness of large amounts of data.

VII PricewaterhouseCoopers, 1998
A survey of markets and customers performed among the largest Scandinavian companies.

IX   Sales Force Automation:
Automation of the sales process and management of the sales force.

X   ERP:
Enterprise Resource Planning.

Chapter 2

The CRM Strategy

"Only the one who goes
his own way, can never be
caught by anyone"

Marlon Brando

This chapter deals with customer loyalty and value. We show how dialogue on the CRM journey replaces traditional segmentation as the enterprise gradually approaches the final goal of *Strategic Customer Relationship Management*. The chapter also discusses ways of increasing customer value by *cross and up-selling (I)* and the active application of segment-oriented campaigns.

Customer loyalty is a necessary but not sufficient condition for creating value as not all loyal customers are profitable. This is why the CRM strategy begins with customer differences, making effective segmentation decisive if the enterprise is to satisfy each customer's specific needs.

To create value for loyal customers, the enterprise must be familiar with both their needs and behaviour. But the enterprise, which is just starting to implement its CRM strategy, will only deal with *accounts and opportunities.* How can it then carry out effective segmentation and build loyalty and value without having established a dialogue with the customer?

The concept of loyalty

Normally we understand "loyalty" to be a positive word. Everyone expects loyalty from a good friend, spouse or colleague. We apply it to people who understand problems and who always make themselves available.

Loyalty can be given to people, enterprises and products and is normally characterised by equality and mutual co-operation.

In international management literature, theories about customer loyalty are a relatively new occurrence. In the last 10 years, interest has risen considerably and today customer loyalty is regarded as the recipe for increasing revenue. There are those who jokingly say, "If the enterprise wants loyalty it can buy a dog". This somewhat defeatist attitude is today being replaced by a more pragmatic approach. Attractive customers feel a sense of loyalty when the relationship is strengthened. In this way, one creates value for the customer who then buys more.

Figure 2.1 shows the correlation between loyalty and value according to the "fried egg" model. The yoke stands for the enterprise's chosen customers - and the CRM strategy, like an egg white, forms a protective and nutritious layer around them.

The idea is that the relationship between customer and enterprise gets stronger as we pass through the different CRM stations on the journey. In this way, customer satisfaction grows, as does the perception of value in the relationship. This reaction leads to an increase in loyalty. If the enterprise continues to sustain the potential for satisfying customer needs and keeps its services in demand, a mutual creation of value emerges and the final goal of *Strategic Customer Relationship Management* is achieved.

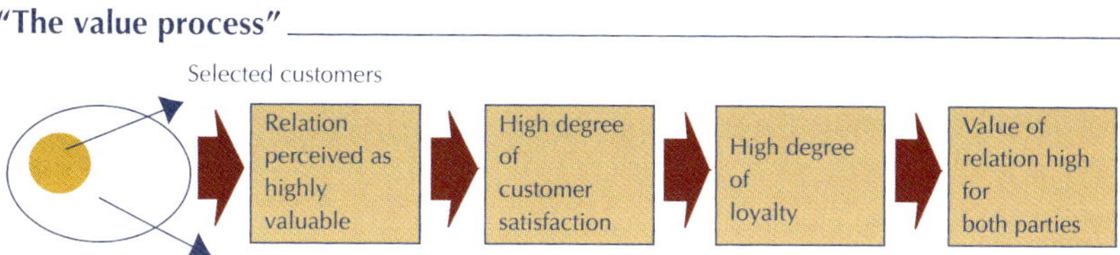

Figure 2.1: The value process

Richard L. Oliver defined the concept of loyalty in this way:

"A deeply held commitment to re-buy or re-patronise a preferred product or service consistently in the future despite situational influences and marketing efforts having the potential to cause switching behaviour."

- Oliver, Richard L., Satisfaction, McGraw-Hill, New York, 1997.

Phases of loyalty

Mutual loyalty cannot be built from one day to the next. The enterprise that has built relationships wins the battle for customers!
Figure 2.2 shows the midway stations for loyalty in CRM.

The cognitive process
The enterprise must first get to know the customer. In this phase, loyalty is considered very weak because it is not based on relationships but solely on products and prices (cognitive). In fact, the customer may switch to a competitor if their offering is better. A good example of this is the fierce price competition in the mobile telephone market.

The affective process
The enterprise engages with customer attitudes both before and after the purchase (affective). It listens to the customer who is gradually getting to know the enterprise. Loyalty is no longer based on price and product alone. Relationship is also becoming a factor, even though there is no guarantee the customer will not seek new pastures. The relationship is solid enough for loyalty to be seen as permanent. False loyalty, however, may be illustrated by the airlines' *"frequent flyer"* programmes where *"loyalty"* is often based on a lack of alternatives rather than satisfaction with the product or relationship.

The conative process

At the final goal, loyalty is based on a high degree of satisfaction. Here the customer will get personally involved in a targeted dialogue with the enterprise. Gradually, as the engagement develops, the bonds between customer and enterprise are strengthened. Here the feeling of customer satisfaction increases and with it loyalty to the enterprise. On the basis of such a relationship, one can speak of "true" loyalty.

Loyalty and the CRM process

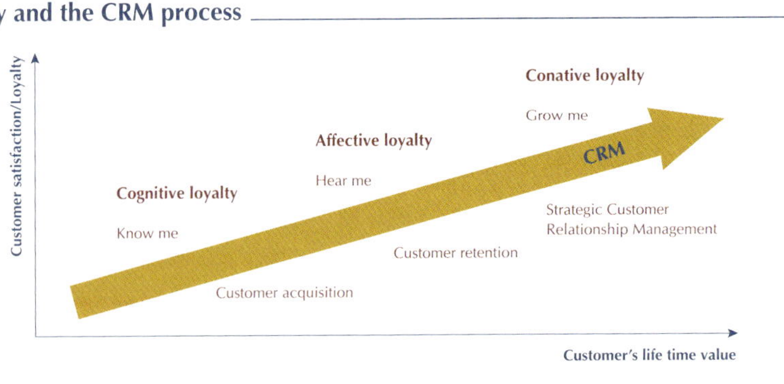

Fig: 2.2: Loyalty and the CRM Process

The loyalty ladder

Both enterprise and customer should receive a positive benefit from the relationship if mutual loyalty is to be achieved - even though on the journey to their common goal both parties will inevitably experience disappointments. The goal of the enterprise in adopting a CRM strategy is to guide both new and current customers up the "loyalty ladder" to the so-called "advocate" stage.

These advocates are living advertisements for the enterprise, praising it and recommending it to others. The prerequisites for this happening are, of course, that all the basic conditions of service, quality, price, etc., are in order. It is impossible to build a loyalty concept if products or services are poor.

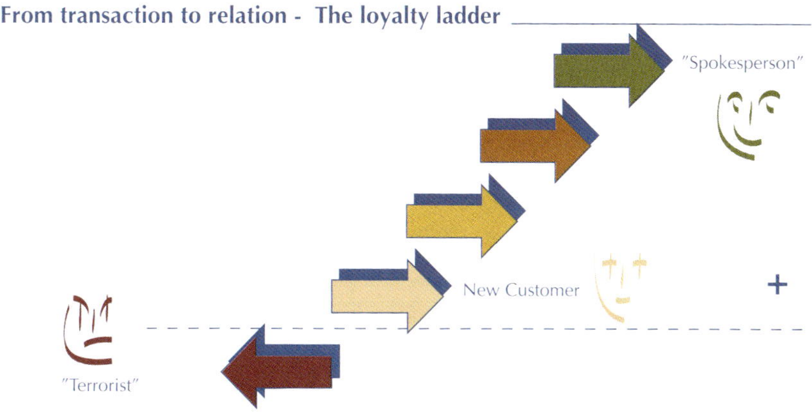

Figure 2.3: The loyalty ladder

The opposite of the advocate is the "terrorist". The terrorist will use every opportunity to publicise negative experiences with the enterprise. It takes the praises of many advocates to offset the negative criticisms created by such terrorists. The enterprise rarely hears about this criticism, so it has little opportunity to correct the mistake. This renders the enterprise poorly equipped in its struggle against terrorists.

When the enterprise comes into contact with a new customer the following holds true:

"The objective is to turn new customers into regularly-purchasing clients, and then to progressively move them through being strong supporters of the company and its products, and finally to being active and vocal advocates for the company thus playing an important role as a referral source."

Source: Payne et al., Relationship Marketing, Butterworth/Heinemann, 1991, Oxford.

Loyalty presupposes mutuality

It is easy to forget that loyalty is a two-way process. Even the best advocate can become a terrorist if trust in the company is weakened or lost.

The traditional form of price setting is a good example. New customers are rewarded and the loyal and faithful ones pay the price. But it should really be the opposite. The logic behind this is that the customer the enterprise already knows requires fewer resources for marketing and administration than "new" customers.

There are many cautionary tales of this in everyday life:
Last year, a monthly magazine ran a Christmas campaign where new subscribers could save DKK 150 in relation to regular customers by subscribing for DKK 398. This irritated the magazine's loyal readers who, on trying to get the same cheaper subscription rate, were told it was impossible. The outcome is that today the magazine has lost many former subscribers because its loyal readers changed from advocates to terrorists.

If only the publisher had thought in terms of "lifetime value", the picture would have been a different one. The advantage of gaining a new customer can rarely compensate for the loss of a loyal one.

Measurement of loyalty

Loyalty will be measured differently depending on where we are in the CRM process. The complexity of these measurements varies considerably depending on what we desire. Is it information on customer satisfaction or economic analyses of earning per individual customer?

Experience shows that loyalty measurements should include, at the very least, a consumption-related measurement and a customer satisfaction measurement.

"Share of Wallet" is often used as the consumption-related measurement of loyalty. It expresses the relation between the customer's actual purchases from the enterprise and the customer's purchasing potential.

An example shows a customer needing house insurance, car insurance, family insurance and accident insurance for a combined premium of DKK 15,000 per annum. The customer, however, has only three of the policies in company 'A' (DKK 10,000), the fourth being in company 'B' (DKK 5,000). If *Share of Wallet* is used as the loyalty indicator, the customer has a 66% loyalty rating for company 'A' and 33% loyalty rating for company 'B'. Company 'A' then has the potential to improve its loyalty rating by 33% and company 'B' by 66%!

A second example shows another family buying basic household items for about DKK 80,000 per annum. They shop primarily in the local supermarket and partly in a supermarket near a kindergarten. The shopping is distributed 60% at the local supermarket and 40% at the one near the kindergarten. How much loyalty, measured by *Share of Wallet*, can be transferred from one supermarket to the other? And what would happen if we could suddenly buy the goods over the Internet at a third supermarket that offers home delivery?

As can be seen, the *Share of Wallet* loyalty indicator fails to take into account whether we are dealing with true or false loyalty. When we speak of false loyalty, as mentioned previously, we mean that there can be situations where the customer is "forced" to use a particular product or specific service benefit. It may be a car repair shop in connection with a car guarantee, or an airline company with the monopoly on a particular route, etc. If the market offers only a limited number of choices, it is easy to give a large part of our business to the enterprise without necessarily being its advocate.

For this reason, *"Share of Wallet"* measurements are often complemented by measurements of customer satisfaction. With this in mind, Pricewaterhouse-Coopers has developed the "Voice of the Customer" concept. The criteria for this customer satisfaction measurement are shown in figure 2.4 (II).

Voice of the customer

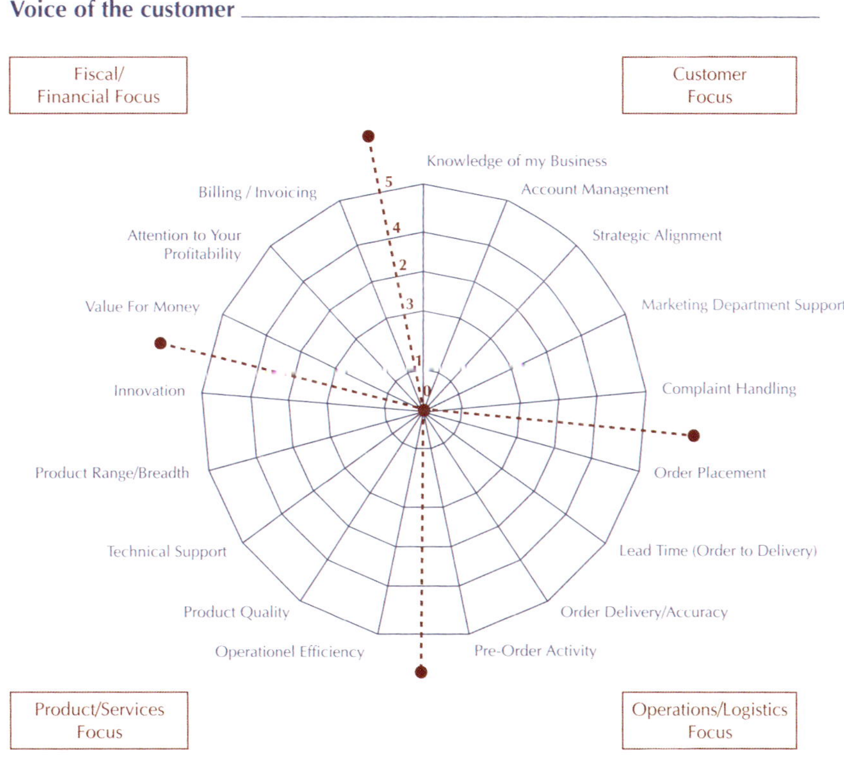

Figure 2.4: Voice of the Customer

Lifetime value

Not all customers have the same value for the enterprise. The decisive factors will always be: Do they seem satisfied and thus loyal? In other words, what is the overall length of the relationship (retention) and how much will the customer buy (lifetime value)?

Many enterprises still focus almost exclusively on new customers. Budgeting, goal-setting and employee goals are all based on this, and the same applies to marketing and price setting. New customers get top priority because they compensate for existing customers who leave the enterprise. Even though these new customers keep the total number at the same level, it is no exaggeration to say that the economic potential of retaining loyal customers is often enormous. This conclusion is not some kind of "hocus-pocus", but rather the state of affairs and should give food for thought.

It will normally be more profitable to keep a customer than acquire a new one. As is shown in figure 2.5, during the normal development of a customer relationship, the enterprise gradually uses fewer resources on administration.

The loyal customer rarely focuses on price alone but instead sees customer relationship in terms of *"value for money"*. In this way, the customer acts as an advocate for the enterprise and thus attracts new customers.

Life time Value - Example

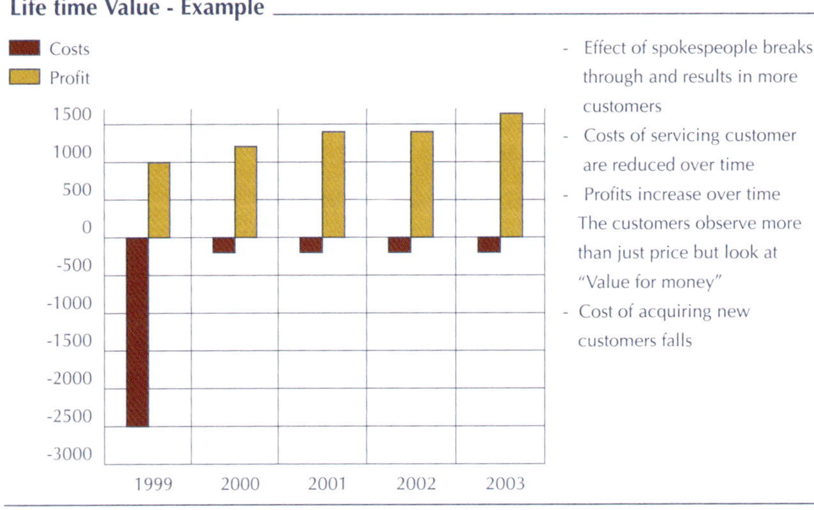

Figure 2.5: The development of lifetime value

Acquiring new customers costs a lot of money. Return on this investment depends to a great extent on how long the customer relationship lasts. Are we speaking of an isolated purchase or the beginning of a new 5-, 10- or 70-year customer relationship?

The retention rate is used to measure customer turnover. It shows how large a percentage of its customer portfolio the enterprise retains yearly. The churn rate, on the other hand, shows how large a percentage of its customer portfolio the enterprise loses yearly.

When an enterprise operates with a *churn rate of 20%*, or a *retention rate of 80%*, it means that it replaces 20% of its customers each year, or in the worst scenario, a total replacement of all its customers over a five-year period. In this case, the period over which the enterprise can generate income from the customer will be five years - the so-called lifetime value.

Retention rate has great significance for the creation of value. It is clear from figure 2.6 that when the enterprise increases the *retention rate* from 80% to 90%, it doubles customer lifetime from five to ten years.

Retention rate

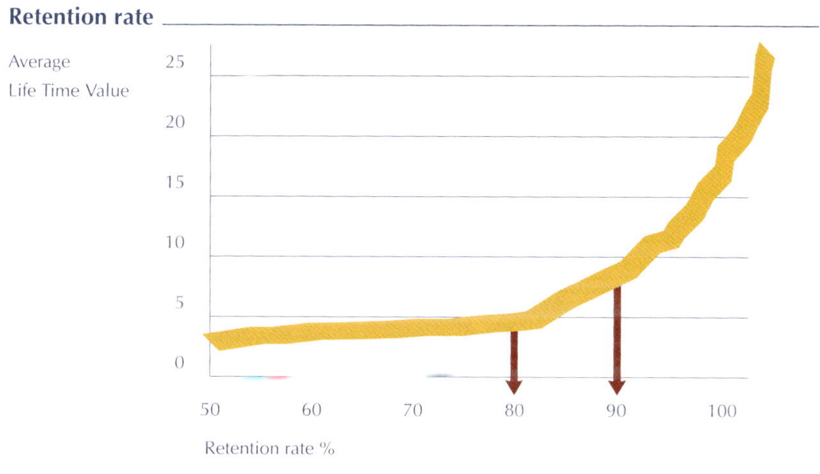

Figure 2.6: Retention rate

To illustrate the effect of an increase in *the retention rate*, figure 2.7 shows the conditions in the mobile telephone market. This market is extremely competitive and characterised by the high acquisition costs and relatively low customer service costs.

As a further example, figure 2.7 estimates income and expenses from a customer portfolio of 100,000 subscribers. Figure 2.8 extends the calculations to explain the economic consequences to the enterprise of diverse *retention rates.* In the calculations, the interest costs and depreciation are not included.

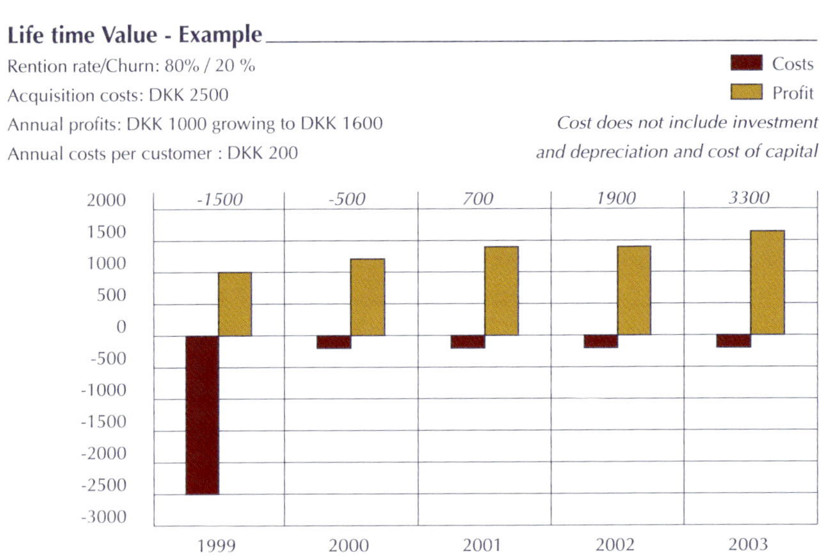

Figure 2.7: Estimated costs in the telecommunications sector

As demonstrated in figure 2.8, it makes a great deal of difference whether the *retention rate* is 70%, 80%, or 90%. The example clearly shows the advantage of retaining existing customers instead of acquiring new ones. There is a marked difference between losing DKK 30 million and earning DKK 400 million! This should be the basis for the ways in which the enterprise prioritises its marketing efforts and allocation of resources.

Retention rate

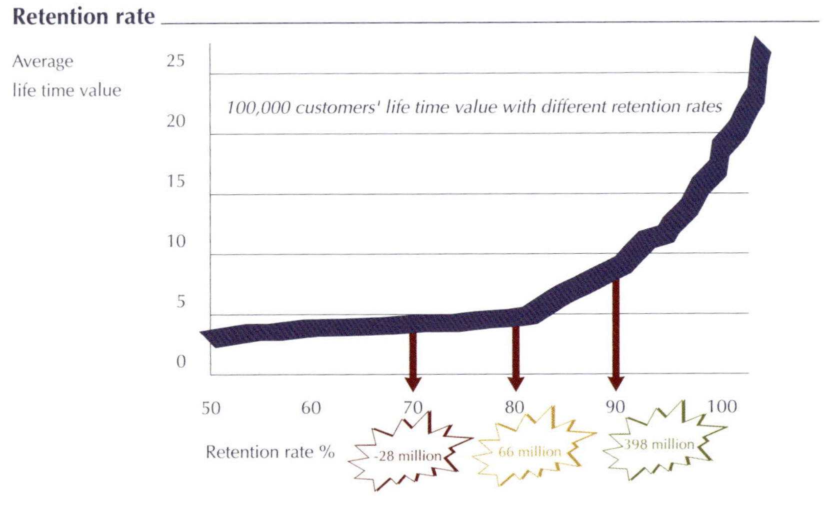

Figure 2.8: Lifetime value with different retention rates for 100,000 customers in the telecommunications sector

From market share to customer share

The transition from market share to customer share (*from market share to share of wallet*) is a prevalent theme in the CRM debate about customer loyalty and lifetime value.

One result of the debate is a growing understanding that a large market share is not equivalent to having loyal customers, including the understanding that enterprise campaigns must shift focus from product, as shown in figure 2.9, to customer, as shown in figure 2.10.

Focus on the product

Who are the best customers to receive to offers/communication?

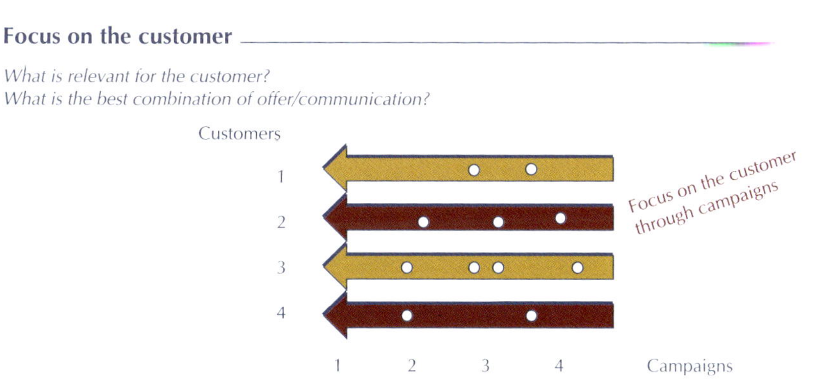

Figure 2.9: Product-oriented campaigns

Focus on the customer

What is relevant for the customer?
What is the best combination of offer/communication?

Figure 2.10: Customer-oriented campaigns

What good does a large market share do for Coca Cola so long as Coca Cola does not come out of the taps in the customers' kitchens? Until this happens, there is still a great deal of potential for Coca-Cola to go after. The example, of course is a parody, but it demonstrates that the issue is to have sufficient knowledge regarding the customer to identify potential needs and sufficient customer knowledge in order to understand the potential of the customer and find out what is relevant for each customer.

What combination of offerings and communication suits the customer best? If one communicates in this way to both profitable and potential customers, are the enterprise's marketing resources utilised effectively? And does the message break through the noise barrier? It is possible to have a dialogue in a normal conversational tone of voice and increase the enterprise's *Share of Wallet*. When this happens, the relevance of the message ensures a creation of value for both parties.

From Share of Wallet to Share of Life!

The debate continues concerning the objectives of CRM strategies. We live in a complex world where we do not function exclusively as individuals. We have many roles and diverse needs depending upon the situations we find ourselves in.

As "multi-individuals", we belong to different segments, depending on the roles we are playing (see figure 2.11). For the multi-individual, *lifetime value* is judged according to the total *lifetime value* of the many different roles we play. Ensuring customer satisfaction and building loyalty in all these roles is a great challenge, in terms of the customer information required and its accessibility in the enterprise.

What good does it do when "the business individual", via a targeted CRM strategy, is made into an advocate for a *frequent flyer* programme if the first trip on tourist class ruins the relationship, turning "the holiday individual'" into a terrorist? It can be fatal to the overall relationship if there is a failure in trust in just one of the many individuals who make up the multi-individual.

Depending on the role, the customer can have numerous relationships and consequently deal through many different channels. This situation makes it more difficult for the enterprise to sustain a good overview of the customer. The complexity highlights the need for CRM systems to ensure integration, knowledge-sharing and a good overview across all channels.

The travel industry and the financial sector are typical multi-individual areas that offer great challenges.

Let us examine a bank customer. The average customer wants easy access to cash via an ATM or local branch office. From home, there should be a link to the bank via a PC and the Internet. In this way, the consumer can manage everyday payment of bills, budget-planning, filing loan applications, etc., in peace and quiet.

The customer has many entry points: The cash dispenser (ATM), the local branch office, PC banking, the loan department, the pension department, the trading department, etc. The challenge to the bank, of course, is to maintain an overview of the customer's overall activities and ensure that the customer is a known and valued person in all the channels.

Social evolution

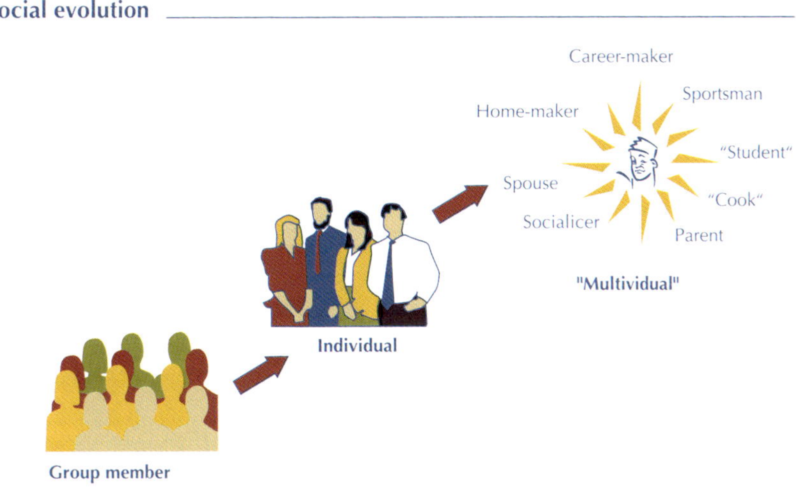

Figure 2.11: From group to multi-individual

Let us take another example from the 'fast moving consumer goods' market (III) - dog food. We have transferred the rationale behind the multi-individual to a supplier of dog food. The dog owner needs to buy dog food and there are many choices on the market. From the supplier's point of view, the customer is a scarcity factor and will always try to develop new, effective solutions to make life easier for the customer. If they succeed, long-term relationships can be built. Thus, the customer is able to get advice and tips about nutrition and health, the chance to buy accessories, the offer of dog training or dog tending during holidays, etc. Should these offers be taken up, a long-term relationship will begin to grow.

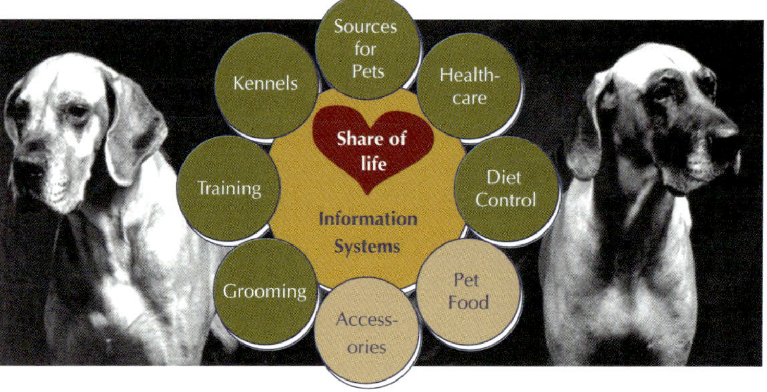

Figure 2.12: Share of life from a pet's point of view

Strategic Customer Relationship Management: "Share of Life"

In figure 2.13 we have brought the concepts together in order to unravel the threads.

On the CRM journey, segmentation constitutes both the start and end point. On the journey, as described in figure 2.13, it just changes character.

Segmentation gradually develops in two dimensions as the CRM strategy is implemented. One dimension is aimed at the fundamentals in order to understand the needs of the multi-individual, to create loyalty by shifting the focus of customer contact from transaction to relationship. The second dimension is aimed at the creation of mutual value in the enterprise and customer relationship, to shift from a product to a customer-oriented solution.

Undoubtedly, these two dimensions depend on each other. Both should be worked on simultaneously to finally reach the enterprise's final goal - *Strategic Customer Relationship Management*. The dialogue between the customer and enterprise has replaced segmentation and the enterprise can now service the customer as a multi-individual, i.e. develop *Share of life*.

New customers will probably enter the product and transaction quadrants. But once CRM is implemented in the enterprise, developing customers will be faster than in the previous end situation where the enterprise had just begun implementation. Another factor that drives developments in relation to the development of new customers is that many of these have probably been recommended by advocates which means that they and the enterprise are on the same wavelength from the start.

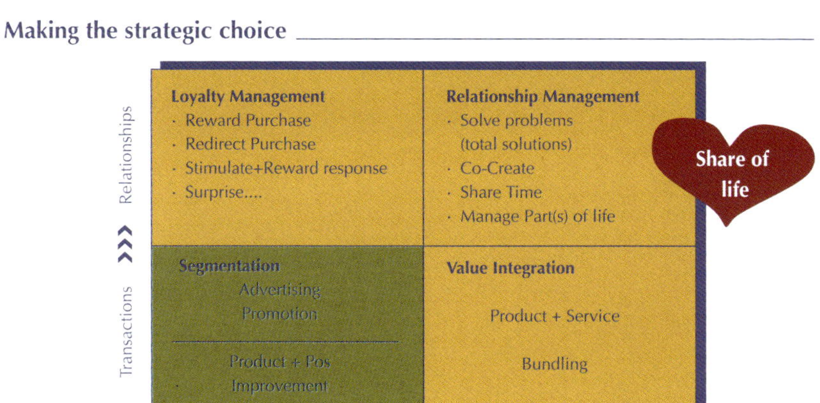

Figure 2.13: From transaction and product to solutions and relationships = Share of life

Who are the "good" customers?

No matter where the enterprise is on its CRM journey, it needs to know about customer loyalty and profitability. Based on this, the enterprise can target its dialogue and further the development of loyalty and *lifetime value* for individual customers, as well as for the whole customer portfolio.

The segmentation model in figure 2.14 describes the following four basic situations in a customer relationship:

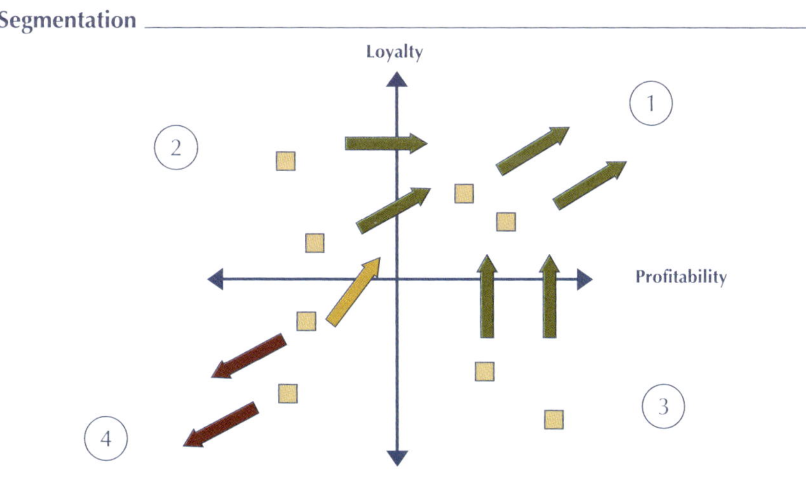

Figure 2.14: All customers are not equal - they require individual treatment.

1. The customer is loyal and profitable - the enterprise focuses on deepening the relationship and strengthening loyalty, and optimising profitability through cross- and up-selling.

2. The customer is loyal but unprofitable - the enterprise should maintain the relationship and secure loyalty because the customer may still become profitable through cross- and up-selling. If not, the customer should be dropped.

3. The customer is profitable but not loyal - the enterprise should in this case focus 100% on strengthening the relationship and loyalty.

4. The customer is not loyal and unprofitable - here it is probably worth considering giving the customer to the competitor.

As shown in figure 2.15, the segmentation model can be used throughout the CRM journey. Loyalty and profitability are the names of axes for the entire process. But loyalty and profitability change on the way as, of course, does the character of the initiatives the enterprise takes up.

In the *Customer Acquisition* phase, loyalty measurement relates to transactions, such as turnover. Measurement of profitability is product related, such as the product's profit margin.

Measuring loyalty in the CRM process

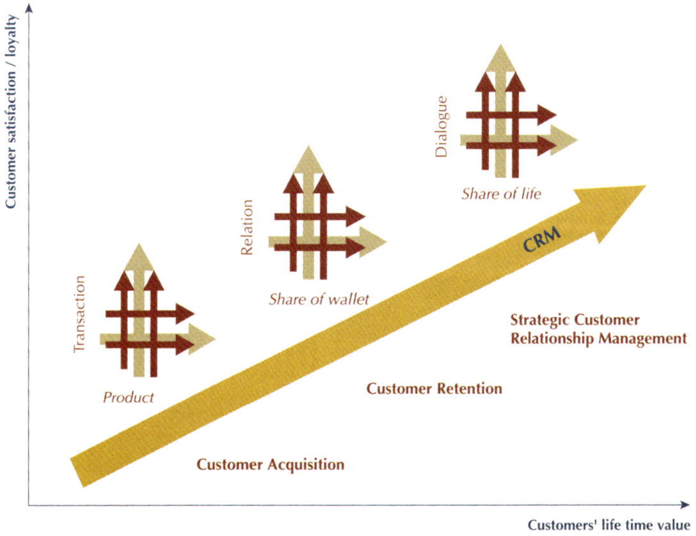

Figure 2.15: Loyalty measurements in the CRM process

In the *Customer Retention* phase, measurement of loyalty changes to being rela-
tionship-oriented using, for example, the customer satisfaction index.
Measurement of profitability changes to being directed at *Share of Wallet*.

When we discuss the *Strategic Customer Relationship Management* phase,
the norms for customer value merge with those of the enterprise - and the
measurement of loyalty will be tied to these. The profitability measurement will
be based on *Share of Life*.

The profit tower discounts, cross- and up-selling

Not all customers create value. As previously mentioned, the enterprise must
focus its resources on those customers who are profitable.

The example in figure 2.16 illustrates this. With the starting point in a large
international enterprise, we have divided customers into five equally large
groups and looked at the profit margin each group generates. The best 20% of
the customers represent nearly 65% of the enterprise's total profit margin, while
the worst 20%, as it were, give no profit. Considered as a whole, we estimate
that about half of the customers give a direct loss. Assuming there is no potential for increasing their loyalty and *Share of Wallet*, the enterprise should drop
these customers as soon as possible.

"The profit tower"

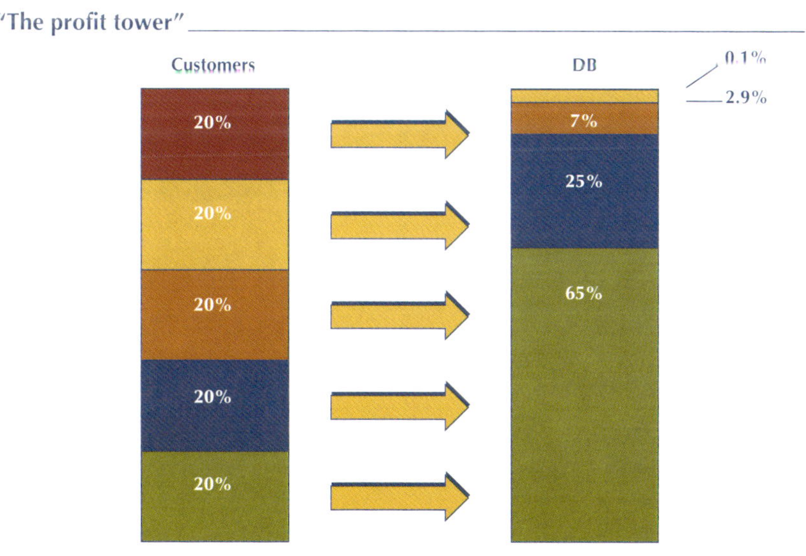

Figure 2.16: The profit tower

In relation to the 80/20 rule, where 20% of customers bring in 80% of the enterprise's profit, the situation described above (65/20) is directly beneficial. This is because the reckoning was made after the customers had been sorted out.

The profit tower gives food for thought. How much does the enterprise really know about its customers? How many of the profitable customers are loyal and how many resources are used on those who are not loyal and unprofitable?

Perhaps non-loyal customers become unprofitable when they are driven through the "discount trap", something that usually takes place when the enterprise lacks customer knowledge.

The classic discount trap as shown in figure 2.17 demonstrates that price is a problematic tool for creating loyalty and retaining customers.

For example, the mobile telephone market is clearly transaction-oriented - and here pricing and discounts are used as tools to create "loyalty", or rather reduce *churn*.

But what is the consequence? Discounts clearly give short-term satisfaction but at the same time are less lucrative. When a competitor comes with a better offer, customer satisfaction wanes. If the telephone company then wants to keep the customer, it must come up with more discounts which, rather than increase company loyalty, make for a less profitable customer.

Segmentation "The Discount Trap"

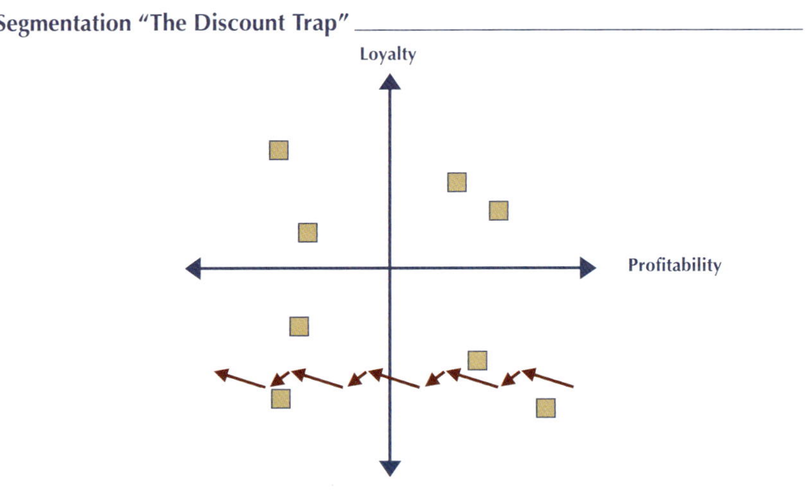

Figure 2.17: The discount trap

The potential of cross-selling

If the enterprise is to improve its position in relation to the profit tower's starting point, it must sell more to customers with potential. In other words, it is much easier and more effective to sell more goods to customers with whom the enterprise already has good relationships. Of course, this means that the enterprise must have knowledge of customer needs and is capable of delivering the goods.

In the model below, a starting point is taken in an enterprise which supplies a range of products in the *business-to-consumer* market and a look at how many of the enterprise's customers buy three of its products, P1, P2 and P3.

The seven different combinations in which these products can be bought are shown in figure 8. 21% buy P1, 14% buy P2, only 2% buy P3, and so on. Out of 100,000 customers, the figure shows that 16,000 buy all three products.

We can choose to interpret this from two different viewpoints. Negatively, it is just too bad. Positively, there is great scope for improvements (figure 2.18).

X sales model with 3 products

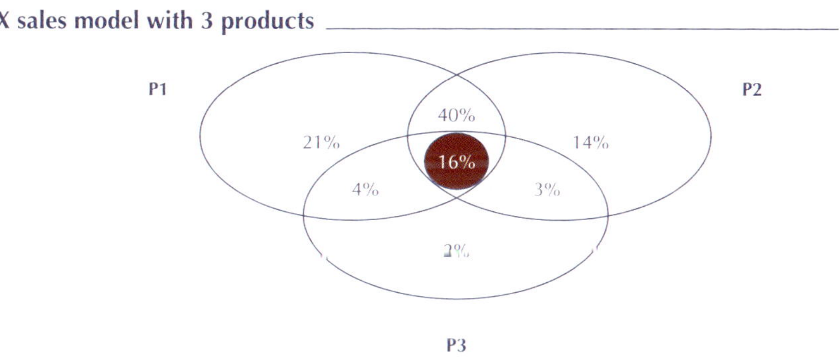

Figure 2.18: The cross-selling model from a specific enterprise

It is also interesting to look at the customer's movements between individual products.

Which customers buy which products? How does a customer relationship get started - and how many products did the customer buy in the end? What is the connection between the number of products purchased and, for example, the customer's "lifetime".

Not surprisingly, there is a connection between the number of products the customer buys and the customer's lifetime with the enterprise. The greater the number of products bought, the longer the lifetime with the enterprise (figure 2.19).

By adding a fourth product to the analysis, we examine how many customers buy all four products.

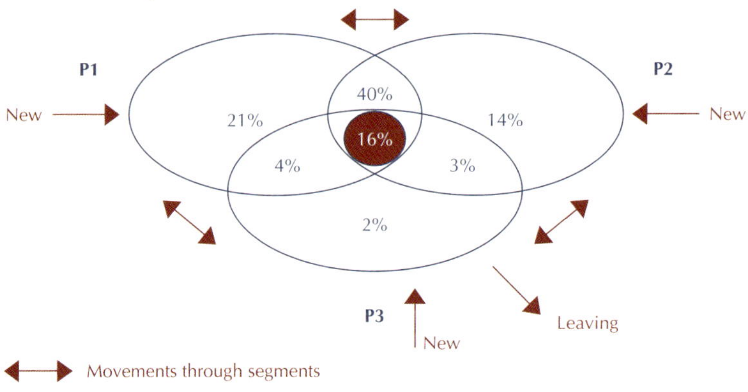

Figure 2.19: The cross-selling model. How are customers gained or lost in relationship to the products?

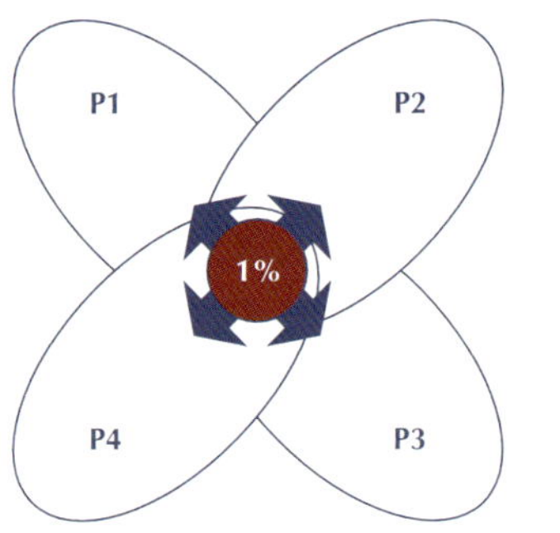

Figure 2.20: The cross-selling model. Only 1% of the enterprise's customers buys four products.

In the above-mentioned enterprise, the figure was only 1%, that is, 1,000 customers out of 100,000. In another enterprise, where we conducted a similar survey, the sales director thought the enterprise had 100,000 customers who bought four products. The correct number was 7,000 customers. This can make one speculate about the potential of CRM. How does one get an overview of the enterprise's customers which will make effective cross-selling possible?

If the enterprise has "a good overview", there will be plenty of opportunities to support and optimise cross-selling and increase value.

Summary of "The Strategy"

The CRM vision can be summarised by the expressions below:

- A holistic picture of the customer

- Regarding customer information as a strategic asset

- Establishing team-based selling as the rule rather than the exception

- Measuring and controlling customer profitability

- Using each customer contact as an opportunity to create loyalty

Questions for the reader:

- How deep is your enterprise's knowledge of the customers?
- How much does your enterprise earn from a new customer?
- How much does your enterprise earn from a current customer?
- Who is the enterprise's most profitable customer?
- Is the enterprise's potential utilised?
- What is the potential of the enterprise's other customers?
- How does the enterprise define loyalty?
- How does the enterprise measure loyalty?
- How loyal are your customers?
- How many customers does the enterprise lose each year?
- How many customers do you keep?
- What is the lifetime value of the enterprise's customers?
- Is it possible to catch a customer who is on his/her way out by means of an "early warning system"?
- Which new customers should you "go" after?
- Can the enterprise build an "ambassador effect"?
- How can you optimise the use of your resources?
- How can the enterprise ensure relevant and targeted communication with customers?
- What goals should your employees have?
- How do you ensure that the organisation shares knowledge about customers?

Notes

I. *Cross-selling*
    On the basis of the current relationships between the enterprise and cus-
    tomers, the ability to sell different and more products to the customer there-
    by improving the enterprise's position.

    Up-selling
    The enterprise focuses on selling the most profitable products that are rele-
    vant for the customer and thereby, indirectly, controls customer demand.

II. *Stanley A. Brown, PricewaterhouseCoopers describes the Voice of Customer
    concept in detail in "Strategic Customer Care". For any further information
    on the subject, inquiries may be sent to PricewaterhouseCoopers.*

III. *The fast moving consumer goods market*
    Market for consumer goods with a high turnover rate.

Chapter 3

What Drives Investments in CRM Software?

"We are facing the largest change in consumer behaviour since World War II. There are individual demands and a growing wish to be treated as the one person you are"

Faith Popcorn

This chapter explores the background for the enterprise acquisition of CRM systems. We examine the scarcity of customers and the increasing demands for targeted, relevant communications in order to break through the so-called "noise" barrier.

Then we will discuss knowledge-sharing about and across customers because it is one of the pillars in any CRM strategy and a crucial factor for the acquisition of a CRM system by any enterprise.

The customer as a scarcity factor

The customer is a scarcity factor. Today, products and services are almost identical - and there is an abundance of suppliers. Take the automobile market for example.

Cars are becoming more and more alike in design and appearance. Every brand of automobile of course has its own image, but this image is becoming weaker and weaker as cars become more and more alike. When a manufacturer begins to equip an inexpensive model with air bags, the competition quickly follows with the same offer. As a result, the price parameter becomes more and more important. Naturally, the consumer is delighted by this very competitive market because it is always a question of utilizing resources optimally. But where is the customer "experience" in all this?

The situation can be described using the "fried egg" model (figure 3.1). The egg yolk is the enterprise's chosen customers. As described above, they buy products and services that are mainly undifferentiated. The whole philosophy behind the CRM strategy is that an egg white must be created which protects and nourishes the yolk. In this way, the enterprise protects its chosen customers from competitors, and the customer receives individual treatment which results in a positive "experience" of services which are otherwise undifferentiated.

"The Fried Egg"

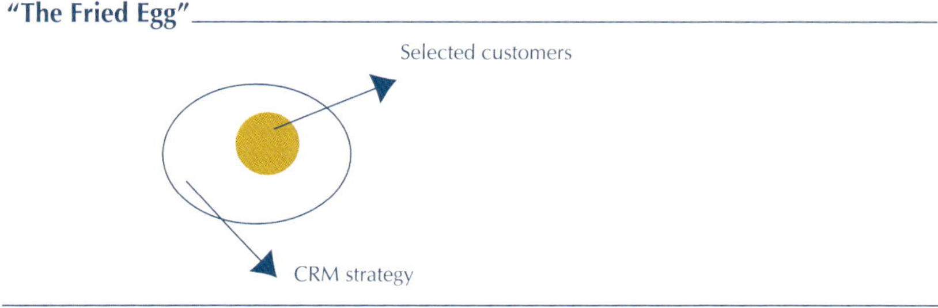

Figure 3.1 "The fried egg"

Demands to communication

In a CRM strategy, communication and dialogue play a central role in creating customer relationships. Enterprise dialogue with the customer (I) indicates how far the enterprise is in the CRM process. How far the enterprise is able to go in the process depends on the functionality and utilisation of the CRM system.

The types of communication used by the enterprise can be divided into 4 main groups:

Communication

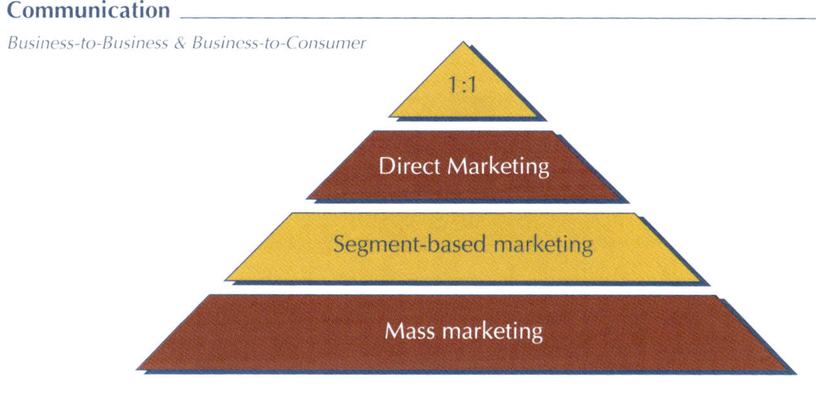

Figure 3.2 The 4 main types of communication

Traditional mass communication includes advertisements in various media such as newspapers, magazines, TV, etc. This type of communication is not particularly targeted, but has a wide reach. It is like watering a dry, newly planted patch of ground - and then hoping something will grow.

Segment-based communication uses the same media plus a simple type of direct mail. It is more targeted in its choice of media and frequency, which is adjusted to the target group. It is like watering the newly planted patch of ground in specific areas, so it is more effective. But the hope is still the same - that something, be it weeds or useful plants, will grow.

Direct marketing is a much more targeted personal type of communication based on the expectation that the customer belongs to a certain segment, determined by certain established criteria. The communication often takes place by mail or e-mail, the Internet or by telephone. In terms of watering the flowerbed, it is much more likely that useful plants will be watered, but no one knows exactly how much water they need. Perhaps they will receive too much water and rot. Or maybe they'll get too little and just dry up. Or perhaps the amount of water will be just perfect so healthy plants begin to grow.

1:1 communication is based on a dialogue between the customer and the enterprise. This often takes place by mail, the Internet, telephone or a salesperson. To continue the analogy, the 1:1 communication is as if all the weeds were pulled up and all the useful seeds were put in a greenhouse where they receive precisely the amount of water and nourishment they need for optimal growth.

This type of communication is extremely targeted, just like giving a plant the precise amount of water and nourishment. And it will usually require the help of computer technology, i.e., a CRM system.

As previously mentioned the level of enterprise operations in relation to a CRM strategy can often be determined from the types of communication the enterprise uses. An understanding of the need for a CRM system becomes clear when we see the complexity which presupposes the full implementation of a CRM strategy. See figure 3.3.

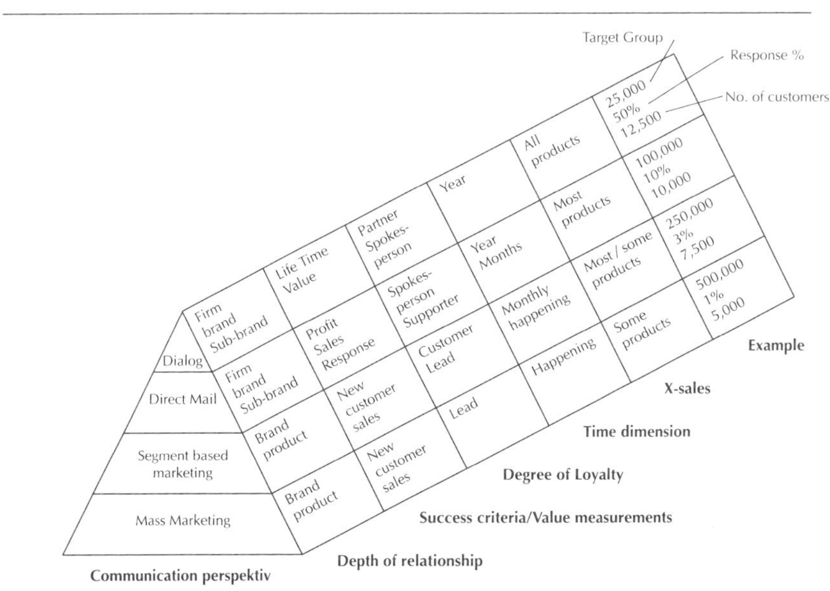

Figure 3.3: The phases of a CRM process with communication as the indicator

When we look at the depth of the relationship between the customer and the enterprise, we find that an enterprise with a 100% implemented CRM strategy will have relationships to the customer, which involve the whole enterprise. At the opposite end of the scale, we find that the depths of relationships are typically oriented around a product.

If we look at the success criteria and value measurements, there is a big difference depending on where in the CRM process the enterprise finds itself. In the genuine CRM enterprise, success criteria will typically be the customer's lifetime value and degree of retention. At the opposite end, the criteria will be sale of products and sales per campaign. If we look at customer satisfaction and loyalty between customer and enterprise, we typically find a large share of "advocates" in cases where the CRM strategy is 100% implemented. Among companies with less of a CRM strategy, there are typically unknown customer leads.

When we look at the time dimension at the beginning of a CRM process, the typical focus will be on campaigns or events within a relatively short time frame. At the other end of the scale, an enterprise that works with customer dialogue will have a time frame that is measured in years. If we look at cross-sales, they are systematised and usually include all products in companies that have 100% implementation of a CRM strategy. While for beginners, the focus is usually on individual products and the selling of them.

The noise barrier

Effective communication and the ability to protect customers are crucial for the individual enterprise. We see an increasing amount of communication in the field of marketing. And when more people are shouting loudly, fewer can hear the message.

A good example is telecommunications. Especially in the mobile telephone market, do we find extensive marketing efforts. Even if the market is constantly growing, the turnover of customers keeps taking place. This means that all suppliers must continually acquire new customers to maintain their position in the market and their level of turnover. The annual accounts from suppliers in this market speak for themselves.

Door-to-door advertising is another good example. We are all familiar with the 10-15 discount newspapers and brochures that come in through the mail slot during the course of a weekend. The growing number of "no advertisements please" signs bears witness to the effectiveness of this type of advertising. The same tendency can also be seen on the Internet where there are now special applications which automatically sort and discard banner ads.

This story has another good example: A famous writer talked about a direct mail campaign by a car company that sells luxury cars in the expensive price range. He received quite a few letters describing the wonders of the car and an invitation to come in for a test drive. He was naturally flattered, but there was just one problem: he didn't have a driver's license.

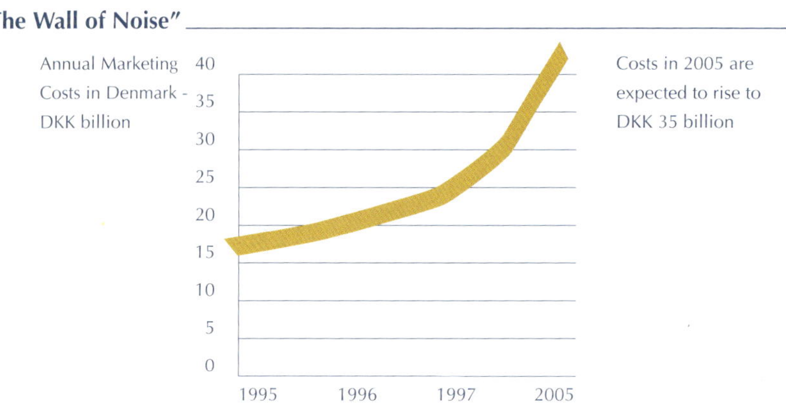

Figure 3.4: The noise barrier, costs
Source: Markedsføring, November 1997

If we look at the intensity of marketing efforts and the resultant development of the cost of marketing in recent years, the expression "noise barrier" is undoubtedly not an exaggeration.

The consequence is ineffective utilisation of resources; in other words, what the enterprise loses on the swings, it must gain on the roundabout.

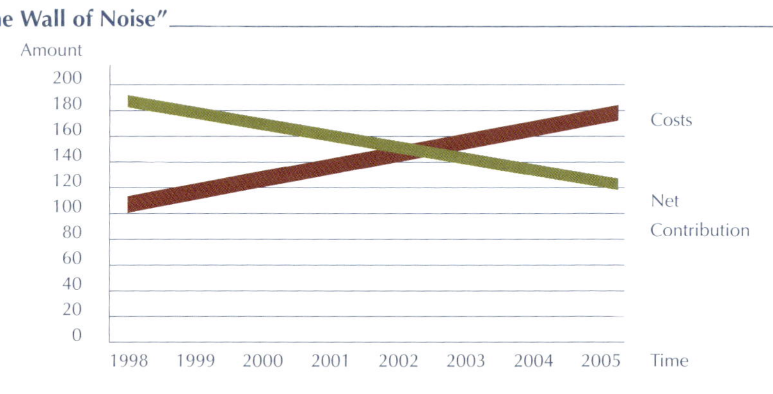

Figure 3.5: The noise barrier. Costs in relation to enterprise earnings

The fact that we still see many companies using mass communications in their marketing is often due to the lack of a clear CRM strategy and the lack of CRM systems to handle more targeted communications. The enterprise cannot just drop out of the mass communications frenzy since it lacks the information it needs about customer needs and preferences to initiate a relevant dialogue.

Often, the customer data which the enterprise already has cannot be used because it is out of date. Or relevant data might quite simply not exist. It is like the dairy products grocer Smith sells: They must be fresh, properly refrigerated and in demand - otherwise they'll just turn sour!

In brief, we can say that the tendency to "shout" more loudly in the hope of being heard can now - thanks to CRM systems - be replaced by normal conversation. One to one dialogue is becoming more and more inexpensive as CRM systems are expanded. The result is increased effectiveness in the utilisation of resources in the enterprise's dialogue with its customers.

Overview of a complex and dynamic marketplace:

Knowledge-sharing

Besides communication, specific knowledge about the customer is the most fundamental element in a CRM strategy. The following is important:

- To create knowledge about the customers
- To expand and make the picture of customers more balanced
- To prepare and analyse the knowledge that has been collected
- To share the knowledge across the organisation and with the customer
- To use the accumulated knowledge to create value for both parties

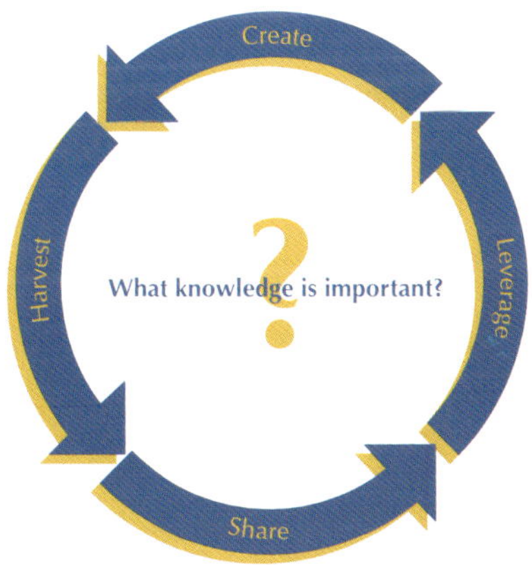

Figure 3.6: CRM systems are the cornerstone of knowledge-sharing

When an enterprise wants to create new value for itself and its customers, having a "good overview" is a key criterion. Mainly because this is the only way the enterprise can ensure that the customer receives optimal individual treatment and service.

In a highly competitive marketplace, the customer is a scarcity factor. In this environment, it is important to utilise every customer contact to retain and develop customer relationships. Every employee in the enterprise is thus responsible for the customer. It is a question of making sure that the customer is satisfied - and of listening to what the customer has in mind. To ensure optimal working conditions, all the information about the customers should be easy to access for all employees in the enterprise.

Managing this knowledge-sharing in the modern enterprise can be a great challenge. And without the use of IT, it is simply impossible. Especially tools such as CRM software, data warehousing and data mining are important elements in a comprehensive CRM system (II).

To build a corporate culture in which knowledge-sharing is the rule rather than the exception places great demands on both enterprise management and employees (III).

Creating more value

Therefore we can conclude that enterprises invest in CRM systems for the following main reasons:

- The customer is a scarcity factor
- The need for effective communication to break through the noise barrier
- The sharing of knowledge in the enterprise

The result is the ability to create more value through an effective targeting of enterprise resources for the basis of its existence - namely the customers.

This is in perfect harmony with the general tendency to focus on a profitable growth of turnover rather than reduce expenditures.

An analysis of the most successful European companies also demonstrates that when turnover increases by 1% more than expected, the value of their shares will rise by an average of 7%. Such an increase in *Shareholder Value* is seldom achieved through cost-cutting alone. No enterprise has ever become successful by cost-cutting alone.

Effective utilisation of enterprise resources is at the heart of CRM and moves the focus from *Share of Market* to relationships, *Share of Wallet* and *Strategic Customer Relationship Management*, also called *Share of Life*.

Questions for the reader:

- How can a CRM system support your company?
- Is your company a noise sender?
- Do the customers know your company?
- Does your company know the customers?
- Is your company's knowledge of customers
  - Up-to-date?
  - Properly stored?
  - In demand?
- Are your company's marketing efforts utilised optimally?
- How many new customers do your marketing efforts produce?
- What does a new customer cost?
- Does your company have set methods and routines which are used when you implement campaigns?
- How are campaigns evaluated?
- How are *"lessons learned"* passed on to the next campaign?

Notes:

I   *As mentioned in Chapter 1*

II   *See figure MIE*

II   *See Chapter 4*

The Challenges
of Introducing CRM

"You should treat your employees
the same way
as you would like to treat
your customers"

Walt Disney

In the previous chapters, we discussed the CRM concept and the enterprise's basis for acquiring a CRM system. CRM deeply affects the way the enterprise functions, and in this chapter we will examine the interaction between a CRM strategy and the enterprise's internal processes. We will also examine the change management required to make the enterprise customer-oriented.

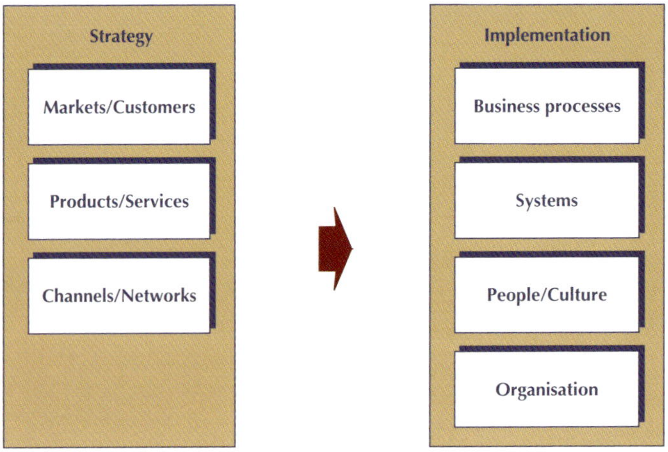

Figure 4.1 CRM: Strategy and implementation

The CRM strategy

The CRM strategy should always be the decisive factor. Far too often, an enterprise begins a CRM implementation process without focusing on the strategy, because the enterprise considers its strategy to be "in place" or "good enough" to build on. Unfortunately, far too often these assumptions prove wrong. Then when the enterprise discovers that its strategy was incorrect, the basis for the success of the CRM implementation also falls apart. Only in the best of cases does the enterprise reach its goal. Usually the implementation period grows longer and longer, while the cost of implementation continues to multiply.

In connection with the preparation of a CRM strategy, it is important (as shown in figure 4.1) to carefully consider how the introduction of CRM will affect the enterprise's markets and customers, products and services - as well as its channels and networks. In the following section, we shall examine these areas.

Markets and customers

The introduction of CRM will quite naturally change the enterprise's view of its markets and customers. Strategically, CRM can open completely new markets and, as a result, the enterprise must say goodbye to that part of its customer portfolio which is not loyal or profitable.

Company management should be aware of this right from the start, when the strategy is being determined. During implementation, it is important, for example, to follow up and thus ensure that the selected line is implemented. One way is to introduce team-based goals (in accordance with the CRM strategy) for the results one wishes to achieve in terms of selected customers.

Products and services

One goal in connection with the introduction of CRM is to create direct links between selected customers and the enterprise's production and the R&D departments. In this way, information concerning the effective use of products and services can be used to optimise efforts in production and R&D. The CRM strategy thus creates the groundwork for improving the enterprise's ability to innovate - and ensures that improvements and renewal of products and services are implemented in accordance with customer needs and preferences.

Channels

Enterprises typically use more than one channel to reach their customers. Some examples of channels are: Sales representatives in the field, call centres, the Internet, the extranet, retail chains, wholesalers, etc
The CRM strategy outlines guidelines for the channels in terms of:

- How customers should be serviced across channels. The enterprise must have a consistent picture of the customer across channels. Likewise, the customer must have a consistent picture of the enterprise across channels.
- How customers are to be supported in choosing the best channel(s) for their needs and preferences.

The CRM strategy is the decisive factor in these situations and determines how far the enterprise will go. Cultural differences across channels, rivalry and channel conflicts can act as direct barriers in relation to the implementation of CRM. Therefore it is important that the enterprise ensures an effective communication of the strategy to everyone involved at an early stage in the process.

Implementation

The above strategic, decision-making areas determine the ambition level of the changes to be implemented. They also set the scene for how the four areas shown in figure 4.2 (business processes, systems, organisation, people and culture) will be affected by the implementation of a CRM strategy. These areas are inter-dependent and, in principle, one cannot change without affecting the other. The chosen method of implementation should provide an overview of these interdependencies - and manage the ways in which they affect one another.

Business processes

The fact that things take time often influences the ambition level in terms of the business process side. The starting point should be a desire to introduce the most effective CRM processes. Conditions such as implementation time frame, resources, the level of employee skills, and the will to change often limit the speed of the process so it can be necessary to divide the implementation into phases.

Consequently, it is a critical success criterion for CRM implementation to determine if and how much enterprise business processes can and will be changed. Which areas will remain unchanged? Which will be automated? And which will be completely replaced by new processes to make the CRM strategy a reality? Automating "the old way of working" will not help the enterprise succeed in the battle for customers.

In order for an enterprise to function smoothly as one unit in terms of its customers, it is a prerequisite that everyone in the enterprise share the same information and knowledge about customers. The introduction of business processes designed for knowledge-sharing is a clear prerequisite for a successful CRM strategy. Enterprise employees must learn to collect, use and share information in order to create real value for the customer (see figure 3.6 for details of the conditions surrounding knowledge-sharing).

It is important, however, to realise that no systems are yet available - in terms of functionality - which are able to fully support the CRM concept. So it is important, right from the start when the strategy is being formulated, to have an eye on possible CRM systems to ensure that the strategy can be implemented in practice. On the other hand, the enterprise should not let itself be controlled by technology - the strategy should be the controlling factor. In other words, the introduction of advanced data warehousing and data mining tools are useless if the enterprise has not reached the stage in the CRM process in which it already has large amounts of data and the need for advanced analyses.

Systems

IT architecture and system performance are two great challenges in connection
with the implementation of CRM. The desire to achieve a consistent and uni-
form treatment of the customer (the enterprise's face to the world) means that
the implementation process must take place across departments and geographi-
cal borders. The enterprise should consider whether its present IT architecture
can support the CRM software system. And also how the CRM system will operate in conjunction with the enterprise's current back office systems. If the enterprise is geographically dispersed, the CRM system should be able to be linked
to several servers and types of servers - and the transmission speed between the
different servers should also be considered. In addition, it must be decided
which information will be considered "local" and which information will be
"global". If the enterprise decides to link to remote workers in the field, can
their PCs handle the amount of data and the data exchange requirements of the
central CRM system?

In Chapter 8, we shall look more closely at the different suppliers of CRM
software - and the flexibility and configuration potential of these systems.

Organisation

The implementation of CRM systems breaks down the boundaries between the
enterprise's customer-related functions and its internal departments. This places
new requirements on the way in which tasks are handled. In this connection, it
is vitally important to the success of a CRM implementation that the necessary
organisational changes are made. Otherwise the CRM solution will not be solid
ly grounded in the enterprise - and organisational barriers will hinder its effectiveness.

After CRM implementation, enterprise operations will be influenced by the
introduction of team-based sales and through the decentralised data collection
of the sales, service and marketing departments. In addition, customer-oriented
employees instead of the support functions will now be feeding information
directly into the CRM system.

The organisation will also be affected by the fact that CRM implementation
brings in new channels such as call centres with all the new job roles, departments and reference lines in the organisation.

People and culture

Ensuring the right corporate culture is without question the greatest single challenge in connection with implementing a CRM strategy.

We have described CRM as the "1 to 1" relationship. The customer, however, as the "multi-individual" has many different relationships to the enterprise. If

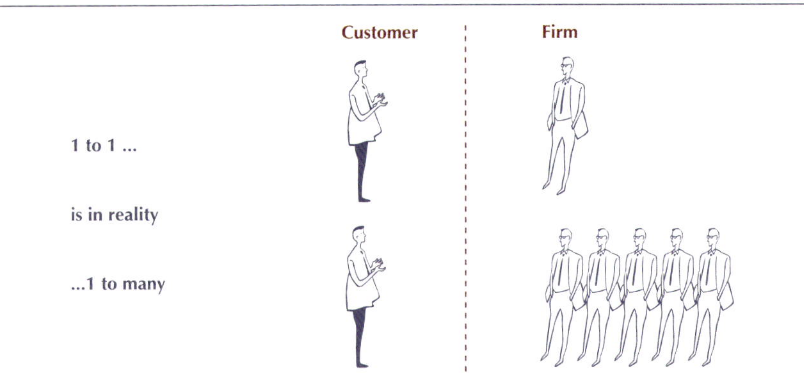

Figure 4.2: 1 to 1 is in reality 1 to many

these relationships are to endure and grow, all employees must meet this
"multi-individual" as a prized and valued customer. In reality, in CRM there are
really "1 to many!" relationships (see figure 4.2).

This "1 to many" relationship and "one face to the world" concept is at the
heart of the cultural change which the enterprise must go through of necessity
to make the CRM strategy a reality. No matter at what point the customer
makes contact with the enterprise, s/he must have the feeling of meeting "one
face". The most important task of management is to guarantee and advocate
this cultural change when CRM is implemented and during the related phases
of change management.

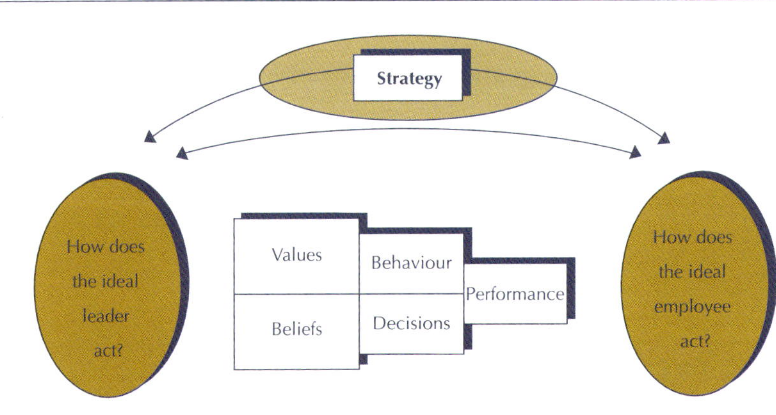

Figure 4.3: The enterprise culture, CRM value basis

Experience demonstrates that enterprises consistently underestimate how comprehensive the requirements of a CRM strategy are to change the enterprise culture. The difference between the present culture and the culture the enterprise is striving towards can be so great that it may be better to divide the implementation into several phases or stages.

Figure 4.3 can be used by the enterprise to set its future cultural goals and to compare them with the present situation.

As part of the process of defining the new culture, a description should be made of the way in which the ideal future employee will act (as part of the team) in showing "one face to the world". The next step should be to describe how management, by means of their behaviour, should act to stimulate the desired attitudes in employees. This description of managerial behaviour refers to the common values and attitudes which enterprise management uses - through his/her actions - to influence the organisation.

The premise here is that if enterprise management is logical and consistent in its behaviour, these actions will affect the behaviour and decision-making processes of the employees.
In this way, the behaviour of employees will be consistent towards the customers and support the CRM strategy.

The development of competencies plays an equally important role in this connection. The CRM strategy usually places the employee in a new and more demanding role. The employee becomes part of a wider perspective in the enterprise and its customer relationships - and this can give rise to the need for the upgrading of professional skills. In extreme cases, the enterprise may have to replace certain employees.

A particularly bad example encountered in England where a retail chain in the early '90s implemented a loyalty concept comprising a loyalty card, among other things. The chain had made the strategic decision to initiate more targeted communication and dialogue with its customers. This meant that focus moved from mass communication to direct mail as knowledge of customers built up. The marketing department with its 26 employees had difficulty adjusting to the change and in the course of one year, all 26 employees were replaced.

To implement such a process is not without challenges. It requires courage and a clear attitude to where we want to go. Or, to avoid drastic consequences, a clear attitude must exist towards change management and HR development.

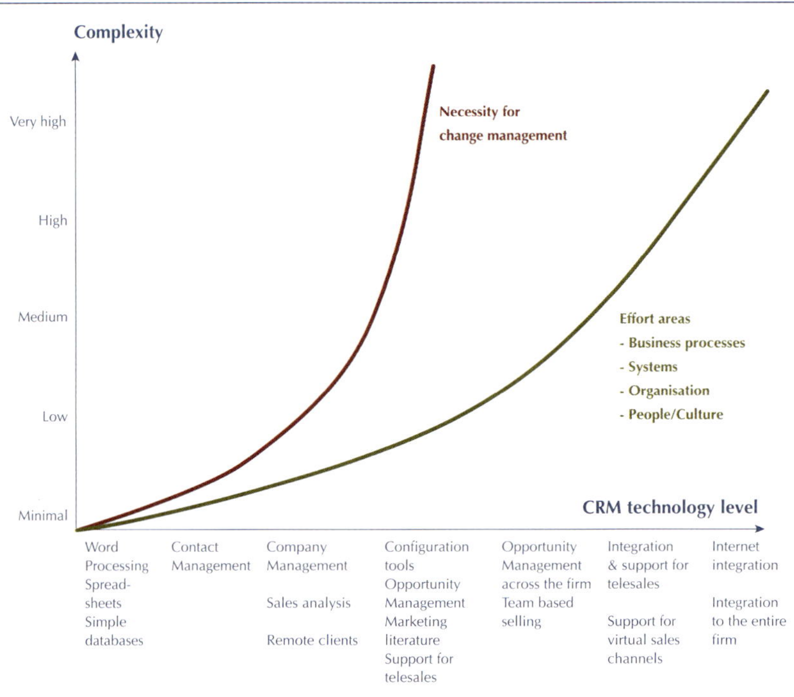

Figure 4.4: Requirements to change management

The following section describes how such changes can be carried out.

Implementation requires effective change management

It would be naive to believe that an investment in CRM software systems alone can change the way an enterprise handles its customers. It often requires comprehensive changes throughout the entire enterprise, which is why strong change management is necessary when CRM is implemented.

The more ambitious a CRM strategy, the more complex is the CRM software that is required. And thus the implementation process also becomes more complex. See figure 4.4. The more technologically advanced the CRM solution is, the greater its influence on the internal dimensions of the enterprise. But in fact, the need for change management is already present even in cases with relatively simple technical levels of CRM solutions.

Experience demonstrates that one of the most common cost-cutting areas in CRM project budgets is change-related activities such as internal communication, team-building, training, etc. As a result of these cuts, the risk associated with CRM implementation becomes unnecessarily high - and the benefits of the CRM investment does not in the final analysis live up to expectations.

In Chapter 5, we offer some guidelines for the implementation of CRM systems. It is our hope that these guidelines, together with the above, will provide inspiration and help improve the implementation of a CRM solution in your company.

Questions for the reader:

- What is your company's CRM strategy?
- How is this CRM strategy expressed in the market, products, service and sales channels?
- Is it necessary to change the corporate culture in relation to the introduction of a CRM project in your company?
- How great an influence does the CRM strategy has on your company's implementation dimensions (processes, systems, people and culture, and organisation)?
- How much of the project's budget has been set-aside for change-related activities?

Chapter 5

The Practical implementation of CRM

"Only the one who
does not try anything in practice,
can avoid mistakes"

Vladimir Lenin

When implementing CRM, there are many pitfalls. Often, the benefits promised by systems suppliers are not realised in practice, even though the "right" system has been chosen.

Why do things sometimes go wrong? And why are many companies not able to achieve the performance breakthrough that lives up to their investments in technology?

Anchoring - many regard the implementation of IT systems as an isolated process within the boundaries of the IT department alone. In practice the implementation projects are change projects that transform the effected part of the company into a new situation. Therefore, it is of utmost importance that the implementation project is anchored within a high level of the organisation and outside the IT department.

Resource needs - the necessary resource allocation of an implementation is usually underestimated. This applies to the number of resources as well as to the qualification needed.

Acceptance, lack of will to change and an over focus on the present situation, instead of the desired future outcome, results in huge extra costs or in the worst case scenario lack of the business improvement planned.

Unrealistic Expectations - normally, following the sale of a CRM system, creates unrealistic expectations with regard to both implementation project as well as business improvements. As a starting point a new system does not deliver any improvement advantages, if the business process, installation, are redesigned simultaneously.

Lack of sufficient training - the importance of a thorough and detailed training programme to the end users is normally overlooked. Furthermore, the cross-functional dependencies result in everybody using the same system and data. At the same time, that the training is planned to take place, the system is being launched. This is at a time when project resources are occupied, that these results are visible after a period of wrong or under-capacity, which in return results in unreliable information from the system. They can easily start a vicious cycle.

What some of these companies forget is that these are just tools which are supposed to help the organisation and its employees to create more value for customers and the owners of the enterprise. In some cases, the technology has quite simply dislodged the organisation and its business processes and employees, which obviously affects the profitability of its investments in technology.

"If, a decade ago, we had had a greater understanding of the business and organisational dynamics of technology, I think we would now have an even greater payback from our investment in it. In my experience, the new systems that work best are those that are aligned not only with the business but also with the way people think and work."

Bob L. Martin, C.E.O. of Wal-Mart Stores
Source: PricewaterhouseCoopers study 1997

Regardless of the extent of the system implementation, it is necessary to have a strong business focus to ensure the necessary change in processes, organisation, people and culture. It is naive to believe that the introduction of a new CRM system will bring improvements if work conditions are left unchanged. The equation below illustrates the problem:

NT +OO = EOO
New Technology + Old Organisation = Expensive Old Organisation

Doing things the same way typically carries marginal improvements. On the other hand changes concerning processes, organisations, people, and culture are determining facts of gaining large effectiveness improvements.

In connection with implementation, the 20 guidelines below can help. These guidelines will be examined under four main categories:

- Business-oriented solutions
- Project management
- Change management
- Implementation strategy and planning

Business-oriented solutions

1. Set precise goals

As mentioned earlier in this chapter, it is important that a CRM solution is business-oriented. This means that the solution should reflect the way in which the enterprise wishes to work in the future. In order to do this, it is necessary to go back to the enterprise's CRM strategy for "guidelines" in order to develop and implement a CRM solution. The CRM strategy should be supplemented with concrete goals which can be used as reference points during the implementation process and which can also function as success criteria for the finished CRM solution.

2. Involve all affected departments

The heads of the departments that are affected by the implementation should be involved. They should, from the start, understand the necessity of reaching an agreement concerning implementation goals since they are externally controlled. At the same time, it should be emphasised that the success of the process depends on the active involvement of the managers. This can be in the form of investing resources (e.g., business specialists) and in their willingness to "sell" the change internally in the organisation.

3. Use the best employees in the enterprise

It is necessary to involve the employees who best understand the business in the process. These business experts, in the role of process owners, must help define and set the business processes in co-operation with the CRM technicians. In other words, they must help define the CRM system's functionality, screen overviews, report formats, etc.

The advantage of involving employees as process owners is that the solution will almost certainly, in terms of functionality, live up to the daily requirements of company users. In addition, these process owners, in conjunction with the department heads, can act as front figures and help sell the change process to the organisation.

Project management

4. Influence the organisation

Change management is a central element in project management. Today CRM software systems build on new ways of thinking, which many organisations do not support. *"Team-based selling"* is a good example because in this type of selling, the sales representatives no longer act as individual hunters, but rather as a party of hunters, supported by the rest of the organisation. Naturally this places new demands on how the sales force co-ordinates sales activities and shares information, which previously was the individual sales representative's "life insurance". If, during the change process, these conditions are not taken into consideration, implementation may meet resistance from employees and the business value of the implementation may be significantly reduced.

5. Co-ordinate with other enterprise initiatives

Project managers are also responsible for co-ordinating the CRM project with other enterprise activities and projects.

In the case of large projects or when several projects are being implemented at the same time, experience shows that using a project manager is a good idea.

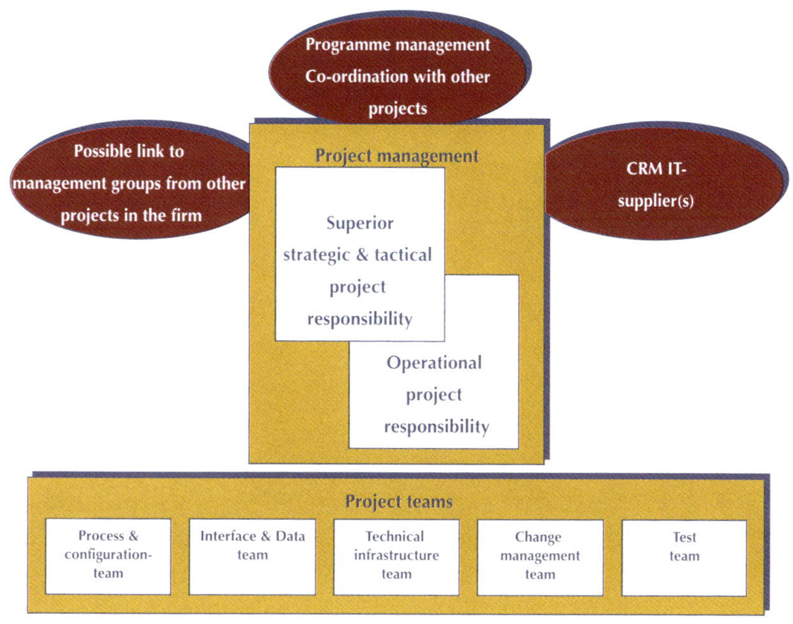

Figure 5.1: Typical project organisation

The project manager's main task is to co-ordinate the different projects such as ERP, e-business and/or CRM projects.

Figure 5.1 shows the organisation of a project that includes both CRM and IT project implementations.

When putting together a project organisation, we must include all the people in the enterprise who are involved in the project. External parties such as CRM-IT suppliers and external consultants should also be included in the project organisation. However, the overall strategic management of the project must always be the responsibility of the enterprise itself.

6. Follow project progress carefully

Despite the fact that good planning is crucial when it comes to ensuring the success of a project, many mistakes are made in this area. Often the enterprise discovers too late that the project plan is not functioning properly. The project may seem to be moving forward because there is a lot of activity - and important deadlines are still far away in the future. Miscalculations may occur, but do not seem serious. Gradually as the project progresses past the various mid-way stations, a picture begins to emerge of the remaining tasks (such as change management); but this does not cause management to assign more employees to the project either. Unfortunately in cases like this, the strategic concept will disappear and the solution will not be sufficiently anchored in the enterprise.

Time after time it has been demonstrated that the unexpected happens. That is why it is necessary to continually follow up and adjust the plan in relation to the original project goals.

There are numerous reasons for project delays. Some are legitimate and good, but others are a direct result of the lack of precise planning or simply no planning at all. Merely to draw up a plan is not necessarily to solve the problem, but it is also of major importance to follow up the plan with work. Said in another way "Plan the work and work the plan".

According to the original project goals, the next step would be to follow up the process improvements in relation to the plan with the necessary adjustments, paying attention to the other adjustments that took place around the project from the beginning.

Keep in mind that there is a difference between spent time and improvements in the project when the time comes to follow up on the project plan.

7. Respect interfaces, conversions and data transfer

The risk of insufficient planning is especially great when it comes to the development of interfaces, converting and transfer of existing data. In some cases, these areas themselves are in fact the project.

If the converted data is not in order and the necessary interfaces do not have sufficient capacity, the system will not take off. Quality insurance of data conversion as well as performance tests of the interfaces must therefore be undertaken as early as possible in the process.

The general performance of the system, including system tests, is another critical point that requires expert know-how. If a sales person in the field is going to be able to obtain the maximum benefit from his/her laptop, the transfer of data must be fast and easy.

In connection with general performance, it is a prerequisite that the hardware has the right dimensions.

8. Wide involvement

Already at an early stage of the project, it is necessary to involve a greater part of the organisation than just the process owners. This is because it requires time to adjust to the changes brought about by CRM. *"Best practice"* shows that best results are achieved if 10-40% of the employees are involved.

Employees can participate in the development work or in hands-on meetings. In this way, they are able to learn about the system and hear how it will affect their daily work.

Consultants who are hired to manage the main part of the development and implementation work must understand and have experience in this CRM implementation phase.

If employees are not involved, it is often difficult to ensure the necessary commitment to using the CRM software system. In the long term, this will affect the survival of the solution. Questions such as ownership of basic data, updating, etc. may also cause many problems if employees do not understand the changes right from the start.

Change management

9. Find a sponsor

The project needs a sponsor whose personal goals are directly linked to the success of the project. The sponsor can help identify the resources and reduce the resistance of employees. In addition, a sponsor ensures that the system will survive once the consultants have left the enterprise.

The best sponsors are often found in top management. Because of their positions, they have enough influence to find the necessary resources and accelerate the decision-making process. At the same time, they are able to co-ordinate the process with other change initiatives and make important decisions. Sponsors are especially effective when changes are to be communicated to employees. By participating actively in the process, they appear as project ambassadors - and when the changes are to be sold internally, these ambassadors can help employees understand the project vision, thus positively influencing employee perception of the project.

10. Speed up progress through a sense of urgency

It is the responsibility of management to create a sense of urgency and decisiveness to give the project the impetus necessary to ensure ongoing progress based on the project vision and guidelines.

Management's direct involvement in the project and ongoing communication about the significance of the CRM initiative is decisive for the success of the project.

11. Make it attractive to participate in the project

In large projects, the changes at times will require the full involvement of certain employees. To create an effective work climate and to make it attractive to participate in the project, employees who are involved should know what their new positions in the organisation will be after the changes. The project must not be used as a place to park "difficult" employees.

12. Communicate continually with interested parties

Communication is one of the most important ingredients when it comes to developing understanding for a CRM solution. From the start, change should be presented as aimed towards the business side and not the IT side. Employees must understand that the enterprise is initiating the project to achieve business benefits in the form of loyalty, cross-sales, improved customer service, etc., and that all activities aim to maintain the competitiveness of the enterprise - and its ability to retain competent employees.

During the project, participants will come into contact with large parts of the organisation - and they are an important group when it comes to communications. All these people should therefore have a good understanding of the whole project and be able to answer general questions such as: 1) Why is this necessary? And 2) how is it going to benefit the company and me?

The following tips sum up our experience with communication:

- When choosing communicators, the enterprise should be selective. These people should be well respected and perceived as reliable sources of information.
- Enterprise "jungle drums" should be avoided because they can be difficult to control.
- Employee understanding of the project must be kept up to date.
- There should be a steady stream of communication. Management should not be afraid to repeat key messages.
- Middle managers are good communicators and at the same time important supporters of the project.
- Areas which employees experience as "insecure" should be identified through communication and HR.
- Employees should have the opportunity to come forward with feedback and ideas through "show & tell" meetings.
- "Picture language" should be used to avoid too many details.
- All information about the project should be collected in a database and made available to all employees.

Communication does not come just from top management and the project team. Employee attitudes and their acceptance of the CRM solution are strongly influenced by other employees in the organisation, for example by a special employee who has the relevant professional and personal qualifications. The project team should therefore at all times throughout the project identify those influential people whose support is necessary for the success of the project. In situations where the person's support is not forthcoming, the team should try to find out what can be done to change that person's attitude.

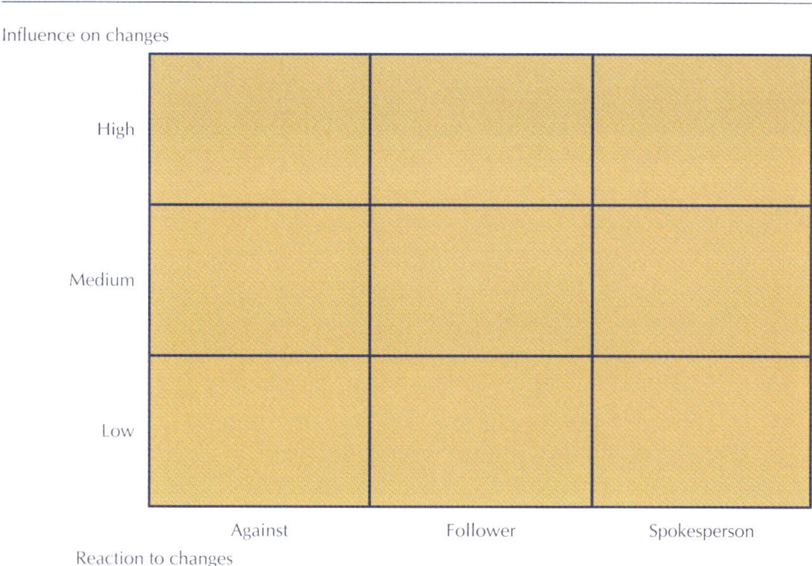

Figure 5.2: Stakeholder Management[1]

In order to send the right messages to the right people, planning of communication must be guided by the individual's position in relation to the project. The model above can be used for this purpose.

The model is based on the expected reactions to change. Advocates of the project should be identified just as individuals, and groups who resist change in relation to the CRM project should be identified. The communication plan should be checked against the knowledge or "power" which these individuals and groups have in relation to the changes. Individuals or organisational units that are found in the upper right hand corner of the chart can be used with advantage as spokespersons. In this way, their position and attitudes can be used to influence other individuals and units in the right direction.

At the same time, those who are high to the left on the chart are an important goal for communication and change management. If their resistance is ignored, it could affect the success of the project.

13. Keep a steady head (stay cool!)
Experience shows that project managers typically go through several emotional phases, as shown in figure 5.3 below.

At the start of the project, participants will be optimistic and generally have high expectations. During this period, expectations should not be raised too much. Management must control employee expectations and not oversell

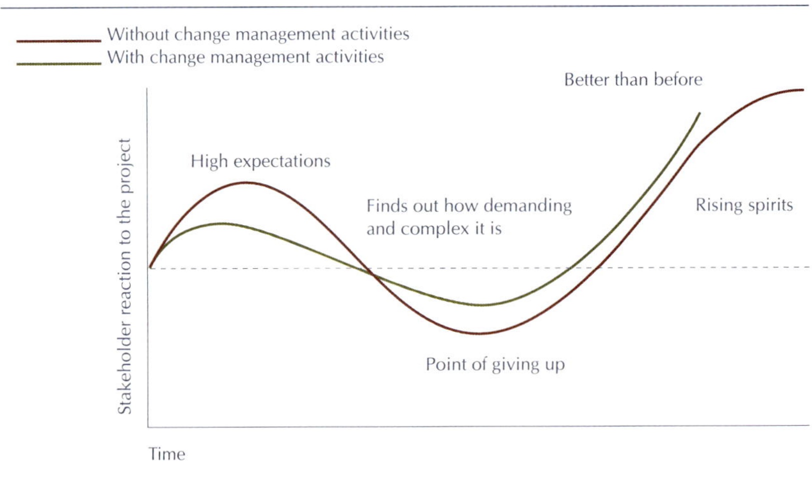

Figure 5.3: Employee reactions to change

the project. These high expectations typically disappear when the parties invol-ved discover how much energy a CRM project demands. In addition, the com-plexity of the project increases at the beginning of the project and this causes a further loss of interest - and in the worst case a sense of defeat. During this phase, communication plays a decisive role. If the enterprise can reap so-called *Quick-Wins* from the project, it is a good idea to save them until this phase of the project to keep up the momentum.

After this defeatist phase, the parties involved have usually passed the first midway stations on the journey. Then the level of expectation rises again as the CRM-IT solution begins to take shape. The dotted line in figure 5.3 shows how a strong focus on change management can influence employee reactions throughout a project. It reduces the fluctuations of the curves and makes imple-mentation more effective.

14. Do not save on training and education

Training both project participants and users is a prerequisite for a successful project. And only through training can the enterprise ensure that all parties in-volved know what to expect in terms of the solution of their particular tasks.

All too often, the enterprise overlooks the fact that not all employees have the necessary general IT skills and that only few understand the CRM concept. The first step of training should therefore give the target audience a business understanding of CRM. After that, attention can be directed towards IT. In par-ticular, lack of IT know-how often creates a situation in which employees feel insecure and unsure of themselves. Rumours about change increase this uncer-tainty - and training becomes ineffective. Planned activities should therefore fully meet employee needs for training. Employees approve of the necessary training when management creates the proper environment for it.

Only few people are able to absorb everything they hear during a traditional training session. Various teaching methods may be used to promote retention of information. Training could take place in the classroom, as *on-the-job*, or as *computer-based* training. When employees learn new skills, their self-esteem increases, they feel more secure and have more self-confidence.

The results of training programmes improve when the teachers actively involve their students. This means that training programmes should be as inter-active as possible - and preferably relate as much as possible to the employees' everyday work situation. And if employees are allowed to test the new enter-prise systems on their own PCs, their sense of familiarity can be increased.

In addition, key employees who become involved in the project must also be trained. If this is not done at an early stage in the process - preferably in connection with the formation of the project team - it will probably be difficult to define enterprise requirements to the new CRM software system.

The implementation strategy and plan

15. Consider using Rapid Application Design (RAD)
Many things must be taken into consideration when defining an implementation strategy. The risks of the various strategies differ greatly, and this is often closely connected to the resources which the enterprise has at its disposal. It is impor-tant, for example, that the project's ongoing design work is evaluated on the basis of how the finished solution will live up to the CRM strategy. Thus it is important to focus on functional requirements and seek a reasonable technical solution. Perhaps not the most advanced solution in the technician's eyes, but a solution that offers a good return on investment (ROI).

In this connection, good results have been achieved with Rapid Application Design (RAD). The RAD method differentiates itself from traditional implemen-tation methods (see the end of this chapter) in that the analysis, design and con-struction phases are carried out simultaneously. In practice this means that no time is wasted in envisioning a final process solution that cannot be supported by the chosen CRM system. In brief, the method comprises small loops in which the individual parts of the CRM processes that are to be supported are described and *re-engineered* when necessary. Immediately afterwards, these processes are tested in relation to the functionality of the selected CRM software system. Next, a pilot is constructed to test user reactions to the selected solu-tion. This process is repeated again and again until all the relevant processes have been covered. To utilise this method requires employees who have a thorough knowledge of process analysis, system design and hands-on experience in system configuration - as well as a complete overview of the extent of the CRM strategy.

16. The profitability of implementation

Choosing to implement a solution in every corner of the organisation is not necessarily optimal. The acquisition of hardware, software, training programmes, the development of local interfaces, etc. requires significant investments. A good tactic is to choose those parts of the organisation that will reap the greatest benefit from implementation and chose them for the first wave of implementation. A carefully selected pilot implementation might well finance the following CRM implementation in the whole organisation.

17. Avoid over-specialised solutions

When the enterprise tries to meet all the demands of functionality that the process owners want to introduce, it runs the risk of customising the CRM software beyond its ability. Very few systems on the market are flexible enough to allow such a high degree of freedom. CRM systems, which are highly customised can quickly become a very costly affair.

It is therefore always a good idea to challenge the demands and specifications of the specialists to see if the same efficiency could be achieved by means of other methods or processes.

Experience shows that those highly customised CRM systems in particular cause difficulties when they are upgraded to later software versions. Many of the CRM-IT suppliers in the analysis section of this book have taken this factor into consideration and have kept the configuration part of their systems separate from the system codes. In this way, all configuration changes are collected in a separate file that can be reused in the new system after an upgrade. Special coded changes will typically be lost in an upgrade of a new version; therefore it is necessary to make a new code once more. Careful documentation of the configuration and changes in code are a vital element in every CRM-IT implementation.

18. Be critical in choice of method

Thanks to its experience with CRM implementation, PricewaterhouseCoopers has prepared a method for integrating IT with the business aspects of a solution. For years PricewaterhouseCoopers has been using a similar method for the implementation of ERP systems.

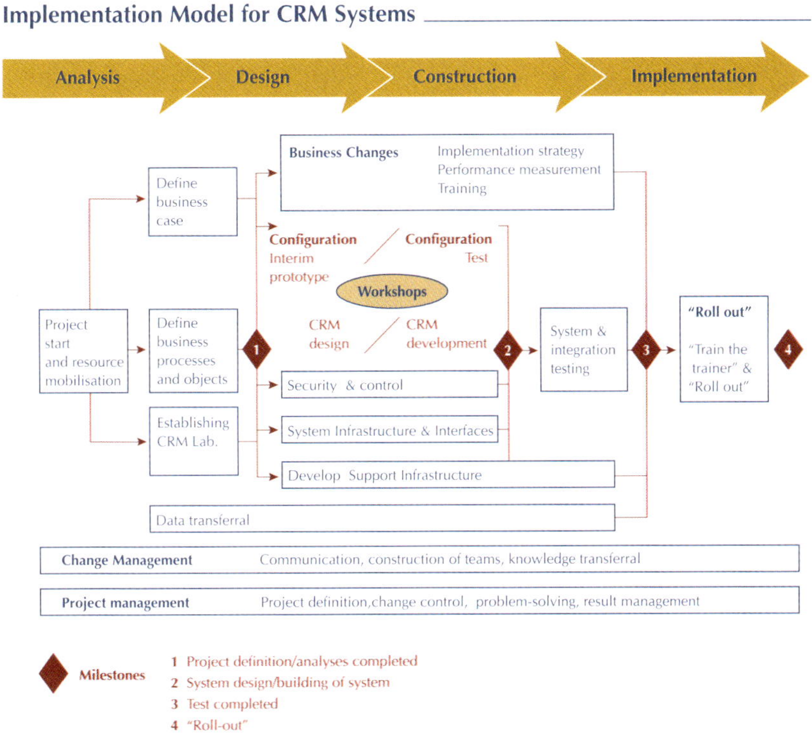

Figure 5.4: CRM System Management Method

19. Prepare implementation waves

In connection with dividing the implementation of CRM into different waves, the different parts of the organisation have a right to know when it will be their turn. Before the start of a wave, time must be set aside for installing the hardware, and the enterprise should be sure that the employees have the necessary CRM and IT skills.

As a forerunner of the project, employees in the selected areas must be made ready for the changes and given the necessary basic understanding of how the project will proceed.

20. Focus on Quick Wins

To promote a willingness to change, top management normally needs to quickly show some *"Quick Wins"* to the organisation to convince employees that the CRM efforts are worth the effort.

Quick Wins are convincing sales arguments for a CRM project to interested parties within the organisation. Thus management often tries to achieve several large *Quick Wins* at the start of a project to create the necessary momentum during the rest of the project period. In some cases, the improved earnings achieved by Quick Wins at the beginning of a project will almost pay for the rest of the project. This highlights the importance of utilising *Quick Wins* effectively.

With the above guidelines in mind, a CRM project is on the right track from the start.

Questions for the reader:

- How many people from top management are part of the CRM project steering group?
- Has a visible connection between the enterprise's overall strategy and the CRM project been established?
- Has the company a clear feeling of the benefits which the CRM implementation can create?
- Is it attractive to participate in the CRM project?
- Is the CRM project co-ordinated with other projects in your company?
- Has a training programme with appropriate modules been developed with the project?
- Does the project group communicate regularly inside the company?
- Does the project make use of the participation of recognised and competent business-oriented employees?
- Does the project try to minimise the extent of company-specific customisation?
- Does the project use a well-proven method - and do the project participants understand it?
- How much money is there in the budget for internal communications?

Notes:

I   *Stakeholder Management*
   - Co-ordination of the attitudes, influence and reactions of interested parties in relation to a CRM project.

II   *ERP systems*
   - Enterprise Resource Planning systems, i.e., the enterprise's transaction or back office systems.

Chapter 6

Beginning the CRM Journey

"Shall we pause now and turn our
back upon the road that lies ahead?
Shall we call this the promised land?
Or, shall we continue on our way?
For: "Each age is a dream that is
dying or one that is coming to birth"

Franklin D. Roosevelt

When the enterprise decides to get aboard the CRM train, a long and exciting journey begins. But if the experience is to be positive, the enterprise must be well prepared. Often, it is marketing, sales or customer service that drive the train forward. But many initiatives get off to a bad start because the initiators have not sold the idea to the organisation (see figure 6.1).

CRM - The "Buy-in" process

Figure 6.1: Typical "Buy in" process in connection with the implementation of a CRM strategy

CRM is a strategic decision which must be led by management and have the full support of the whole enterprise. It is therefore crucial for management to anchor the decision and set aside enough resources for the organisation to work seriously with CRM.

Everyone in the enterprise should know about the decision - and it should be made clear what its significance is for the enterprise and the individual employees. The next step is to inform enterprise suppliers as to what the implementation means for them and what expectations and demands will be placed on them in the future.

Many enterprises choose to seek advice from a consulting company when introducing a CRM strategy. Others start the process by choosing possible suppliers, and thereby let the systems control the strategy or, more correctly, let the strategy be adapted to the systems.

If the process is introduced in the latter way, a lot of time is soon spent on product information about the respective systems. All things considered, this is not relevant in a starting phase. Focus should be on the enterprise's strategy - and on what this will demand of the enterprise's business processes. Only later should requirements to the system be considered. Only then can the enterprise begin to look at the systems and suppliers. Once the system has been chosen, implementation can begin.

The enterprise must have resources to carry through the process. Generally, it is a good idea to get inspiration from others who have worked with CRM. It is expensive to acquire this experience by yourself. What is important is to get started, create competitive advantages and harvest the results.

The enterprise should expect investment in software to be multiplied by a factor of two to three. If DKK one million is invested in software, another DKK two to three million should be calculated in connection with the implementation. All this becomes part of the basis of calculation in a cost/benefit analysis. Experience shows that we often underestimate the investment, while overestimating the benefits.

Figure 6.2 below outlines a typical process consisting of a preliminary analysis and the implementation itself. The process ensures the above-mentioned "buy in" from management, employees and business partners.

It is a good idea to bring in consultants for both the preliminary analyses and the implementation. The consultant can function as a sparring partner and bring to the enterprise expert knowledge about the CRM concept. Also during implementation, the consultant can bring practical knowledge concerning systems installation and contribute a method to ensure effective and successful implementation in the enterprise.

Initiating the process

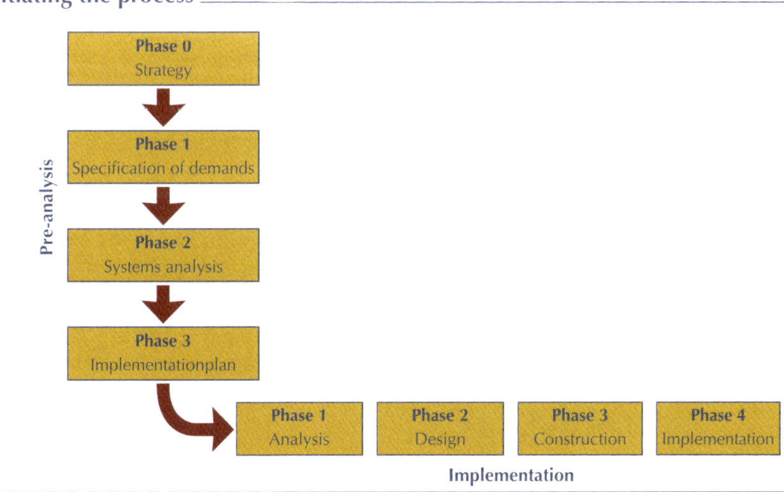

Figure 6.2: Preliminary analysis and implementation phases for a CRM concept

The preliminary analysis contains the strategy, requirements and specifications, the systems analysis, and the implementation plan.

Strategy

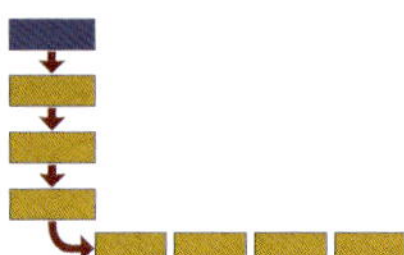

Method: - Interview
- Workshops

Purpose: - Create a CRM strategy for the firm's
"good" overview
- Estimate cost/benefit for the firm when
implementing CRM
- Identify key factors of success:
- Business processes
- Systems
- People & culture
- Organisation
- Identify critical change factors

Result: - Input for specification of demands
concerning the choice of CRM
system including a budget estimate

Specification of demands

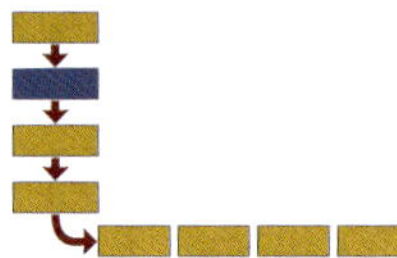

Method: - Interview
- Workshops

Purpose: - Transform the CRM strategy into general
business processes in order to establish
demands for the CRM software
- Establish basis for deciding on a choice of system,
including:
- Connection between cost/benefit
- Match against functional and technical criteria

Result: - Foundation for a CRM systems analysis/
choice of CRM system

Systems analysis

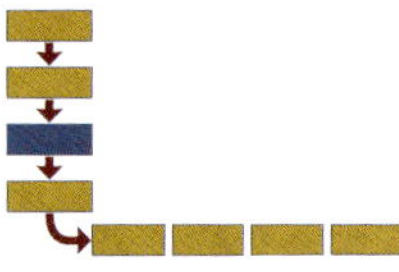

Method: - Interview with suppliers of CRM-systems
- Workshops

Purpose: - Create a foundation for the firm's choice
of CRM system

Result: - The firm is capable of choosing a specific
CRM software system

Implementation plan

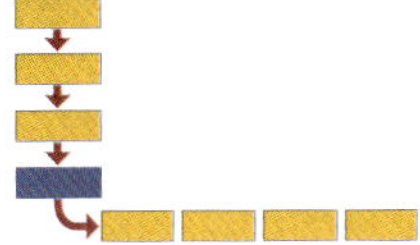

Method: - Interview
 - Workshops

Purpose: - Establishment of a project plan with definitions of:
 - Tasks
 - Milestones
 - Use of resources
 - Describe the organisational structure of the
 project including underlying co-operative relations
 between the firm and external suppliers,
 e.g. consultants
 - Describe a plan for change management, including:
 - Roll-out
 - Training/education
 - Set up framework for the project economy

Result: - Decision on a GO / NO GO for the CRM software
 project based on cost/benefit and
 detailed project/ roll-out plan

Implementation Model for CRM Systems

Questions for the reader:

- Who takes the initiative for CRM concepts in your enterprise?
- Is the management group prepared to support the project through budgeting and human resources?
- How will you cope with the extra strain needed to implement the project?
- Can the enterprise improve sales by, for example, 3% by implementing CRM?
- How quickly could these improvements take place?
- What are the enterprise success criteria?
- Can the enterprise manage the process alone or should it draw on the knowledge and experience of consultants?

Chapter 7

Guidelines for Choosing a Supplier

"Wanting to be a doctor
is wanting to suffer"

Søren Kierkegaard

The market for CRM software has experienced explosive growth in the last few years, with a marked rise in the demand in software for the automation of sales, marketing and service processes. This growth has simultaneously been paralleled by major changes in the supplier side of the market.

Whereas the market was once characterised by many small and relatively undifferentiated suppliers, the tendency today appears to be towards a more concentrated market. Small suppliers offer niche solutions in specific CRM areas, while the big suppliers offer systems solutions with a broader functionality.

The growing focus on CRM software has meant that the global ERP suppliers, like SAP, Baan and Oracle, now promote their own CRM solutions. Other ERP suppliers such as PeopleSoft and J. D Edwards have chosen to enter into official partnership with leading CRM suppliers and thus offer a third party CRM solution which is integrated with their own ERP systems.

In the relationship between supplier and user, it is vital to ensure a certain consensus on the main criteria, which both user and supplier prioritise in the CRM system. As a rule, if the supplier's key criteria correspond with the users', it will be easier to enter into a dialogue.

When choosing a supplier, a user naturally focuses on the actual system, its functionality, price, etc. However, there should also be a strong awareness of the supplier's personal attitude to CRM and commitment to his customers. Some suppliers of the CRM systems have traditionally focused on the sale of software licenses and paid less attention to after-sales customer care. However, a few individual suppliers have modified their payment systems and bonus principles to include long-term performance measurements such as customer satisfaction.

In an analysis of the criteria for choosing suppliers, the Gartner Group has found that from now on there will be a marked difference in the way users and suppliers prioritise the various important aspects in the evaluation of a new system. For example, the user will give high priority to service and support systems, while the supplier will prioritise the opposite.

Criteria for evaluating suppliers ______________________________

Key criteria (year 2002)	User priority	Supplier priority
Functionality	1	4
Longevity	2	1
Service and support	3	6
Architecture and technology	4	3
Design and technology	4	3
Vision	6	7
Partnership	7	2

Source: GartnerGroup Dec., 1998

Choice of CRM supplier

Most CRM systems are very flexible, and for users it can often be difficult to detect where the enterprise gets the best return on investment. To ensure the enterprise gets the maximum utilisation of the systems, here are some guidelines on choosing a CRM software supplier.

These guidelines are divided into five areas:

- Strategy
- Business processes
- Organisation and culture
- Functionalities
- CRM supplier

In relation to figure 6.2 in the previous chapter, the above five areas deal with issues under the headings of requirements/specification and system analysis.

Strategy

1. Agreement between enterprise and supplier
It is a prerequisite for successful co-operation with a software supplier that the supplier has taken his/her own medicine and wants to establish a long-term relationship with customers. In addition, the supplier should support the enterprise's long-term CRM strategy and goals. Make sure this is in order before co-operation is established.

2. Requirements to functionality

A part of the enterprise's CRM strategy will centre on which contact points, or channels to the customer, a CRM software system should support. It could be systems meant to support, for example, the direct sales force, a customer service centre, a web site and, if necessary, external business partners. In relation to the choice of a CRM system, this may mean quickly to discard systems which do not support the chosen channels. Similarly, the selection or rejection of marketing, sales or service functionalities may mean the selection or rejection of certain systems. (See the "Marketing Intelligence Enterprise" model shown in figure 8.1, Chapter 8).

Business processes

3. Does the CRM software system support the enterprise's business processes?
Put pressure on the supplier to ensure that the system supports your enterprise's CRM processes. Unfortunately, this is not always a plain and simple task.

Many CRM software suppliers will always claim that their system supports most of the enterprise's CRM processes. But how much configuration and customisation will be needed for the CRM system to support the processes? Can the system support the processes in an "out-of the box" version entirely without customisation? Will the system need simple configurations - or will the system need coding? These considerations are relevant both in relation to the labour needed for system implementation as well as for future system upgrades in which direct coding and, in some cases, configurations will be lost. Keep in mind that over-specialised solutions should be avoided (see guideline number 17, Chapter 5).

Organisation and culture

4. Involve users in the choice of system
A CRM software system is simply a tool, which is why it will be the employees who decide whether the system works. Therefore, the needs and preferences of future users should be integrated into the process of choosing a system. At times, it is employees in the IT department who "test" and try out the systems instead of the future users. This often leads to the selection of highly technical solutions; business-oriented solutions are often given a lower priority. Involving users at an early stage also has the advantage of making it easier to anchor ownership of the CRM project and the CRM software system in the enterprise.

Insist that the supplier give a demonstration to key employees of a CRM system that is customised to the enterprise and its requirements.

5. User friendliness and flexibility

It is taken for granted today that a CRM system should be user-friendly and flex-ible. Most CRM suppliers use Windows-based systems with a "web-like" inter-face. This does not in itself mean that the system will be user-friendly. User-friendliness means the system can be used intuitively and that the succession of functions is straightforward in relation to enterprise work processes. It should be mentioned in this connection that most systems can be configured to reflect the work processes. The question is simply to what extent it needs to be done, how long it will take, and how many resources will be used for it.

Test user-friendliness by means of CRM systems demonstrations and ask for references where the question of user-friendliness is specifically addressed.

6. Training programmes

A successful implementation of a new CRM system demands employee training. It is crucial that the supplier or hired consultants help the enterprise through this important part of the process. When an employee masters a system it does not necessarily mean that the learning process has been easy. Even though the supplier may say that "you're just a click away from all the information" and the system is easy to operate, it can still take several weeks to learn.

Who can provide training and how much does it cost? Training programmes can be a costly item in relation to the total CRM investment!

Functionality

7. Technology: Take the long view

It could be said, somewhat pointedly, that the rapid development of CRM soft-ware systems means that the moment they become available for sale they are already obsolete. For example, many CRM systems are in a transition phase where traditional client/server solutions are developing towards full browser-based solutions, where access to the application is exclusively via the Internet. Does the supplier have a vision for how the system will develop during the next few years? And does the supplier have the ability needed to carry out these innovations?

8. The cross-border solution

If the CRM solution is to be implemented across national borders, demands will be made to the supplier's CRM system as well as to the supplier's own sales and service organisation. The CRM system should, for example, be able to con-solidate customer data across borders and work with various currencies (includ-ing the Euro) and foreign languages. To ensure implementation and ongoing support of the CRM system, it is desirable that the supplier has a service organisation in the country in question, just as it is desirable to have implementation consultants with hands-on experience at all locations.

Ask the supplier for references on international implementations and on the possibility for consultancy help in this area.

9. Integration with existing software systems

Integration with other enterprise systems has become the rule rather than the exception with CRM implementations. For example, it may be necessary in marketing, sales and services to gather information on customer credit rating from the finance system and, when checking delivery times, to gather information from the warehouse, production and distribution systems. If the enterprise already uses a back office system (ERP) from a supplier who also offers a front office system, it would be natural to investigate these, that is if they have passed through the eye of a needle during the process of choosing a system. The decisive question, then, is whether the solution has the functionalities that match the enterprise's needs.

The majority of CRM suppliers claim that they can integrate with practically all systems, but in practice such a claim should be taken with a grain of salt. Ask for references of existing solutions and for the enterprise's development plans in the area of integration.

Another area that must be touched upon is re-scheduled releases.

Ask for references, running of solutions along with any development plans of an integration area from the supplier.

The IT supplier

10. References

References are the CRM supplier's most important marketing tool and are used in that way! One should not get dazzled by "famous" names on a reference list. Just because a system is used by a major, well-known company, it does not necessarily mean the CRM system is suited to your enterprise. Find out the number of users in the reference. Even though the supplier may refer to an enterprise with 5,000 employees, it is not certain that the system itself is used by more than 10 people. Use the references - and contact the enterprises. Find out about their experience with the CRM system and their co-operation with the CRM software supplier. If possible, visit the names on the reference list and quiz the employees on the system's strengths and weaknesses.

11. Recognised branch and industry solutions

Many CRM software suppliers have specialised in diverse industry solutions that cater to the needs of different branches. As a user, by choosing such "best practice" solutions, you can achieve considerable savings compared to the choosing of a system, which has never before been used in the industry in question. Especially in the CRM systems market, which to all intent and purposes is still in the developmental phase, the well-tested CRM solutions will often eliminate the problems typically experienced during a first-time implementation. Ask for a reference for a live demonstration of an industry solution. Some CRM software suppliers base industry solutions on one installation in the industry in question, whereas other suppliers have more demanding criteria for what they call an industry solution.

The large CRM suppliers normally have many different industry solutions that have been worked out in collaboration with management consulting firms. PricewaterhouseCoopers has in this way collaborated with several CRM software suppliers on the development of industry solutions.

12. Support and service

The support and service of the installed system is a major factor. As a user, it is often crucial that help is never further away than the nearest telephone. Can you get support on the Internet or by e-mail, and is it possible to come in contact with support 24 hours a day (a hot-line with a "follow the sun" principle)? In the worst-case scenario, if the system goes down and the enterprise needs assistance, how is it provided? Price-setting and costs of CRM software suppliers' support and service are further factors which must be taken into account when choosing a system supplier. Moreover, research should be made as to whether the system supplier has the capacity and resources to implement and maintain a satisfactory service level, or whether it would be better to get support and service from a consulting firm.

13. The supplier's financial and business status

The supplier's financial situation says little about the system itself, but a lot about the supplier's own future. Key economic figures will reveal whether the supplier's business is sound and whether it earns enough money to continue investing in its system. Key figures and the supplier's basis of existence are, of course, crucial if the CRM project is to continue for a prolonged period as, for example, with a global CRM roll-out. In such cases, you must be very certain of the supplier's soundness.

14. The supplier's business partners

The implementation part of CRM software systems is a significant and important part of a CRM project. Experience shows that the greatest chance of risk and error in a CRM project typically occurs during implementation. As a result, many CRM software suppliers have found it expedient to work with and build alliances with leading consulting firms. These partnerships normally include joint development and training facilities as well as joint marketing activities. The advantage of this is that the consulting firms' experience with system implementation minimises the risk during the implementation phase, and the CRM software suppliers can focus on their core competence, to develop CRM software systems, while entrusting the rest to experienced consultants.

Ask the supplier if he/she has relationships with leading consulting firms and ask for common references.

15. Price versus performance

In addition to all the points above, a judgement will always have to be made concerning the system's performance versus its acquisition price. Depending on the enterprise's needs, different CRM system types will be of interest.

For some, a Rolls Royce solution will be the only possibility because of the complexity of the work processes, the size of the enterprise and the need for global application. In such cases, focus will inevitably fall on the large, global CRM software suppliers.

On the other hand, other enterprises may need only a stand-alone solution with minimal functionality in just one country.

Another factor in CRM investment is the time horizon. For some enterprises, it can be most advantageous to begin with a smaller solution and then, after a few years, upgrade to a larger system. On the other hand, some enterprises choose a solution with a large, all-inclusive CRM system from the start. Alternatively, other enterprises may choose a large system for the head office and for the largest subsidiaries, and a smaller solution for the more peripheral and smaller subsidiaries. What is important in relation to these choices is that the different solutions work together without any problems.

All the above considerations must be included when choosing a supplier to ensure that the CRM solution, or solutions, support the enterprise's long-term CRM strategy.

Questions for the reader:

- What are your enterprise's systems requirements?
- How well do you know the CRM software market?
- Which suppliers are you focusing on?
- Who in the enterprise will participate in defining the requirements and specifications of the new system?
- What are your expectations to ROI for the new system?
- Will the enterprise use external experts in connection with the implementation of the new system?
- In what areas will the system first be implemented?
- Can you live with a supplier who covers only 80% of your needs, if this solution only costs half of that of a supplier who can meet your need 100%?

Chapter 8

Supplier Analysis

"The important thing
is not to stop questioning"

Albert Einstein

The market for IT-based, integrated marketing, sales and service systems - known as CRM systems - is characterised by a few global and many local suppliers. Our supplier analysis includes both the global market leaders and the most important suppliers in the Nordic markets.

The analysis examines the most important differences in the selected systems and classifies the systems functionalities in relation to enterprise-specific requirements. These classifications are guidelines which should be followed up by demonstrations from the suppliers - and supplemented by thorough cost-benefit analyses. In addition, it is a good idea to consult experts in the area because this can save both time and money.

Setting limits

There are many types of suppliers in the market for integrated marketing, sales and service systems. Many of the smaller providers are niche-oriented, and several of them have specialised in specific sales channels such as telemarketing, one-to-one sales in the field, and Internet sales. Other suppliers try to cover all the areas of the selling function, i.e., marketing, sales and service.

Normally, CRM software systems are divided into the main areas of sales, service and marketing as follows:

- Marketing systems which focus on campaign management and communications, etc.
- Sales systems which support sales personnel, budgets, meeting and resource planning, analysis tools, technology-driven one-to-one marketing/dialogue, direct marketing, mail-merging, etc.
- Service and support systems which include Internet services, call centre systems, tele-systems, field services, etc.

As can be seen in PricewaterhouseCoopers' Market Intelligent Enterprise technology model in figure 8, marketing, sales and service systems touch all functionalities from customer contact point to interface to back office system and data warehousing.

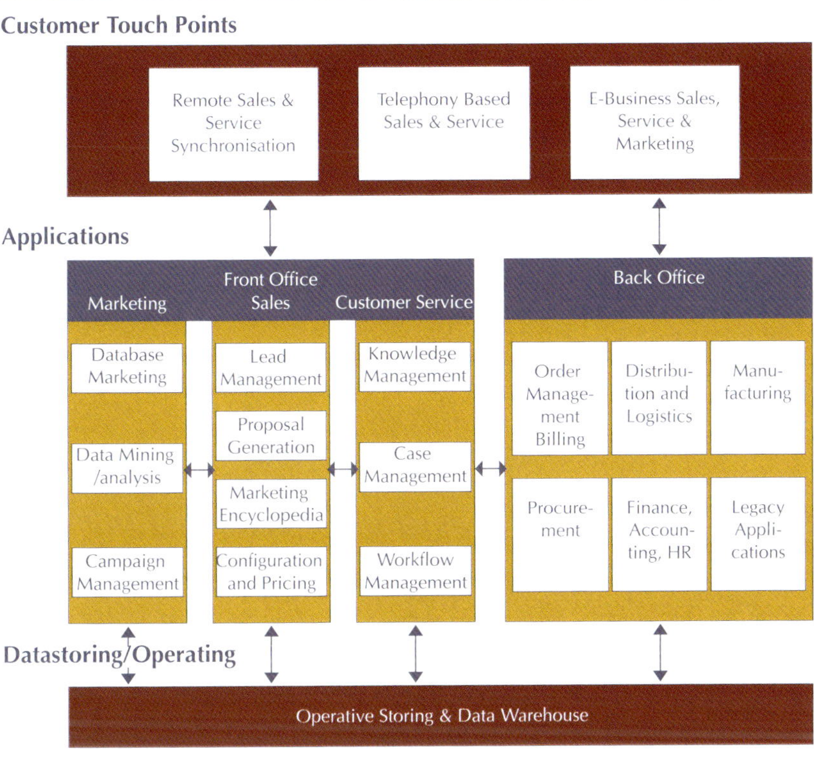

Figure 8.1: MIE model

Source: PricewaterhouseCoopers The Market Intelligent Enterprise (SM)

Most CRM systems offer functions which extend across marketing, sales and service. In the supplier analysis, the CRM systems are mapped out according to the following business-based main groups:

- Segmentation
- Campaigns
- Leads
- Customer data
- Product configuration and contract management
- Marketing tools
- Sales Force Automation
- Resource management
- Analysis tools
- Forecasts

- Other functionalities
- Internet
- Telemarketing, Call Centre and Help Desk

As mentioned in Chapter 7, the choice of system should not just be based on the system's functionality, but also on numerous other important elements such as customer references, training, and educational support. It is also important that the system supports the enterprise's current software and hardware. That is why we have made the following system and enterprise evaluations a part of the analysis.

About the supplier:
- Year founded/year launched
- Strategy
- Number of employees
- Training programmes

About the system/products:
- Back office integration (supported by mainstream technology)
- Database supporting
- Price
- Product development
- Number of users
- Product customisation/development
- User-friendliness

History of use:
- Customer references
- Consultant support/including agreements

The supplier analysis does not include systems which are mainly designed for retailers. In addition, the field service aspect has been toned down in this study. As a result, the following functionalities have not been examined:

- POS Systems
- Shelf space management
- Field service logistics
- Field service implementation
- Category management
  - Product return on investment analysis
  - Product promotion management
  - Cost management

- Product-mix optimisation
- Management of product introductions

The supplier analysis focuses primarily on sales and marketing activities, and secondly on service activities. This implies that the analysis is concentrated on what could be called Customer Service - a service or support which is normally conducted by phone.

This means that all functions and processes that are included in a traditional service are not covered. Therefore, the listed functionalities are only marginally used, if used at all.

- Functionality for handling warrantees and claims.
- Functionality for handling service contracts including coverage.
- Functionality for handling existing installations. (Installed Based Management).
- Functionality for billing of services e.g. quarterly subscription payments along with payments that are not covered by the service agreement.
- Functionality for handling service logistics e.g. spare parts, warehouses, receipt of products for repairs, etc.
- Functionality for handling field service e.g. driving, mounting.
- Functionality for handling in house service e.g. 10000 km check-ups and/or repairs.

Some of the analysed systems offer solutions to the above listed items.

The suppliers in this analysis are listed in the table below:
- Abalon
- Baan
- Caesar
- CDM
- Clarify
- Core Point
- Dialog Manager
- MultiMark
- Oracle Applications
- Prime Response
- SAP
- Siebel
- Software Innovation
- Vantive

Main Groups: How and when can a CRM software system be a benefit?
In the supplier analysis, we have divided the system functionalities into business-based main groupings instead of the systems' main modules - marketing, sales and service. This business-based division makes it much easier to compare the different suppliers in relation to the needs the enterprise is trying to meet via the chosen system.

In the following, we describe each of the individual business-based main groups which will typically be examined when the enterprise, in the pre-analysis stage, tries to identify what the CRM effort should be targeted towards in the beginning:

Main group	Segmentation
CRM software supports	- Relevant communication with customers - Effective utilisation of marketing resources, e.g. more targeted campaigns - Knowledge about the enterprise's customer base - Differentiated service for profitable and non-profitable customers

The noise barrier shows that most enterprises do not use their marketing resources optimally.

Superfluous advertisements come pouring into customer mail boxes. Customers receive advertisements for products they already have and companies get too little response to their efforts. Companies send super offers to "hit and run" customers or are unable to follow up on profitable opportunities in their customer base such as opportunities for extra sales, etc.

Many of these situations could be improved or avoided if companies become more aware of their customers and their needs.

Many CRM software systems offer functions that make it possible for marketing departments to determine the customer groups that should be contacted in connection with a campaign. In this way, the enterprise avoids sending letters to people who have already bought the product or do not need it. This saves marketing resources and improves the image of the enterprise in the customer's eyes.

Segmentation is also of central importance when the enterprise is deciding which customers are core customers and which are not profitable. All customers are not equal. An ABC classification makes it possible to differentiate efforts to the different customer groups. Based on this, one can aim the enterprise's service resources (which are not unlimited) towards the most profitable customers.

Main group	Campaigns
CRM software supports	- Fast and effective campaigns - Integrated and targeted campaigns across enterprise departments - Effective use of marketing budgets - Control and knowledge of the effectiveness of campaigns - Resource management - Utilisation of knowledge from previous campaigns and improved information gathering - Fast reaction to customer opportunities and problems

The CRM system's campaign management tool helps companies maintain control over their efforts towards customers.

A campaign can promote sales, loyalty or just image creation. A campaign can be directed towards a specific customer group for a short period of time or it can go on "forever" and be directed towards all types of customers.

At the beginning of a campaign, a lead is just a potential buyer. Then, depending upon how the lead reacts to diverse efforts (sales calls, customer brochures, phone calls, etc.), the campaign can either end (with or without a sale) or it can move on to the next activity (more information, another sales call, phone calls, cross-selling, etc.).

All activities in the campaign should be filed in a campaign history database where the information can be retrieved and used in connection with later dealings with the customer.

Some CRM systems automatically start a campaign when a specific situation arises. This type of automatic campaign management is a powerful tool for immediately taking advantage of possible sales opportunities or for discovering potential risks of losing a customer. An example might be: An important customer has not purchased anything during the month when the company normally makes purchases. The campaign could then, for example, include a phone call from the key account manager to the enterprise. Perhaps it has even been entered into the system that the key account manager under certain conditions must report to his/her superiors in the enterprise. In addition, a time frame can be included for each part of a campaign. If a deadline is exceeded, a co-ordinator can be notified to follow up on the message. If the contact person is on holiday, the system can be programmed to notify another person. In this way, the system can deal with any problems before they arise and help the enterprise avoid situations which might result in the loss of a customer.

Campaigns are often launched by the marketing department where employees have an intuitive or experience-based knowledge as to which type of campaigns are most beneficial to the enterprise's selling efforts. Supported by a CRM software system, this valuable enterprise resource can be freed to deal with other sales-promoting activities and creative tasks. The support of the CRM system can help in many ways. For example it can ensure that campaigns run perfectly; it can help with analyses of completed campaigns; it can save and reuse knowledge from previous campaigns, and it can ensure consistency in communications from sales personnel, in call centres, letters, e-mails, on the Internet, when invoicing, etc. The application manages analyses, resource management, time frames, information sharing, etc.

Main group	Leads
CRM software supports	- Understanding where in the sales process leads are lost and won - Uncovering enterprise strengths and weaknesses - and competitiveness - Division of leads to sales personnel - Budgeting and precise forecasts of earnings - Control of sales force/more effective sales personnel - Identification of leads

A lead is a potential sales opportunity. A lead can be a previous customer or a completely new customer. Leads are normally given to the sales person or sales team that will follow-up the opportunity and hopefully make a sale.

Leads are followed in a CRM system via a sales funnel. See figure 8.2

Figure 8.2: An example of a sales funnel

At the wide end of the funnel, sales opportunities or leads are registered. Then they are registered every time the lead moves further along in the sales process, for instance, after the first meeting with the customer, after identifying the customer's needs, after giving an offer, after negotiations, and finally after the sale. Throughout the sales process, every potential sales opportunity and probable likelihood of making a sale are registered. This information can be used for sales forecasts by the individual salesman/woman or can be used to make forecasts for the whole enterprise. In addition, the causes and the position of competitors are also registered in connection with won or lost sales.

All this brings about a better understanding of the enterprise's strengths and weaknesses. At the same time, information is obtained as to how well the different members of the sales force manage the various types of leads, which also makes it possible to improve the division of customers among the sales force.

Main group	Customer data
CRM software supports	- Ability to collect the knowledge the enterprise gains from dialogue with customers - Utilisation of the knowledge the enterprise already has - Access to customer knowledge and history and a broad cross-functional use of this knowledge - Loyal customers and relationships with these customers

The customer database is at the heart of the CRM software system and it is the place where all the knowledge which the enterprise has about customers must be registered. Often individual salesmen/women have this information but do not share it with others.

For the customer, it is highly stressful to have to explain a problem over and over again every time s/he speaks to a new employee in the company. If information about customers (e.g. correspondence, scheduled meetings, meeting results, products of interest, problems, strategies toward customers, etc.) is stored in the CRM system instead of in the sales person's head, then the groundwork has been laid for consistent, trouble-free and professional treatment of customers.

Main group	Product configuration and contract management
CRM software supports	- Configuration of products, ability to make offers and draw up contracts quickly - Fewer faults in the product configuration/more professional management of product and price options - Precise delivery dates and service agreements - Options for price differentiation and customer-specific discounts - Preparation of contracts

The CRM system's product and price configuration function make it possible to put together products depending on customer preferences, enabling the enterprise to give price estimates quickly and effectively. This rapid processing of customer inquiries is one of the most important criteria in a customer's decision to make a purchase. A good example could be a bicycle, which the customer wants to assemble him/herself by choosing the specific model, colour, gears, etc. Configuring a PC is another good example.

There are two types of systems for configuring. The hierarchy system which operates with fixed criteria - and the dynamic system in which there is no limitation to the list of criteria (but where there are still limitations in the configuration options - for example that a 22″ wheel cannot be put on a small bicycle). The dynamic model offers better interaction with the customer because it can start with whatever is the most important for the customer and then select the other criteria after that.

Certain enterprises offer a graphic presentation of the finished products. This means, for example, that the customer can see how the finished bicycle s/he has assembled will look.

In the same way, the CRM contract system makes it possible to prepare contracts, including discounts and service agreements, quickly. Again this means less work for the sales force, product managers and middle management. At the same time, the customer perceives his/her treatment by the enterprise as fast, competent and fair.

Main group	Marketing tools
CRM software supports	- Collection of knowledge about marketing history - Utilisation of knowledge about competitors - Setting up and managing customer satisfaction analyses - Generating direct mail and one-to-one marketing

In our analysis, marketing tools cover a number of CRM applications. All these applications have one thing in common - they support the marketing department in the daily analyses and tasks which are necessary for optimal planning, and strategy. These tasks can be extremely varied and encompass setting up customer satisfaction analyses, managing the logistics of marketing materials, managing information about competitors, and analysing the competitive situation. In addition, these marketing tools support mail merging, which can give the customer an experience of receiving a personalised service, based on the customer's specific situation.

Main group	Sales Force Automation
CRM software supports	- Interaction between sales force and enterprise - Exchange of information between sales force and enterprise - Overview for the sales force of own budgets, sales, etc. - Contact to CRM applications from the field

The customer's most important contact point to the enterprise is often its sales representative, so it is important that these give the customer optimal service. This can be supported by giving the sales force access to the CRM system via laptops so that the necessary information is available during sales calls. This support improves dialogue and ensures better time management. It also improves correspondence and customer service (faster information and offers). The result: Increased earnings per sales representative.

Main group	Resource management
CRM software supports	- Planning of meetings, routes and time - Logistics - Expense management

Experience shows that the sales force typically spends 20% of its time on sales meetings and 80% on planning, transportation, reports, etc. The CRM system can change this with better planning, more effective route planning, a more efficient division of customers in the sales force, better segmentation - all of which will reduce the amount of administrative work.

Main group	Analysis tools
CRM software supports	- Budget-making - The basis for strategy planning

It is important to collect the information generated by customer contacts. This knowledge is the basis of the creation of value in CRM relationships. This is why it is important to be able to utilise this information - and here analysis tools play an important role.

Main group	Forecasts
CRM software supports	- Forecasts

When the enterprise has collected knowledge about leads, the lead's potential purchases, success rate per campaign and probable earnings, etc. it is possible to prepare far more accurate forecasts than previously. Forecasts support production management, purchasing, HR management, etc. and this improved forecasting ability can translate into significant savings for the enterprise.

Main group	Other functions
CRM software supports	- Miscellaneous

Many suppliers offer special functions in their systems. They can obviously be the reason for selecting one system instead of another. Some of these functions, such as the multi-currency option and data security, could be essential parameters for even considering the system.

Main group	Internet
CRM software supports	- Creating Internet sites - Using the Internet as an integrated part of campaigns and marketing efforts - Receiving and registering payment via the Internet - Sending letters via e-mail - Collecting information via the Internet

Telephones, letters and personal contact are increasingly being replaced by the Internet. Via the Internet, the enterprise can reach customers all over the world easily and cheaply.

As a result, some CRM software systems offer Internet options so the enterprise can quickly and easily set up Web pages (both graphics and direct links to campaign tools) with no programming. A few systems can actually create individual screen dumps depending on the customer who is logging in. In this way, the Internet brings together two previous contradictions: One is the ability to reach customers all over the world from a centralised point - and the other is the ability to offer service that is tailored to the individual.

Main group	Telemarketing, Call Centre and Help Desk
CRM software supports	- Better and faster telephone management of customers - Better and more professional dialogue with customers - Better and faster solutions to customer problems - More effective use of time in Call Centres and Help Desks - Less time spent answering e-mails - More effective use of Telemarketing, Call Centre and Help Desk employees - More telephone sales via cross-selling - Improved collection and use of customer data

Enterprise telephone services often create customer dissatisfaction. Customers are constantly being sent from one person to another. The customer cannot get the answer s/he is looking for and meets employees with no knowledge of his/her personal data. Perhaps a customer waits for weeks for a promised reply. Or calls back and discovers that their file has disappeared, so s/he has to start all over again.

A CRM software system can help many of these problems. For example, it is possible to integrate computer and telephone (CTI computer) so there is a direct connection to the person responsible when the call comes in. The first time the customer encounters someone, this person already has the customer's personal data on the screen. This gives fast and professional handling of incoming calls.

Another option a CRM software system can offer in this area is the ability to solve technical problems. Some systems can actually create solution models by themselves, based on previous cases. For example: If 90% of the people calling in have problems starting their PCs because they forgot to plug them in, this will be the first question the CRM system will suggest that the service employee asks the caller. When the most common cause of problems changes, the system will change the model from which the service employee is using to ask questions.

A similar system is available for answering e-mails. It is also possible for some CRM applications to analyse the contents of incoming e-mails and automatically choose the answer which is appropriate. This obviously saves time.

The unequal flow of incoming calls to a call centre is another problem some enterprises face. During certain hours, customers must wait a long time before their calls are answered; during other hours call centre employees have little or nothing to do. By means of "blending", a CRM application can send employees other tasks such as a telemarketing assignment, when they are not occupied with incoming calls. This gives optimal utilisation of resources. There are even systems that can forecast a call centre's workload and set up timetables and working hours for employees, based on this.

Optimising the whole process around telephone contact with customers creates more satisfied and loyal customers.

Method and source criticism
The supplier analysis covers 14 systems. PricewaterhouseCoopers prepared a fixed questionnaire to avoid having the suppliers define CRM functionality in relation to their own system applications.

To make the study as precise and consistent as possible, we visited all the suppliers and, in most cases, we received a demonstration and the opportunity to discuss their systems. For some of the systems, we have our own system expertise and experience. Generally speaking, there are the following uncertainties in the analysis:

- Some of the suppliers could not demonstrate some functionalities "live" because they had not been configured or set up in their demo version - so we had to rely on the supplier's statements.

- Some of the suppliers showed certain functionalities by means of a PowerPoint presentation - which makes it difficult to assess the real performance of the functionality.

- CRM software is developing so rapidly that new functionalities have been developed since our interviews. Some suppliers are more aggressive than others with respect to the functionalities they expected to have ready by the time this book was published. We have chosen to remain neutral in our judgement as to the extent in which they will live up to their promises - so these assertions are entirely the supplier's responsibility.

- Some suppliers in certain areas felt that a specific functionality could easily be programmed, but our assessment is that installing an optimal, integrated solution is an arduous task. On these points, we have chosen to accept the suppliers' statements, but suggest that the enterprise demand to see a "live" version and even a reference list showing how a given functionality was previously installed.

In general, the analysis gives an overview of the different systems. We suggest that the 3-4 CRM systems are chosen that seem the most interesting and we request "live" demonstrations of these.

Signs and symbols

In the following analysis, the system functions and technical specifications are described. Each section begins with a short introduction to the company, made by the company, including the following:

1) A description of the company and its vision
2) A management summary of the system the company offers
3) A reference list
4) Ownership and equity capital, company address and Web site

Next follows an analysis of the company's CRM software systems. The following symbols are used:

√	When the functionality is available
(√)	When the functionality meets almost all the requirements we made (see the appendix for more details). It can also indicate that the task was accomplished in a way not specified in the established parameters.
t	Tailoring
-	When the functionality does not exist
*1	The functionality is achieved via integration to Excel spreadsheets
*2	The functionality is achieved via integration to MS Outlook
*3	The functionality is achieved via integration to MS Project
*4	The functionality is achieved via integration to SAS
*5	The functionality is achieved via integration to Crystal Reports
*6	The functionality is achieved via integration to Active X
*7	The functionality is achieved via integration to External Workflow tools
*8	The functionality is achieved via integration to IBM tools
*9	The functionality is achieved via integration to Cognos Cube
*10	The functionality is achieved via integration to Sp-expert, etc.
*11	The functionality is achieved via integration to Actuate
*12	The functionality is achieved via integration to Selling Point
*13	The functionality is achieved via integration to Vignette
*14	The functionality is achieved via integration to Analyzer
*15	The functionality is achieved via integration to BW
R3	The functionality is found in SAP R/3 - but not as a stand-alone CRM solution
OR	The functionality is found in Oracle - but not as a stand-alone CRM solution
NA	Not available

The columns in the analysis describe 1) the main function, 2) product qualities, or 3) the technical specification which is being investigated. These three areas are described by the following different symbols:

Function

This model is a miniature edition of PricewaterhouseCoopers's Market Intelligence Enterprise (MIE) model. The upper rectangle is empty because it covers customer contact technologies. The other 10 squares describe each of the main elements of a CRM system. The areas in the MIE which the function touches are shaded.

Product qualities

This symbol indicates the qualities of a CRM product that do not specifically relate to the system's functions. These "product qualities" are factors which should be just as important in the decision-making process as the system's functions. These factors include price, product development, user-friendliness, and the industry-specific solutions that are available.

Technical specifications

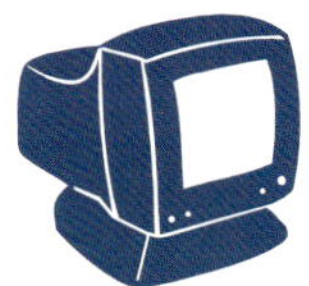

Technical specifications are another decision-making parameter. It is important to investigate if the system fits the enterprise's present hardware and software so that the enterprise has an idea of how large the extra expenditures will be when using one CRM software solution rather than another. Likewise, the degree of integration with other enterprise systems is an important parameter because it determines how well the system will function and if it is problem-free for users.

Abalon

Company Overview

ASTEA INTERNATIONAL AB (Astea International AB has just changed its name to Industri Matematik Abalon AB. We will market the company under the name Abalon AB) is a knowledge and specialist company owned by Industri-Matematik registered on NASDAQ as IMIC. Industri-Matematik bought Astea International AB from Astea International Inc on January 1, 1999. Astea International Inc wanted to focus on Service Management solutions, and Astea International AB (modern IT solutions for Customer Relations Management Systems) was therefore sold. Astea International Inc is now focusing on its core business around Service Management Solutions. Astea International AB, formerly known as Abalon AB, was established in 1988. We develop standard solutions for CRM (Customer Relationship Management). We also develop customer specific solutions for CRM as an add-on to our existing standard products and we carry out marketing consulting. As consultants we are often called in to investigate, analyse, act as a speaking partner, trainer and temporary boost to an organisation's competence in our areas of expertise.

Vision

Abalon AB's Mission is to supply the most innovative software solutions for efficient management of your interactions with your market and customers.

Management Summary

The combined Industri-Matematik and Abalon capabilities redefine supply chain and front-office applications by bringing together the strategic processes in revenue generation in one solution, including marketing automation, sales management, order capture, global fulfilment and service management. The joint solution will enable companies to acquire, develop and retain customers more profitably by effectively managing the complete life cycle of their business interactions.

Industri-Matematik will integrate Abalon Customer Management Solution (CIS) software, which supports sales, marketing, service and call centre operations, with its Advanced Supply Chain Execution Suite for managing customer-driven fulfilment in complex logistics environments. Both products support the multi-language, multi-currency environments of global companies and provide e-commerce capabilities that allow companies to collaborate with customers and partners.

Abalon CMS software supports the complete customer management cycle, from identifying prospects and winning business to maintaining ongoing relationships that generate repeat business. It is a suite of integrated, modular applications that provide marketing automation, technically assisted sales activities and customer support, including call centre operations. The software maintains a central repository for all information about customers, business partners, competitors and suppliers, allowing companies to respond quickly and accurately to customer inquiries.

The software uses object-oriented programming that makes it extremely adaptable to changes in organisations. It supports Microsoft Windows, Web-based and Java clients to extend applications across and outside the organisation. The fact that Abalon supports Java-based clients makes it easy and cost-effective for companies to conduct business over the Web. The software further includes comprehensive tools that allow companies to measure the performance and profitability of their products – helping them connect business strategies to supply chain operations.

References

Telia, Sonofon, Eirsell, Communitel, Telnordia, Smartone, VLT, ASG, Göteborgs Energy, Lyse Energy Interkraft, Resco Utbilding, LärData, IFL, Spray, Mind Innovative, Bredbandsbolaget, Sun Microsystems, SCO, Fritidsresor, Stena Line, NCC, ABB, Ericsson.

Ownership and Equity

IM Inc owns 100% of IM Abalon AB, formerly Astea International AB.

Addresses

www.abalon.com

Sweden	*Denmark*
Industri-Matematik Stockholm	Abalon Danmark
Kungsgatan 12-14	Trekronergade 126 H, 3. sal
Box 7733	DK-2500 Valby
S-103 95 Stockholm	Denmark
Sweden	Phone +45 70 13 13 30
Phone +46 8 676 50 00	

Supplier analysis – Abalon

Segmentation

√	1)	Automatic electronic ABC categorisation based on criteria defined by the company
√	2)	Possibility of manual categorisation (override of automatic categorisation)
√	3)	Segmentation can be based on different criteria based on the specific "territory". Furthermore, the possibility of a customer being A customer in one "territory" and B customer in another is also an issue
(√)	4)	Automatic warnings at low levels of activity on dimensions defined by the company
√	5)	Basic profiling tools (AND, OR, LIKE, NOT LIKE, *, -, +, /)
√	6)	Reuse of earlier group profiles in new profile definitions
√	7)	"Drop-down-box" or equivalent with predefined database field information for and creation of group profiles

Campaigns

√	1)	Campaign can consist of a number of different tasks in a pre-defined order
√	2)	Costing on campaigns on more than one dimension
-	3)	Display campaigns and activities using graphic tools like flowcharts
√	4)	Management of several parallel campaigns
√	5)	Campaign surveillance tools
√	6)	"Event triggers"
√	7)	"Assistants" (already programmed "event triggers") for user level
√	8)	Automatic generation of next step in a campaign
√	9)	Budgeting tool to calculate viability of planned campaigns
*9	10)	Graphic tools to show results
-	11)	Possibility of seeing a list of all active campaigns incl. time-horizon
√	12)	Estimation and measuring of campaigns earnings efficiency
√	13)	Distribution of leads to campaign teams

Leads

√	1)	Management and creation of leads
√	2)	Calculation of success-rates on leads
√	3)	Status for leads' placing in a sales process
(√)	4)	Graphic tool that shows how many leads there are on each step of a sales funnel
√	5)	Possibility of attaching one or more competitors to a lead
√	6)	Status for leads' purchasing potential and the probability of the sale coming through
√	7)	Manual salesman assignment to leads
√	8)	Automatic salesman assignment to leads

Customer Data	√	1) Customer data table with the firms' own defined fields
	√	2) Possibility of more than one address per customer
	√	3) Possibility of attachments to customer database of previous e-mails, letters, documents (a so-called customer log)
	√	4) Registration of all previous meetings/contacts with customers including outcome
	√	5) Registration of own sales strategy and tactics towards each customer
	√	6) Registration of customers' goals, visions and key success factors
	√	7) Search possibilities on data on several dimensions simultaneously (for example area and age)
	-	8) Word/text search tool
	√	9) Registration and measurement of the customers' product interests over time
	√	10) Hyperlink to relations
Product Configuration and Contract Management	-	1) Product configuration from offline PC (being frequently replicated)
	-	2) Configuration of product by use of a hierarchic (one-way) system
	-	3) Configuration of product by use of a full dialogue (dynamic) system
	-	4) Configuration with circumstances, e.g. max price
	-	5) Calculation of delivery date of configured product/availability check
	-	6) Possible from offer to create order including data needed for invoicing
	-	7) Visualisation for customer of the product configuration online/via Internet
	-	8) Visualisation for the customer of the product configuration via print
	√	9) Verification of price offer from internal organisation
	√	10) Contract management tool
	√	11) Possibility of more than one price list for one product based on customer seniority, area, season, etc.
	-	12) Service level agreements integrated with contract processing
	√	13) Discounting tools supporting contract creation
	-	14) Possibility of maintaining configurations without the use of programming
Marketing Tools	-	1) Library for storing marketing material (folders, brochures, etc.)
	√	2) Historical product/price information library
	(√)	3) Competitor Information System
	(√)	4) Tool for customer satisfaction analysis
	-	5) Management and registration of materials (e.g. banners, stickers, etc.) from current and previous campaigns
	√	6) Possibility of mass-generated direct mail/mail-merging

Sales Force Automation	√	1) Online data transfer from workstation to databases
	√	2) Batch data transfer from workstation to databases
	√	3) Possibility of quick synchronisation of offline laptops
	√	4) Possibility of integration with PDA or the like via MS Outlook
	-	5) Possibility of taking orders/making sales online via PDA to the CRM application
	√	6) Graphs for salesman comparing actual sales to budget
Resource Management	√	1) Planning calendar for each salesman
	√	2) Possibility of booking a meeting on a calendar without the salesman's acceptance
	√	3) Shared calendars (across several users)
	√	4) Graphical calendar
	*2	5) Possibility of setting alarms for meetings
	√	6) Management of activities per user/customer/company/contact person
	√	7) Possible for a customer to be member of numerous territories
	√	8) Possibility of geographic, product type, and industry "territories"
	-	9) Geographic route planning
	-	10) Salesman resource planner
	*1	11) Registration of CRM related costs for each customer (e.g. travel costs for sales visits and marketing contribution costs etc.)
	-	12) Front office logistics (storage repair, spares holding etc.)
Analysis Tools	√	1) Flexible report-generator for sales
	√	2) Flexible report-generator for marketing
	√	3) Flexible report-generator for service and support
	√	4) Standard Executive Information System incl. graphics
	*9	5) Advanced budgeting tools (includes e.g. fixed and variable calculation methods based on data from previous seasons, salesmen efficiency rates, etc.)
Forecasts	√	1) Product forecasts (sales per month/year)
	√	2) Revenue forecasts (revenue per month/year)
	√	3) Roll-ups of forecasts across numerous organisations
	√	4) Support for user-defined forecast dates
	√	5) Roll-ups and forecasts on several levels in a firm

Other functionalities	√	1)	Push technology for information-gathering on the Internet (active search on words)
	√	2)	Active Briefing
	√	3)	Multiple currencies
	√	4)	Euro compliant
	√	5)	Supports electronic scrollbar
	√	6)	Security system that defines user-clearance
	-	7)	Quick-print of document without having to open the application supporting the document
	-	8)	Personal correspondence templates
	√	9)	Full integration to word-processing and spreadsheet applications (automatic merging into these from the CRM-system), e.g. OLE technology (Object Link Enabling)
	√	10)	Guide functions for using the application ("Wizards")
	(√)	11)	Integrated fax tool that works seamless, as part of the application
Internet	√	1)	Automatic assignment of leads from the Internet
	√	2)	Tool for creating web-sites with predefined links to CRM database fields and interactive fields to CRM application
	-	3)	Tool for creating web-sites with "drop-down-box" or equivalent with "drag-and-drop" graphics
	√	4)	Possibility for web-site differentiation dependant on customer logging in
	√	5)	Integrated e-mail tool that works seamless, as part of the application
	-	6)	Support for electronic payment
Telemarketing, Call Centre and Help-Desk	√	1)	Automatic dialling facilities (Predictive Dialling)
	√	2)	Computer-Telephony Integration (CTI) enabled/supportive
	√	3)	Application (through integration of CTI) enables routing possibilities of customer calling in, e.g. customer to specific operator, "A" customer first in queue, etc.
	√	4)	Use of electronic scripts for telemarketing or response for Call Centre/guided dialogue management
	-	5)	Dialogue management with a neural network/adaptive learning
	√	6)	Cross-sales functions
	-	7)	"Neural" inbound e-mail answering tool
	-	8)	Calculation/prognosis of inbound call frequency during the day
	-	9)	Scheduling device for Call Centre operators (Schedule Planner)
	(√)	10)	Technical problem resolution system
	-	11)	"Trouble-Ticketing" – a system for requesting service
	√	12)	Blending of Telemarketing and Call Centre function. That is the possibility of the system assigning telemarketing tasks to vacant operators during less busy periods

Price	1)	**Price per user:** *If Windows client app. SEK 6,000 per user. If web based client app. SEK 4,000 per user. Server engine needed for about SEK 100,000 per Abalon customer*
	2)	**Annual license per user:** *No*
	3)	**Installation and maintenance:** *Installation of standard configuration app. 2 days (SEK 14,000). Maintenance and support costs app. 14% of the license fee per year.*
Product Development	1)	**Annual new versions:** *2x*
	2)	**Users in the Nordic countries:** *500 (Denmark)*
	3)	**Global users incl. Nordic Countries:** *15,000*
	4)	**Planned new applications/functions within the next six months:**
	-	*Account Sales*
	-	*Customer Contact Centre*
	-	*Event Management/Course Booking*
	-	*Highly configurable, early warnings, built-in forecasting tools, trends, planning, ongoing sales, bulletin board functionality within the sales team*

Support	√	1)	Hot-line
	-	2)	24-hour hot-line
	√	3)	Education Centre
	-	4)	Internet help

Ease of use

User-friendly Interface

√	1)	Danish version
√	2)	Swedish version
√	3)	Norwegian version
√	4)	Finnish version
t	5)	German version
√	6)	English version
t	7)	French version
√	8)	Spanish version
t	9)	Other versions:

Industry Solutions

The following Industry Solutions are offered:

- *Bank and Finance*
- *Telecommunications*
- *IT (System providers)*
- *Energy sector*

Platforms and Architecture

√	1)	Unix
√	2)	Win NT
√	3)	Win 95/98
-	4)	OS/2
-	5)	Mainframe, e.g. MVS
√	6)	MAC
-	7)	Netscape
√	8)	Internet explorer
√	9)	Full Web-based Architecture (Total O MB Thin Clients)
-	10)	Partial Web-based Architecture
√	11)	Client/Server-based Architecture
√	12)	Runs Client/Server over WAN
√	13)	Runs Client/Server over Dialup

Configuration of CRM-System

	1)	Programming language: *C++*
	2)	Possibility for the firm to develop its own display: *High*
	3)	Scalability from no. of users: *1*
		to no. of users: *100,000+*
√	4)	Automatic generation of connections between data fields
√	5)	When upgrading software customer-specific configurations are not lost
√	6)	The systems IT structure supports global operations with several servers

---

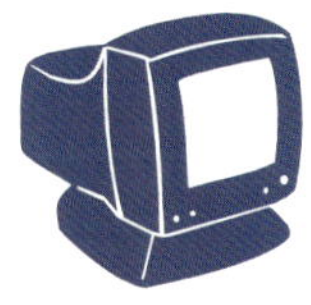

Databases

√	1)	Oracle
(√)	2)	Sybase
√	3)	Informix
-	4)	Scalable SQL
√	5)	MS SQL
-	6)	IBM DB2
-	7)	Access
-	8)	Ctree

Integration

√	1)	Pre-built SAP Interface
-	2)	Pre-built Oracle Interface
-	3)	Pre-built Peoplesoft Interface
-	4)	Pre-built Baan Interface
-	5)	Pre-built JD Edwards Interface
-	6)	Other pre-built Interfaces
√	7)	Supports Application Program Interfaces or equivalent
√	8)	Supports Object Link Enabling technology or equivalent
√	9)	Tool for creation of Interfaces without the use of programming
√	10)	Integration to 3rd party data providers, incl. D&B

Hardware

Minimum requirements for workstation

Processor:	*Pentium 100*
RAM:	*24 MB RAM*
Free harddisk space:	*1 MB*

Baan

Company Overview

Baan Front Office is a leading international supplier of CRM solutions that assist organisations in identifying, establishing and servicing customers based on a durable partnership. There are approx. 200 employees in Europe plus approx. 400 employees in the USA, including approx. 100 employees in the European Competence Centre in Copenhagen. Baan Front Office sells solutions that are independent of existing frameworks. In this connection they have a standard offer of an interface to SAP and Baan.

Vision

Think Global -Throughout the world we wish to be perceived as a primary supplier of complete Customer Relationship Management (CRM) solutions to companies striving to provide superior customer satisfaction.

Act Local – In collaboration with our business partners, we strive to deliver optimum return on investment through industry specific applications and business knowledge.

Simplicity & Integration – We would like to be seen as the best in our business, based on world-class integrated CRM products and rapid implementation.

Management Summary

Baan Front Office offers a number of IT solutions that are all basically working to improve the company's customer-related activities. The solutions are divided into the following main categories:

BaanSales: A tool that supports the company by handling business opportunities, account management, communication between salespeople, tele sales and marketing. BaanSales increases the salespeople's productivity by ensuring that the right activity is carried out at the right time. Furthermore, it minimises the time spent on administrative tasks, hereby increasing the time available for the salespeople to be used in dialogue with the company's customers/ potential customers. BaanSales supports several kinds of sales channels, including direct, indirect and partner sales models.

BaanConfiguration: BaanConfiguration is a revolutionary step forward in connection with sales configuration. It allows the salesman to assemble even very complex products and services quickly and safely to satisfy the customer's unique demands. The company's distributors and customers can also use BaanConfiguration through the Internet. Baan Configuration is the main component in the BaanInteractive-Selling-BIS, an ISS (Interactive Selling Solution) which in combination with a product catalogue and a business offer generation tool ensures that the salesman can generate offers to customers/ lead customers with a guarantee that the executive and production parts of the company are able to deliver the offered products and services. Thus it is ensured that products or services that the company cannot deliver are not sold, and that the company's products and services are sold at the optimum and simultaneously fulfil the customer's needs.

BaanCallCenter. As a natural part of the Baan Front Office solutions, the Baan Company has a strategy for CallCentre functionality, which is designed to ensure that the company stays in close contact with its customers, be it in the sales or support function. The Baan CallCenter will contain functions for tele-marketing, customer service and support.

References

AT&T, Delta Airlines, Fujitsu, Hewlett Packard, KPN Dutch Telecom, Nortel Networks, Volvo, Construction Equipment, Volvo Trucks, Barclays Bank, Grundfos (DK), Scandinavian Mobility Internationality (DK), Wittenborg (DK), Sabroe (DK), Epoke (DK), Nera (N), ABB Robotics (S), Partek (F).

Ownership and Equity

Baan Front Office is a division of the Baan Company. The Baan Company is one of the market leaders in the delivery of software solutions for middle-market and large national and international companies. The Baan Company delivers a full range of "best-in-class" component-based software solutions within Customer Management, Corporate Management and Operations Management.

The company was established in Holland in 1978 and has today 5,000 employees globally with head offices in Putten in Holland and Reston, Virginia in the USA. Furthermore, direct and indirect sales channels are attached operating in 80 countries. Baan Nordic A/S has head office in Herlev and a salesoffice in Vejle. The Baan Company's net capital as at 98/12/31: $156,760,000

Addresses

www.baan.com

Denmark	*Sweden*	*Norway*	*Finland*
Baan Nordic A/S	Baan Nordic AB	Baan Nordic AB	Baan Nordic AB
Hørkær 12A	Aniaraplatsen 4	Vollsveien 13c	Metsänneidonkuja 8
DK-2730 Herlev	S-191 21 Sollentuna	Spektrin Trio	FI-02130 ESPOO
Phone +45 44 88 56 00		N-11324 Lysaker	

Supplier analysis – Baan Front Office

Segmentation

- 1) Automatic electronic ABC categorisation based on criteria defined by the company
- 2) Possibility of manual categorisation (override of automatic categorisation)
- 3) Segmentation can be based on different criteria based on the specific "territory". Furthermore, the possibility of a customer being A customer in one "territory" and B customer in another is also an issue
- 4) Automatic warnings at low levels of activity on dimensions defined by the company
- 5) Basic profiling tools (AND, OR, LIKE, NOT LIKE, *, -, +, /)
- 6) Reuse of earlier group profiles in new profile definitions
- 7) "Drop-down-box" or equivalent with predefined database field information for and creation of group profiles

Campaigns

- 1) Campaign can consist of a number of different tasks in a pre-defined order
- 2) Costing on campaigns on more than one dimension
- 3) Display campaigns and activities using graphic tools like flowcharts
- 4) Management of several parallel campaigns
- 5) Campaign surveillance tools
- 6) "Event triggers"
- 7) "Assistants" (already programmed "event triggers") for user level
- 8) Automatic generation of next step in a campaign
- 9) Budgeting tool to calculate viability of planned campaigns
- 10) Graphic tools to show results
- 11) Possibility of seeing a list of all active campaigns incl. time-horizon
- 12) Estimation and measuring of campaigns earnings efficiency
- 13) Distribution of leads to campaign teams

Leads

- √ 1) Management and creation of leads
- √ 2) Calculation of success-rates on leads
- √ 3) Status for leads' placing in a sales process
- √ 4) Graphic tool that shows how many leads there are on each step of a sales funnel
- √ 5) Possibility of attaching one or more competitors to a lead
- √ 6) Status for leads' purchasing potential and the probability of the sale coming through
- √ 7) Manual salesman assignment to leads
- √ 8) Automatic salesman assignment to leads

Customer Data	√	1)	Customer data table with the firms' own defined fields
	√	2)	Possibility of more than one address per customer
	√	3)	Possibility of attachments to customer database of previous e-mails, letters, documents (a so-called customer log)
	√	4)	Registration of all previous meetings/contacts with customers including outcome
	√	5)	Registration of own sales strategy and tactics towards each customer
	√	6)	Registration of customers' goals, visions and key success factors
	√	7)	Search possibilities on data on several dimensions simultaneously (for example area and age)
	√	8)	Word/text search tool
	√	9)	Registration and measurement of the customers' product interests over time
	√	10)	Hyperlink to relations
Product Configuration and Contract Management	√	1)	Product configuration from offline PC (being frequently replicated)
	-	2)	Configuration of product by use of a hierarchic (one-way) system
	√	3)	Configuration of product by use of a full dialogue (dynamic) system
	√	4)	Configuration with circumstances, e.g. max price
	√	5)	Calculation of delivery date of configured product/availability check
	√	6)	Possible from offer to create order including data needed for invoicing
	√	7)	Visualisation for customer of the product configuration online/via Internet
	√	8)	Visualisation for the customer of the product configuration via print
	√	9)	Verification of price offer from internal organisation
	√	10)	Contract management tool
	√	11)	Possibility of more than one price list for one product based on customer seniority, area, season, etc.
	√	12)	Service level agreements integrated with contract processing
	√	13)	Discounting tools supporting contract creation
	√	14)	Possibility of maintaining configurations without the use of programming
Marketing Tools	√	1)	Library for storing marketing material (folders, brochures, etc.)
	√	2)	Historical product/price information library
	√	3)	Competitor Information System
	-	4)	Tool for customer satisfaction analysis
	√	5)	Management and registration of materials (e.g. banners, stickers, etc.) from current and previous campaigns
	√	6)	Possibility of mass-generated direct mail/mail-merging

Sales Force Automation	√	1) Online data transfer from workstation to databases
	√	2) Batch data transfer from workstation to databases
	√	3) Possibility of quick synchronisation of offline laptops
	√	4) Possibility of integration with PDA or the like via MS Outlook
	-	5) Possibility of taking orders/making sales online via PDA to the CRM application
	√	6) Graphs for salesman comparing actual sales to budget
Resource Management	*2	1) Planning calendar for each salesman
	*2	2) Possibility of booking a meeting on a calendar without the salesman's acceptance
	*2	3) Shared calendars (across several users)
	*2	4) Graphical calendar
	*2	5) Possibility of setting alarms for meetings
	√	6) Management of activities per user/customer/company/contact person
	√	7) Possible for a customer to be member of numerous territories
	√	8) Possibility of geographic, product type, and industry "territories"
	-	9) Geographic route planning
	-	10) Salesman resource planner
	-	11) Registration of CRM related costs for each customer (e.g. travel costs for sales visits and marketing contribution costs etc.)
	-	12) Front office logistics (storage repair, spares holding etc.)
Analysis Tools	√	1) Flexible report-generator for sales
	-	2) Flexible report-generator for marketing
	-	3) Flexible report-generator for service and support
	√	4) Standard Executive Information System incl. graphics
	*1	5) Advanced budgeting tools (includes e.g. fixed and variable calculation methods based on data from previous seasons, salesmen efficiency rates, etc.)
Forecasts	√	1) Product forecasts (sales per month/year)
	√	2) Revenue forecasts (revenue per month/year)
	√	3) Roll-ups of forecasts across numerous organisations
	√	4) Support for user-defined forecast dates
	√	5) Roll-ups and forecasts on several levels in a firm

Other functionalities	√	1)	Push technology for information-gathering on the Internet (active search on words)
	√	2)	Active Briefing
	√	3)	Multiple currencies
	√	4)	Euro compliant
	√	5)	Supports electronic scrollbar
	√	6)	Security system that defines user-clearance
	√	7)	Quick-print of document without having to open the application supporting the document
	√	8)	Personal correspondence templates
	√	9)	Full integration to word-processing and spreadsheet applications (automatic merging into these from the CRM-system), e.g. OLE technology (Object Link Enabling)
	(√)	10)	Guide functions for using the application ("Wizards")
	√	11)	Integrated fax tool that works seamless, as part of the application
Internet	√	1)	Automatic assignment of leads from the Internet
	√	2)	Tool for creating web-sites with predefined links to CRM database fields and interactive fields to CRM application
	√	3)	Tool for creating web-sites with "drop-down-box" or equivalent with "drag-and-drop" graphics
	√	4)	Possibility for web-site differentiation dependant on customer logging in
	√	5)	Integrated e-mail tool that works seamless, as part of the application
	-	6)	Support for electronic payment
Telemarketing, Call Centre and Help-Desk	√	1)	Automatic dialling facilities (Predictive Dialling)
	-	2)	Computer-Telephony Integration (CTI) enabled/supportive
	-	3)	Application (through integration of CTI) enables routing possibilities of customer calling in, e.g. customer to specific operator, "A" customer first in queue, etc.
	-	4)	Use of electronic scripts for telemarketing or response for Call Centre/guided dialogue management
	-	5)	Dialogue management with a neural network/adaptive learning
	-	6)	Cross-sales functions
	-	7)	"Neural" inbound e-mail answering tool
	-	8)	Calculation/prognosis of inbound call frequency during the day
	-	9)	Scheduling device for Call Centre operators (Schedule Planner)
	-	10)	Technical problem resolution system
	-	11)	"Trouble-Ticketing" – a system for requesting service
	-	12)	Blending of Telemarketing and Call Centre function. That is the possibility of the system assigning telemarketing tasks to vacant operators during less busy periods

Price	1)	Price per user: *Depends on modules and number of users*
	2)	Annual license per user: *Depends on modules and number of users*
	3)	Installation and maintenance: *Depends on modules and number of users*

Product Development	1)	Annual new versions: *2-3 incl. Service Packs*
	2)	Users in the Nordic countries: *600+*
	3)	Global users incl. Nordic Countries: *50,000+*
	4)	Planned new applications/functions within the next six months:
	-	*Call Centre*
	-	*Campaign Management*
	-	*Telemarketing*
	-	*Helpdesk & Support*

Support	√	1)	Hot-line
	√	2)	24-hour hot-line
	√	3)	Education Centre
	√	4)	Internet help

Ease of use

Baan Sales runs on a browser. Strong integration to Microsoft Outlook. General screen layout like MS Outlook. Possible to navigate through hyperlinks. Baan Configuration works with select and press key – and graphic support.

(√)	1)	Danish version
t	2)	Swedish version
t	3)	Norwegian version
t	4)	Finnish version
√	5)	German version
√	6)	English version
√	7)	French version
√	8)	Spanish version
√	9)	Other versions: *Dutch, Italian, Portuguese*

Industry Solutions

The following Industrial Solutions are offered:

Platforms and
Architecture

√	1)	Unix
√	2)	Win NT
√	3)	Win 95/98
-	4)	OS/2
-	5)	Mainframe, e.g. MVS
-	6)	MAC
√	7)	Netscape
√	8)	Internet explorer
√	9)	Full Web-based Architecture (Total O MB Thin Clients)
-	10)	Partial Web-based Architecture
√	11)	Client/Server based Architecture
√	12)	Runs Client/Server over WAN
√	13)	Runs Client/Server over Dialup

Configuration of
CRM-System

1) Programming language: *VB6, C++*

2) Possibility for the firm to develop its own display: *High*

3) Scalability from no. of users: *NA*

      to no. of users: *NA*

√	4)	Automatic generation of connections between data fields
√	5)	When upgrading software customer-specific configurations are not lost
√	6)	The systems IT structure supports global operations with several servers

Databases

√	1)	Oracle
-	2)	Sybase
√	3)	Informix
-	4)	Scalable SQL
√	5)	MS SQL
-	6)	IBM DB2
-	7)	Access
-	8)	Ctree

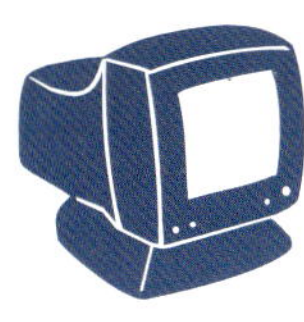

Integration

√	1)	Pre-built SAP Interface
-	2)	Pre-built Oracle Interface
-	3)	Pre-built Peoplesoft Interface
√	4)	Pre-built Baan Interface
-	5)	Pre-built JD Edwards Interface
-	6)	Other pre-built Interfaces
√	7)	Supports Application Program Interfaces or equivalent
√	8)	Supports Object Link Enabling technology or equivalent
√	9)	Tool for creation of Interfaces without the use of programming
√	10)	Integration to 3rd party data providers, incl. D&B

Hardware

Minimum requirements for workstation

Processor:	*Pentium 233*
RAM:	*64 MB RAM*
Free harddisk space:	*100 MB*

Caesar Business Systems

Company Overview

Caesar has about 80 employees in offices in Stockholm, Gothenburg, Huskvarna, Malmö and Oslo. One fourth of the staff works with product development. Caesar is a fully-owned subsidiary in the Linné Group, which is quoted on the Stock Exchange in Stockholm. The focus of the group is to offer the corporate sector an IT tool that secures an efficient dialogue with the markets. This is done via two business areas: Consultants and Products, of which Caesar represents the Product part. Totally, the group has about 500 employees.

Vision

The business idea of Caesar is to develop, sell and implement standard programs for sale, marketing and management functions to enhance efficiency and create value in the daily work.

Caesar's task is via the Caesar-concept (programs and service) to increase the competitive effect and enhance the negotiation force of the commissioners. The concept should yield tangible effects in the form of increased value and efficiency in the commissioner's work with sales, marketing and service.

Management Summary

Caesar offers a business strategic program portfolio which gives complete IT-support to the sales, marketing and management functions. Caesar's basic idea is that the customers should be able to start from any level they choose within the frames of Caesar's product structure and successively build up a complete sales and marketing system. Caesar's products consist of the following modules:
Caesar Säljverktyg 4.1 (Sales Tool), Caesar Affärsverktyg 4.1 (Business Tool), Caesar Kampanjverktyg 4.1 (Campaign Tool), Caesar Affärsnavigator 4.1 (Business Navigator) and Caesar Administrationsverktyg 4.1 (Administration Tool).

To give the customers the best conditions for success, Caesar has since 1998 developed an implementation method that builds on the following advisory services:
- Project management – A well-documented, detailed project plan administered by Caesar with the purpose of controlling the implementation process for Caesar's customers.
- Priority analysis – The purpose of this analysis is to map what the organisation considers to be important to improve in the present situation. Future users are involved in the process.

- CRM-analysis – The CRM-analysis is a simplified process analysis primarily dealing with the customers' sales and marketing processes.
- Goal formulation – The goals of the project are formulated on the basis of the priority analysis and the management's vision for IT-support of the business processes.
- Structuring of market information – Based on the goal formulation, Caesar and the customer determine what information to store in order to create and activate a business database.
- Technical support – Caesar offers technical support in the following areas: Check of the technical infrastructure, adjustment of Caesar's applications, installation and data import/export
- Training – Caesar offers training to the users. This is a central means to reach the customers' goals with the implementation of Caesar.
- Follow-up priority analysis – A final analysis answers whether the original goals have been fulfilled.

References

ABB Sverige (company agreement), AGA AB, Norden, AssiDomän, BASF AB, Elekta Instrument AB, Ericsson Cables AB, Ericsson Radio Access AB, ESAB AB, GE Capital Equipment Finance AB, Goodyear Svenska AB, Maersk Line – A.P. MØLLER, Posten Norge, Saab Opel Sverige AB (group agreement), SBAB, SEB/Trygg-Hansa, Semcon Engineering West AB, SMHI, Statoil Norden, Svenska Mässan, Teracom AB, W.L. Gore & Associés, WM-Data (company agreement).

Ownership and equity

Caesar is a fully owned subsidiary in the Linné Group which is quoted on the Stock Exchange in Stockholm. The biggest shareholder in the Linné Group is Telenor Venture.

Addresses

Internet: www.cas.se

Göteborg, head office

Kungsportsavenyn 18

S-411 36 Göteborg

Phone +46-31-817700

Stockholm

Södra Långgatan 21

S-169 59 Solna

Phone +46-8-4701250

Malmö

Grimsbygatan 24

S-211 20 Malmö

Phone +46-40-306830

Oslo

Waldemar Thranes Gate

N-0175 Oslo

Phone +47-2203-2770

Supplier analysis – Caesar Business Systems

Segmentation

-	1) Automatic electronic ABC categorisation based on criteria defined by the company
√	2) Possibility of manual categorisation (override of automatic categorisation)
√	3) Segmentation can be based on different criteria based on the specific "territory". Furthermore, the possibility of a customer being A customer in one "territory" and B customer in another is also an issue
√	4) Automatic warnings at low levels of activity on dimensions defined by the company
√	5) Basic profiling tools (AND, OR, LIKE, NOT LIKE, *, -, +, /)
-	6) Reuse of earlier group profiles in new profile definitions
√	7) "Drop-down-box" or equivalent with predefined database field information for and creation of group profiles

Campaigns

√	1) Campaign can consist of a number of different tasks in a pre-defined order
√	2) Costing on campaigns on more than one dimension
-	3) Display campaigns and activities using graphic tools like flowcharts
√	4) Management of several parallel campaigns
√	5) Campaign surveillance tools
-	6) "Event triggers"
-	7) "Assistants" (already programmed "event triggers") for user level
√	8) Automatic generation of next step in a campaign
√	9) Budgeting tool to calculate viability of planned campaigns
√	10) Graphic tools to show results
-	11) Possibility of seeing a list of all active campaigns incl. time-horizon
√	12) Estimation and measuring of campaigns earnings efficiency
√	13) Distribution of leads to campaign teams

Leads

√	1) Management and creation of leads
√	2) Calculation of success-rates on leads
√	3) Status for leads' placing in a sales process
-	4) Graphic tool that shows how many leads there are on each step of a sales funnel
√	5) Possibility of attaching one or more competitors to a lead
√	6) Status for leads' purchasing potential and the probability of the sale coming through
√	7) Manual salesman assignment to leads
√	8) Automatic salesman assignment to leads

Customer Data	√	1)	Customer data table with the firms' own defined fields
	√	2)	Possibility of more than one address per customer
	√	3)	Possibility of attachments to customer database of previous e-mails, letters, documents (a so-called customer log)
	√	4)	Registration of all previous meetings/contacts with customers including outcome
	√	5)	Registration of own sales strategy and tactics towards each customer
	√	6)	Registration of customers' goals, visions and key success factors
	√	7)	Search possibilities on data on several dimensions simultaneously (for example area and age)
	-	8)	Word/text search tool
	√	9)	Registration and measurement of the customers' product interests over time
	√	10)	Hyperlink to relations
Product Configuration and Contract Management	-	1)	Product configuration from offline PC (being frequently replicated)
	-	2)	Configuration of product by use of a hierarchic (one-way) system
	-	3)	Configuration of product by use of a full dialogue (dynamic) system
	-	4)	Configuration with circumstances, e.g. max price
	-	5)	Calculation of delivery date of configured product/availability check
	-	6)	Possible from offer to create order including data needed for invoicing
	-	7)	Visualisation for customer of the product configuration online/via Internet
	-	8)	Visualisation for the customer of the product configuration via print
	-	9)	Verification of price offer from internal organisation
	√	10)	Contract management tool
	√	11)	Possibility of more than one price list for one product based on customer seniority, area, season, etc.
	-	12)	Service level agreements integrated with contract processing
	√	13)	Discounting tools supporting contract creation
	-	14)	Possibility of maintaining configurations without the use of programming
Marketing Tools	-	1)	Library for storing marketing material (folders, brochures, etc.)
	√	2)	Historical product/price information library
	√	3)	Competitor Information System
	-	4)	Tool for customer satisfaction analysis
	-	5)	Management and registration of materials (e.g. banners, stickers, etc.) from current and previous campaigns
	√	6)	Possibility of mass-generated direct mail/mail-merging

Sales Force Automation	√	1)	Online data transfer from workstation to databases
	-	2)	Batch data transfer from workstation to databases
	-	3)	Possibility of quick synchronisation of offline laptops
	√	4)	Possibility of integration with PDA or the like via MS Outlook
	√	5)	Possibility of taking orders/making sales online via PDA to the CRM application
	√	6)	Graphs for salesman comparing actual sales to budget.
Resource Management	*2	1)	Planning calendar for each salesman
	*2	2)	Possibility of booking a meeting on a calendar without the salesman's acceptance
	*2	3)	Shared calendars (across several users)
	*2	4)	Graphical calendar
	*2	5)	Possibility of setting alarms for meetings
	√	6)	Management of activities per user/customer/company/contact person
	√	7)	Possible for a customer to be member of numerous territories
	√	8)	Possibility of geographic, product type, and industry "territories"
	-	9)	Geographic route planning
	-	10)	Salesman resource planner
	√	11)	Registration of CRM related costs for each customer (e.g. travel costs for sales visits and marketing contribution costs etc.)
	-	12)	Front office logistics (storage repair, spares holding etc.)
Analysis Tools	√	1)	Flexible report-generator for sales
	√	2)	Flexible report-generator for marketing
	√	3)	Flexible report-generator for service and support
	√	4)	Standard Executive Information System incl. graphics
	√	5)	Advanced budgeting tools (includes e.g. fixed and variable calculation methods based on data from previous seasons, salesmen efficiency rates, etc.)
Forecasts	√	1)	Product forecasts (sales per month/year)
	√	2)	Revenue forecasts (revenue per month/year)
	√	3)	Roll-ups of forecasts across numerous organisations
	√	4)	Support for user-defined forecast dates
	√	5)	Roll-ups and forecasts on several levels in a firm

Category	✓		
Other functionalities	-	1)	Push technology for information-gathering on the Internet (active search on words)
	√	2)	Active Briefing
	√	3)	Multiple currencies
	√	4)	Euro compliant
	-	5)	Supports electronic scrollbar
	√	6)	Security system that defines user-clearance
	-	7)	Quick-print of document without having to open the application supporting the document
	√	8)	Personal correspondence templates
	√	9)	Full integration to word-processing and spreadsheet applications (automatic merging into these from the CRM-system), e.g. OLE technology (Object Link Enabling)
	√	10)	Guide functions for using the application ("Wizards")
	√	11)	Integrated fax tool that works seamless, as part of the application
Internet	-	1)	Automatic assignment of leads from the Internet
	-	2)	Tool for creating web-sites with predefined links to CRM database fields and interactive fields to CRM application
	-	3)	Tool for creating web-sites with "drop-down-box" or equivalent with "drag-and-drop" graphics
	-	4)	Possibility for web-site differentiation dependant on customer logging in
	√	5)	Integrated e-mail tool that works seamless, as part of the application
	-	6)	Support for electronic payment
Telemarketing, Call Centre and Help-Desk	-	1)	Automatic dialling facilities (Predictive Dialling)
	-	2)	Computer-Telephony Integration (CTI) enabled/supportive
	-	3)	Application (through integration of CTI) enables routing possibilities of customer calling in, e.g. customer to specific operator, "A" customer first in queue, etc.
	-	4)	Use of electronic scripts for telemarketing or response for Call Centre/guided dialogue management
	-	5)	Dialogue management with a neural network/adaptive learning
	-	6)	Cross-sales functions
	-	7)	"Neural" inbound e-mail answering tool
	-	8)	Calculation/prognosis of inbound call frequency during the day
		9)	Scheduling device for Call Centre operators (Schedule Planner)
	-	10)	Technical problem resolution system
	-	11)	"Trouble-Ticketing" – a system for requesting service
	-	12)	Blending of Telemarketing and Call Centre function. That is the possibility of the system assigning telemarketing tasks to vacant operators during less busy periods

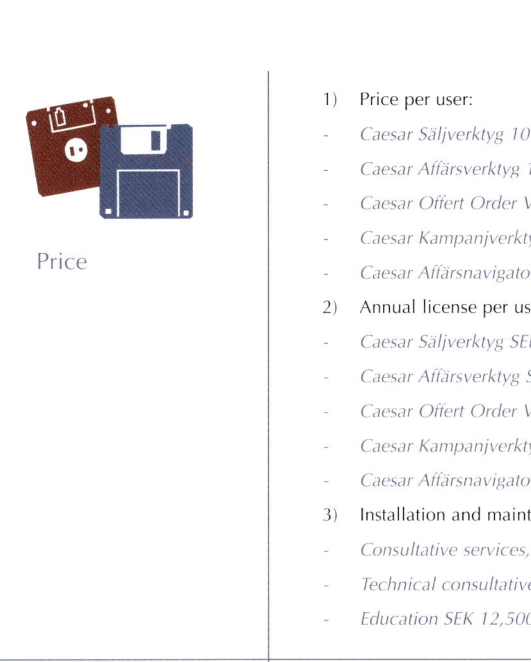

Price

1) Price per user:

- *Caesar Säljverktyg 10 users SEK 85,000 + SEK 3,000 per extra user*
- *Caesar Affärsverktyg 10 users SEK 85,000 + SEK 8,000 per extra user*
- *Caesar Offert Order Verktyg SEK 5,000 per user*
- *Caesar Kampanjverktyg SEK 10,000 per user*
- *Caesar Affärsnavigator SEK 10,000 per user*

2) Annual license per user:

- *Caesar Säljverktyg SEK 1,395*
- *Caesar Affärsverktyg SEK 1,395*
- *Caesar Offert Order Verktyg SEK 595*
- *Caesar Kampanjverktyg SEK 1,395*
- *Caesar Affärsnavigator SEK 3,000*

3) Installation and maintenance:

- *Consultative services, project management SEK 995*
- *Technical consultative services SEK 995*
- *Education SEK 12,500 per day*

Product Development

1) Annual new versions: *2 x*
2) Users in the Nordic countries: *20,000*
3) Global users incl. Nordic Countries: *21,000*
4) Planned new applications/functions within the next six months:

- *Telemarketing module*
- *Web Interface*
- *E-Business*
- *Customer Service/Field-service*

Support

-	1) Hot-line
-	2) 24-hour hot-line
√	3) Education Centre
√	4) Internet help

Ease of use

One of the core elements of Caesar's strategy is ease of use. As an evidence of this Caesar was elected as "Best in Test" in the periodical "Mikrodatorn 1997" on the basis that "Caesar wins on ease of use". An important parameter is the Windows user-interface. Another parameter is user groups and reference groups appointed by Caesar, which continually provide new ideas for Caesar's products.

√	1)	Danish version
√	2)	Swedish version
√	3)	Norwegian version
t	4)	Finnish version
t	5)	German version
√	6)	English version
t	7)	French version
t	8)	Spanish version
t	9)	Other versions:

Industry Solutions

The following Industryl Solutions are offered:

- *Caesar has an object in the database with relations to almost all other objects in the database. This is used for the development of industry specific solutions.*

Platforms and Architecture

-	1)	Unix
√	2)	Win NT
√	3)	Win 95/98
-	4)	OS/2
-	5)	Mainframe, e.g. MVS
-	6)	MAC
-	7)	Netscape
-	8)	Internet explorer
-	9)	Full Web-based Architecture (Total 0 MB Thin Clients)
-	10)	Partial Web-based Architecture
√	11)	Client/Server based Architecture
√	12)	Runs Client/Server over WAN
√	13)	Runs Client/Server over Dialup

Configuration of CRM-System		1) Programming language: *Visual C++* 2) Possibility for the firm to develop its own display: *High* 3) Scalability from no. of users: *1* to no. of users: *1000 +*
	-	4) Automatic generation of connections between data fields
	√	5) When upgrading software customer-specific configurations are not lost
	√	6) The systems IT structure supports global operations with several servers
Databases	√	1) Oracle
	-	2) Sybase
	-	3) Informix
	-	4) Scalable SQL
	√	5) MS SQL
	√	6) IBM DB2
	√	7) Access
	-	8) Ctree
Integration	-	1) Pre-built SAP Interface
	-	2) Pre-built Oracle Interface
	-	3) Pre-built Peoplesoft Interface
	-	4) Pre-built Baan Interface
	-	5) Pre-built JD Edwards Interface
	-	6) Other pre-built Interfaces:
	√	7) Supports Application Program Interfaces or equivalent
	√	8) Supports Object Link Enabling technology or equivalent
	√	9) Tool for creation of Interfaces without the use of programming
	√	10) Integration to 3rd party data providers, incl. D&B
Hardware		Minimum requirements for workstation Processor:　　　　　　　*Pentium 75* RAM:　　　　　　　　　*16 MB RAM* Free harddisk space:　 *20 MB + the size of the replicated database*

CDM Gruppen A/S

CDM Gruppen A/S

Company Overview

CDM Gruppen A/S was established in 1986 and has 68 employees in Denmark.

Vision

To be able to conduct a meaningful dialogue with all the people of the world regarding fulfilment of needs. The CDM Gruppen A/S ensures through information technology, services and consultancy assistance that our customers obtain the largest possible success by optimisation of parts of the entire sales and marketing function with specific focus on the dialogue processes.

Management Summary

CDM works within most areas of dialogue processes with their customers. CDM's core areas are divided as follows:

Sales systems: Sales and Marketing, Campaign management, Call Centre, Telemarketing, Quality management, Internet, Customer service and Support. The CDM Sales System covers a company's demands for modern sales and marketing. Just as a professional finance system collects and refines data from a number of functions such as administration, finance, stock etc., the CDM Sales System is the perfect choice for a total software solution for the sales function. The CDM Sales System consists of Windows based software systems – powerful tools for optimisation of the different aspects of the sales function ensuring considerable improvement of the company's competitiveness. The CDM Sales System consists of several independent systems that can be 100% integrated.

Consulting: Strategic Planning, Development of the sales organisation, MQA Certification, Turnkey Projects, Call Centre, Internal Telemarketing, Support Organisation

Human Resources: Recruitment, Education through NLP, Telemarketing, Sales, Management, and Personal Development.

Telemarketing bureau: Market scanning, ABC categorisation, and Satisfaction analysis, meeting arrangements, Follow-up on seminars, telephone sales.

WebWorkers: Integration between databases and homepages, Homepage design, Web business, Loyalty programs, GroupWare on the Internet.

Staffing Agency: Hiring out of databases co-ordinators, Supervisors and TM-assistants.

References
TeleDanmark, Fujitsu, Naturgas Syd, McCann Fokus, BRF Kredit, Radissson SAS, Alm. Brand, Telia, Groupe Schneider, Scandlines, DFDS, H&M, Posten SDS, Astra, SCA, Xerox.

Ownership and Equity
CDM Holding owns the company 100%.

Addresses
www.cdm.dk

Taarbæklund	*Frichsparken*
Strandvejen 781	Søren Frichs Vej 42B
DK-2930 Klampenborg	DK-8230 Åbyhøj
Denmark	Denmark
Phone +45 39 96 01 00	Phone +45 86 15 84 86
Fax +45 39 96 01 01	Fax +45 86 15 57 39

Supplier analysis – CDM Gruppen A/S

Segmentation

√	1)	Automatic electronic ABC categorisation based on criteria defined by the company
√	2)	Possibility of manual categorisation (override of automatic categorisation)
√	3)	Segmentation can be based on different criteria based on the specific "territory". Furthermore, the possibility of a customer being A customer in one "territory" and B customer in another is also an issue
√	4)	Automatic warnings at low levels of activity on dimensions defined by the company
√	5)	Basic profiling tools (AND, OR, LIKE, NOT LIKE, *, -, +, /)
(√)	6)	Reuse of earlier group profiles in new profile definitions
√	7)	"Drop-down-box" or equivalent with predefined database field information for and creation of group profiles

Campaigns

√	1)	Campaign can consist of a number of different tasks in a pre-defined order
√	2)	Costing on campaigns on more than one dimension
*3	3)	Display campaigns and activities using graphic tools like flowcharts
√	4)	Management of several parallel campaigns
√	5)	Campaign surveillance tools
√	6)	"Event triggers"
√	7)	"Assistants" (already programmed "event triggers") for user level
√	8)	Automatic generation of next step in a campaign
√	9)	Budgeting tool to calculate viability of planned campaigns
*3	10)	Graphic tools to show results
*3	11)	Possibility of seeing a list of all active campaigns incl. time-horizon
√	12)	Estimation and measuring of campaigns earnings efficiency
√	13)	Distribution of leads to campaign teams

Leads

√	1)	Management and creation of leads
√	2)	Calculation of success-rates on leads
√	3)	Status for leads' placing in a sales process
√	4)	Graphic tool that shows how many leads there are on each step of a sales funnel
√	5)	Possibility of attaching one or more competitors to a lead
√	6)	Status for leads' purchasing potential and the probability of the sale coming through
√	7)	Manual salesman assignment to leads
√	8)	Automatic salesman assignment to leads

Customer Data	√	1) Customer data table with the firms' own defined fields
	√	2) Possibility of more than one address per customer
	√	3) Possibility of attachments to customer database of previous e-mails, letters, documents (a so-called customer log)
	√	4) Registration of all previous meetings/contacts with customers including outcome
	√	5) Registration of own sales strategy and tactics towards each customer
	√	6) Registration of customers' goals, visions and key success factors
	√	7) Search possibilities on data on several dimensions simultaneously (for example area and age)
	√	8) Word/text search tool
	√	9) Registration and measurement of the customers' product interests over time
	√	10) Hyperlink to relations
Product Configuration and Contract Management	-	1) Product configuration from offline PC (being frequently replicated)
	-	2) Configuration of product by use of a hierarchic (one-way) system
	-	3) Configuration of product by use of a full dialogue (dynamic) system
	-	4) Configuration with circumstances, e.g. max price
	-	5) Calculation of delivery date of configured product/availability check
	-	6) Possible from offer to create order including data needed for invoicing
	-	7) Visualisation for customer of the product configuration online/via Internet
	-	8) Visualisation for the customer of the product configuration via print
	√	9) Verification of price offer from internal organisation
	√	10) Contract management tool
	t	11) Possibility of more than one price list for one product based on customer seniority, area, season, etc.
	-	12) Service level agreements integrated with contract processing
	√	13) Discounting tools supporting contract creation
	-	14) Possibility of maintaining configurations without the use of programming
Marketing Tools	√	1) Library for storing marketing material (folders, brochures, etc.)
	-	2) Historical product/price information library
	(√)	3) Competitor Information System
	√	4) Tool for customer satisfaction analysis
	-	5) Management and registration of materials (e.g. banners, stickers, etc.) from current and previous campaigns
	√	6) Possibility of mass-generated direct mail/mail-merging

Sales Force Automation	√	1)	Online data transfer from workstation to databases
	√	2)	Batch data transfer from workstation to databases
	√	3)	Possibility of quick synchronisation of offline laptops
	√	4)	Possibility of integration with PDA or the like via MS Outlook
	-	5)	Possibility of taking orders/making sales online via PDA to the CRM application
	√	6)	Graphs for salesman comparing actual sales to budget
Resource Management	√	1)	Planning calendar for each salesman
	√	2)	Possibility of booking a meeting on a calendar without the salesman's acceptance
	√	3)	Shared calendars (across several users)
	√	4)	Graphical calendar
	*2	5)	Possibility of setting alarms for meetings
	√	6)	Management of activities per user/customer/company/contact person
	√	7)	Possible for a customer to be member of numerous territories
	√	8)	Possibility of geographic, product type, and industry "territories"
	-	9)	Geographic route planning
	-	10)	Salesman resource planner
	√	11)	Registration of CRM related costs for each customer (e.g. travel costs for sales visits and marketing contribution costs etc.)
	-	12)	Front office logistics (storage repair, spares holding etc.)
Analysis Tools	*5	1)	Flexible report-generator for sales
	*5	2)	Flexible report-generator for marketing
	*5	3)	Flexible report-generator for service and support
	t	4)	Standard Executive Information System incl. graphics
	√	5)	Advanced budgeting tools (includes e.g. fixed and variable calculation methods based on data from previous seasons, salesmen efficiency rates, etc.)
Forecasts	√	1)	Product forecasts (sales per month/year)
	√	2)	Revenue forecasts (revenue per month/year)
	√	3)	Roll-ups of forecasts across numerous organisations
	√	4)	Support for user-defined forecast dates
	√	5)	Roll-ups and forecasts on several levels in a firm

	-	1) Push technology for information-gathering on the Internet (active search on words)
	√	2) Active Briefing
	√	3) Multiple currencies
	√	4) Euro compliant
	-	5) Supports electronic scrollbar
Other functionalities	√	6) Security system that defines user-clearance
	√	7) Quick-print of document without having to open the application supporting the document
	√	8) Personal correspondence templates
	√	9) Full integration to word-processing and spreadsheet applications (automatic merging into these from the CRM-system), e.g. OLE technology (Object Link Enabling)
	-	10) Guide functions for using the application ("Wizards")
	√	11) Integrated fax tool that works seamless, as part of the application
	√	1) Automatic assignment of leads from the Internet
	√	2) Tool for creating web-sites with predefined links to CRM database fields and interactive fields to CRM application
	√	3) Tool for creating web-sites with "drop-down-box" or equivalent with "drag-and-drop" graphics
Internet	√	4) Possibility for web-site differentiation dependant on customer logging in
	√	5) Integrated e-mail tool that works seamless, as part of the application
	√	6) Support for electronic payment
	√	1) Automatic dialling facilities (Predictive Dialling)
	√	2) Computer-Telephony Integration (CTI) enabled/supportive
	√	3) Application (through integration of CTI) enables routing possibilities of customer calling in, e.g. customer to specific operator, "A" customer first in queue, etc.
	√	4) Use of electronic scripts for telemarketing or response for Call Centre/guided dialogue management
Telemarketing, Call Centre and Help-Desk	-	5) Dialogue management with a neural network/adaptive learning
	√	6) Cross-sales functions
	-	7) "Neural" inbound e-mail answering tool
	-	8) Calculation/prognosis of inbound call frequency during the day
	-	9) Scheduling device for Call Centre operators (Schedule Planner)
	-	10) Technical problem resolution system
	-	11) "Trouble-Ticketing" – a system for requesting service
	√	12) Blending of Telemarketing and Call Centre function. That is the possibility of the system assigning telemarketing tasks to vacant operators during less busy periods

Price	1) Price per user: *DKK 2,500 – 9,000 depending on number of modules* 2) Annual license per user: *dependant on number of modules* 3) Installation and maintenance: *dependant on number of modules*
Product Development	1) Annual new versions: *1x* 2) Users in the Nordic countries: *7,500* 3) Global users incl. Nordic Countries: *10,000* 4) Planned new applications/functions within the next six months: - *e-commerce solution/incl. visual showrooms*
Support	√ 1) Hot-line (√) 2) 24-hour hot-line √ 3) Education Centre √ 4) Internet help
Ease of use	*User-friendly Interface* √ 1) Danish version √ 2) Swedish version √ 3) Norwegian version √ 4) Finnish version √ 5) German version √ 6) English version √ 7) French version √ 8) Spanish version √ 9) Other versions: *Italian, Polish*

Industry Solutions

The following Industry Solutions are offered:

- *Medical*
- *Telecom*
- *Marine*
- *(Building and Construction)*

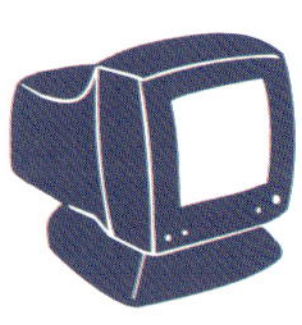

Platforms and Architecture

-	1)	Unix
√	2)	Win NT
√	3)	Win 95/98
-	4)	OS/2
-	5)	Mainframe, e.g. MVS
-	6)	MAC
-	7)	Netscape
-	8)	Internet explorer
-	9)	Full Web-based Architecture (Total O MB Thin Clients)
√	10)	Partial Web-based Architecture
√	11)	Client/Server-based Architecture
√	12)	Runs Client/Server over WAN
√	13)	Runs Client/Server over Dialup

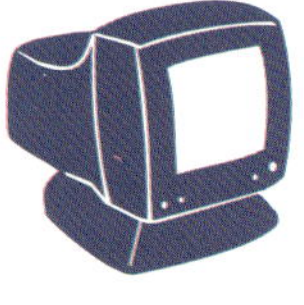

Configuration of CRM-System

1) Programming language: *Smalltalk*

2) Possibility for the firm to develop its own display: *High*

3) Scalability from no. of users: *1*

       to no. of users: *1000+*

√	4)	Automatic generation of connections between data fields
√	5)	When upgrading software customer-specific configurations are not lost
√	6)	The systems IT structure supports global operations with several servers

Databases

√	1)	Oracle
√	2)	Sybase
√	3)	Informix
-	4)	Scalable SQL
√	5)	MS SQL
√	6)	IBM DB2
-	7)	Access
-	8)	Ctree

Integration

-	1)	Pre-built SAP Interface
-	2)	Pre-built Oracle Interface
-	3)	Pre-built Peoplesoft Interface
-	4)	Pre-built Baan Interface
-	5)	Pre-built JD Edwards Interface
-	6)	Other pre-built Interfaces
√	7)	Supports Application Program Interfaces or equivalent
√	8)	Supports Object Link Enabling technology or equivalent
√	9)	Tool for creation of Interfaces without the use of programming
√	10)	Integration to 3rd party data providers, incl. D&B

Hardware

Minimum requirements for workstation

Processor:	*Pentium 133*
RAM:	*32 MB RAM*
Free harddisk space:	*20 MB*

Clarify

Company Overview

Clarify was founded in 1990 in San Jose, CA, in the heart of Silicon Valley. Clarify has more than 560 employees and has offices in the United States, Europe and Asia. Over the past years, Clarify has grown at an incredible rate of 3,844 percent, which has landed the company in a top-three position within the front office/customer interaction software industry. Clarify continually invests more in research and development than any other front-office vendor, a focus that has made it the technology leader in the industry.

Vision

Leading companies around the world use Clarify solutions to orchestrate every aspect of the customer life cycle across their front-office operations, including call centres, sales and marketing, customer service, quality assurance, field service, logistics and help desks. When these entities operate independently of each other, they often create chaos and, as a result, customer dissatisfaction. Clarify solves this problem. Our solutions unite your approach to customers, promote the collaboration that nurtures customer loyalty, and serve your unique business needs. And because customer loyalty drives down the cost of sales and increases revenues, Clarify can provide a critical competitive advantage.

Management Summary

Clarify offers an award winning set of integrated applications that allows to proactively manage customer interactions, and capitalize on the opportunities they present. Clarify is a leading provider of automated, customer-centric business solutions that integrate "front office" functions, improve productivity and, ultimately, increase competitiveness.

Clarify's integrated suite of customer interaction software provides a single source for all customer information. eFrontOffice acts as a lever of the latest database, Web, mobile and intelligent software agent technology to make sure that every customer interaction is personal, consistent, knowledge-based and shared across the customer organisation.

eFrontOffice offers comprehensive functionality that allows the customer to automate specific processes and increase employee productivity. Products are available as an integrated suite, or as separate modules:

- ClearCallCenter
- ClearSales
- ClearSupport
- Clear Helpdesk
- ClearLogistics
- ClearContracts
- ClearQuality
- ClearEnterprise Traveler
- ClearEnterprise e.link

References:
ADP, Amoco Corporation, British Telecom, Cisco Systems, Compaq, Ericsson, GE of USA, Georgia-Pacific, Hewlett-Packard, MCI, Microsoft Corporation, Prudential, Procter & Gamble, Sprint PCS, Toyota and Transamerica Corporation.

Ownership and Equity:
Traded as Nasdaq: CLFY.

Addresses:
www.clarify.com

Germany

Clarify GmbH

Weltenburger Strasse 70

81677 Munich

Germany

Phone +49-89-92-404-164

Fax +49-89-92-404-167

Email: info.germany@clarify.com

United Kingdom (EMEA Headquarters)

Clarify Ltd.

Clarify Court, London Road

Reading RG6 1BW

England

Phone +44-118-9-299-200

Fax +44-118-9-299-201

Supplier analysis – Clarify

Segmentation

√	1) Automatic electronic ABC categorisation based on criteria defined by the company
√	2) Possibility of manual categorisation (override of automatic categorisation)
√	3) Segmentation can be based on different criteria based on the specific "territory". Furthermore, the possibility of a customer being A customer in one "territory" and B customer in another is also an issue
√	4) Automatic warnings at low levels of activity on dimensions defined by the company
√	5) Basic profiling tools (AND, OR, LIKE, NOT LIKE, *, -, +, /)
-	6) Reuse of earlier group profiles in new profile definitions
√	7) "Drop-down-box" or equivalent with predefined database field information for and creation of group profiles

Campaigns

√	1) Campaign can consist of a number of different tasks in a pre-defined order
√	2) Costing on campaigns on more than one dimension
-	3) Display campaigns and activities using graphic tools like flowcharts
√	4) Management of several parallel campaigns
√	5) Campaign surveillance tools
√	6) "Event triggers"
√	7) "Assistants" (already programmed "event triggers") for user level
√	8) Automatic generation of next step in a campaign
√	9) Budgeting tool to calculate viability of planned campaigns
*6	10) Graphic tools to show results
√	11) Possibility of seeing a list of all active campaigns incl. time-horizon
√	12) Estimation and measuring of campaigns earnings efficiency
√	13) Distribution of leads to campaign teams

Leads

√	1) Management and creation of leads
√	2) Calculation of success-rates on leads
√	3) Status for leads' placing in a sales process
-	4) Graphic tool that shows how many leads there are on each step of a sales funnel
√	5) Possibility of attaching one or more competitors to a lead
√	6) Status for leads' purchasing potential and the probability of the sale coming through
√	7) Manual salesman assignment to leads
√	8) Automatic salesman assignment to leads

Customer Data	√	1)	Customer data table with the firms' own defined fields
	√	2)	Possibility of more than one address per customer
	√	3)	Possibility of attachments to customer database of previous e-mails, letters, documents (a so-called customer log)
	√	4)	Registration of all previous meetings/contacts with customers including outcome
	√	5)	Registration of own sales strategy and tactics towards each customer
	√	6)	Registration of customers' goals, visions and key success factors
	√	7)	Search possibilities on data on several dimensions simultaneously (for example area and age)
	√	8)	Word/text search tool
	√	9)	Registration and measurement of the customers' product interests over time
	√	10)	Hyperlink to relations
Product Configuration and Contract Management	√	1)	Product configuration from offline PC (being frequently replicated)
	√	2)	Configuration of product by use of a hierarchic (one-way) system
	√	3)	Configuration of product by use of a full dialogue (dynamic) system
	√	4)	Configuration with circumstances, e.g. max price
	√	5)	Calculation of delivery date of configured product/availability check
	√	6)	Possible from offer to create order including data needed for invoicing
	√	7)	Visualisation for customer of the product configuration online/via Internet
	-	8)	Visualisation for the customer of the product configuration via print
	√	9)	Verification of price offer from internal organisation
	√	10)	Contract management tool
	√	11)	Possibility of more than one price list for one product based on customer seniority, area, season, etc.
	√	12)	Service level agreements integrated with contract processing
	√	13)	Discounting tools supporting contract creation
	√	14)	Possibility of maintaining configurations without the use of programming
Marketing Tools	√	1)	Library for storing marketing material (folders, brochures, etc.)
	√	2)	Historical product/price information library
	√	3)	Competitor Information System
	-	4)	Tool for customer satisfaction analysis
	√	5)	Management and registration of materials (e.g. banners, stickers, etc.) from current and previous campaigns
	√	6)	Possibility of mass-generated direct mail/mail-merging

Sales Force Automation	√	1) Online data transfer from workstation to databases
	√	2) Batch data transfer from workstation to databases
	√	3) Possibility of quick synchronisation of offline laptops
	√	4) Possibility of integration with PDA or the like via MS Outlook
	-	5) Possibility of taking orders/making sales online via PDA to the CRM application
	-	6) Graphs for salesman comparing actual sales to budget
Resource Management	*2	1) Planning calendar for each salesman
	*2	2) Possibility of booking a meeting on a calendar without the salesman's acceptance
	*2	3) Shared calendars (across several users)
	*2	4) Graphical calendar
	*2	5) Possibility of setting alarms for meetings
	√	6) Management of activities per user/customer/company/contact person
	√	7) Possible for a customer to be member of numerous territories
	√	8) Possibility of geographic, product type, and industry "territories"
	-	9) Geographic route planning
	-	10) Salesman resource planner
	√	11) Registration of CRM related costs for each customer (e.g. travel costs for sales visits and marketing contribution costs etc.)
	√	12) Front office logistics (storage repair, spares holding etc.)
Analysis Tools	√	1) Flexible report-generator for sales
	√	2) Flexible report-generator for marketing
	√	3) Flexible report-generator for service and support
	-	4) Standard Executive Information System incl. graphics
	√	5) Advanced budgeting tools (includes e.g. fixed and variable calculation methods based on data from previous seasons, salesmen efficiency rates, etc.)
Forecasts	√	1) Product forecasts (sales per month/year)
	√	2) Revenue forecasts (revenue per month/year)
	√	3) Roll-ups of forecasts across numerous organisations
	√	4) Support for user-defined forecast dates
	√	5) Roll-ups and forecasts on several levels in a firm

Other functionalities	-	1)	Push technology for information-gathering on the Internet (active search on words)
	-	2)	Active Briefing
	√	3)	Multiple currencies
	-	4)	Euro compliant
	-	5)	Supports electronic scrollbar
	√	6)	Security system that defines user-clearance
	√	7)	Quick-print of document without having to open the application supporting the document
	-	8)	Personal correspondence templates
	√	9)	Full integration to word-processing and spreadsheet applications (automatic merging into these from the CRM-system), e.g. OLE technology (Object Link Enabling)
	-	10)	Guide functions for using the application ("Wizards")
	√	11)	Integrated fax tool that works seamless, as part of the application
Internet	√	1)	Automatic assignment of leads from the Internet
	-	2)	Tool for creating web-sites with predefined links to CRM database fields and interactive fields to CRM application
	-	3)	Tool for creating web-sites with "drop-down-box" or equivalent with "drag-and-drop" graphics
	-	4)	Possibility for web-site differentiation dependant on customer logging in
	√	5)	Integrated e-mail tool that works seamless, as part of the application
	-	6)	Support for electronic payment
Telemarketing, Call Centre and Help-Desk	√	1)	Automatic dialling facilities (Predictive Dialling)
	√	2)	Computer-Telephony Integration (CTI) enabled/supportive
	√	3)	Application (through integration of CTI) enables routing possibilities of customer calling in, e.g. customer to specific operator, "A" customer first in queue, etc.
	√	4)	Use of electronic scripts for telemarketing or response for Call Centre/guided dialogue management
	-	5)	Dialogue management with a neural network/adaptive learning
	√	6)	Cross-sales functions
	√	7)	"Neural" inbound e-mail answering tool
	-	8)	Calculation/prognosis of inbound call frequency during the day
	-	9)	Scheduling device for Call Centre operators (Schedule Planner)
	√	10)	Technical problem resolution system
	√	11)	"Trouble-Ticketing" – a system for requesting service
	√	12)	Blending of Telemarketing and Call Centre function. That is the possibility of the system assigning telemarketing tasks to vacant operators during less busy periods

Price	1) Price per user: *£3000 list price per concurrent user (full function)* *£375 for web user* 2) Annual license per user: *none* 3) Installation and maintenance: *dependant on service options*
Product Development	1) Annual new versions: *2 major releases* 2) Users in the Nordic countries: *40 firms* 3) Global users incl. Nordic Countries: *700 firms* 4) Planned new applications/functions within the next six months: - *eCommerce suite within the product* - *thin web client* - *enhancements across all front office modules*
Support	√ 1) Hot-line √ 2) 24-hour hot-line √ 3) Education Centre √ 4) Internet help
Ease of use	*User-friendly Interface* t 1) Danish version t 2) Swedish version t 3) Norwegian version t 4) Finnish version √ 5) German version √ 6) English version √ 7) French version t 8) Spanish version √ 9) Other versions: *Kanji*

Industry Solutions

The following Industry Solutions are offered:

- *Clarify CommCentre for Telecommunications*

Platforms and
Architecture

√	1)	Unix
√	2)	Win NT
√	3)	Win 95/98
-	4)	OS/2
-	5)	Mainframe, e.g. MVS
-	6)	MAC
√	7)	Netscape
√	8)	Internet explorer
√	9)	Full Web-based Architecture (Total O MB Thin Clients)
-	10)	Partial Web-based Architecture
√	11)	Client/Server-based Architecture
√	12)	Runs Client/Server over WAN
√	13)	Runs Client/Server over Dialup

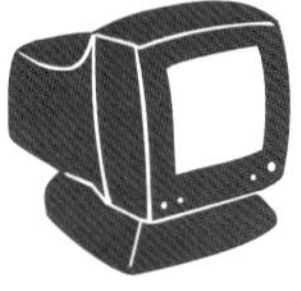

Configuration of
CRM-System

1)	Programming language: *ClearExtensions*
2)	Possibility for the firm to develop its own display: *High*
3)	Scalability from no. of users: *1* to no. of users: *30,000+*

√	4)	Automatic generation of connections between data-fields
√	5)	When upgrading software customer-specific configurations are not lost
√	6)	The systems IT structure supports global operations with several servers

---

Databases

√	1)	Oracle
√	2)	Sybase
-	3)	Informix
√	4)	Scalable SQL
√	5)	MS SQL
-	6)	IBM DB2
-	7)	Access
-	8)	Ctree

Integration

-	1)	Pre-built SAP Interface
-	2)	Pre-built Oracle Interface
-	3)	Pre-built Peoplesoft Interface
-	4)	Pre-built Baan Interface
-	5)	Pre-built JD Edwards Interface
-	6)	Other pre-built Interfaces
√	7)	Supports Application Program Interfaces or equivalent
√	8)	Supports Object Link Enabling technology or equivalent
√	9)	Tool for creation of Interfaces without the use of programming
√	10)	Integration to 3rd party data providers, incl. D&B

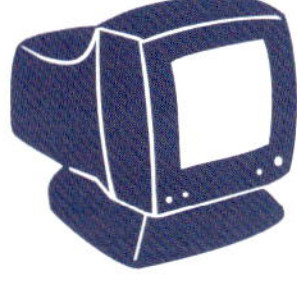

Hardware

Minimum requirements for workstation

Processor:	*Pentium*
RAM:	*32 MB RAM*
Free harddisk space:	*25 MB*

Corepoint Technologies

Company Overview

Corepoint Technologies is part of IBM.

Vision

Customer Relationship Management is a broad term generally applied to any means taken to improve customer service. But that is not the case with Corepoint. Our definition moves beyond traditional CRM to a new vision, based on new approaches for managing customer relationships for competitive advantage and differentiation. This approach, enabled by e-business technology, aims at managing the customer "holistically," by providing consistent value-added experiences to the customer through a single long-running dialogue. And through this dialogue, you can deal with each customer as an individual, supported by the ability to recall and reference all previous interactions with each customer, and to customise product offerings if and when necessary to accommodate each customer's needs and preferences.

That is the vision of the Corepoint Customer Relationship Solutions. A customer-focused business solution that works across your entire enterprise. And it can be your point of difference, your competitive advantage, by becoming a company known to its customers for the ability to respond to needs and accommodate requests, a company well deserving their patronage, a company to which they will become loyal.

Management Summary

The Corepoint Suite is a world-class, integrated software product solution that helps your organisation manage customer relationships. Corepoint is as open as it is comprehensive, addressing the needs of marketing and sales, all the way to customer service and follow-up. The suite is not only complete but also flexible, allowing you to select only the product packages that fit the needs of your organisation. Universal access makes it easy for your customers to be in contact with your company through many different channels (i.e. telephone, web email) in both assisted (person-to-person) or unassisted (self-service) modes. The suite's robust, cross-platform technologies make the system easy to implement and easy to use. Best of all, the suite puts the information right at hand so that the user can respond quickly and intelligently to customers as well as be proactive in addressing future customer needs. The Corepoint Suite includes:

Corepoint Sales Products: Sales products that help you maximise revenue by serving customers where, when and how they desire.

Corepoint Marketing Products: Products that help you select profitable customer segments, and execute effective marketing campaigns to increase sales revenue.

Corepoint Service Products: Products that help you resolve customer inquiries in a fast, consistent and accurate manner.

Corepoint Support Products: Products that help your customers get maximum value from the products they purchase.

Corepoint Foundation Products: Products that serve as the foundation for building powerful business applications.

Corepoint Universal Access Products: Products that allow your customers to interact with your company through personal assistance or self-service, whether via the phone, Internet or any other electronic means.

Corepoint Enterprise Connections Products: Products that make your front-office, back-office and other systems work together in concert to serve customers better, faster and more effectively.

Corepoint Relationship Management Products: Products that help you manage and use information to better serve your customers' personal needs and expectations.

In addition, Corepoint provides a specific set of solutions for the Finance Industry, Corepoint Banking Solutions. This includes solutions for the Branch (both service & sales), the contact centre and the Web.

References

ANZ Bank, ABN AMRO, Bank of Scotland, Eastern Energy, Fuji Bank, Konica, Mannheimer, Postbank, Bank One, Pacific Bell, Best Buy, Key Corp, PNC Bank, Sprint, Telecom New Zealand, Unibank

Ownership and Equity

Corepoint Technologies is part of IBM

Addresses

www.corepoint.com

Headquarters	*European Headquarters:*
9025 North River Road	Rosanne House
Indianapolis, IN	Bridge Road East
USA: 46240-7622	Welwyn Garden City
Phone (800) COREPNT (800 267-3768)	Hertfordshire, AL8 6UB
	England
	Phone +44 1707 363111

Supplier analysis – Corepoint Technologies

Segmentation

(√)	1)	Automatic electronic ABC categorisation based on criteria defined by the company
√	2)	Possibility of manual categorisation (override of automatic categorisation)
√	3)	Segmentation can be based on different criteria based on the specific "territory". Furthermore, the possibility of a customer being A customer in one "territory" and B customer in another is also an issue
(√)	4)	Automatic warnings at low levels of activity on dimensions defined by the company
√	5)	Basic profiling tools (AND, OR, LIKE, NOT LIKE, *, -, +, /)
-	6)	Reuse of earlier group profiles in new profile definitions
-	7)	"Drop-down-box" or equivalent with predefined database field information for and creation of group profiles

Campaigns

(√)	1)	Campaign can consist of a number of different tasks in a pre-defined order
(√)	2)	Costing on campaigns on more than one dimension
-	3)	Display campaigns and activities using graphic tools like flowcharts
(√)	4)	Management of several parallel campaigns
√	5)	Campaign surveillance tools
(√)	6)	"Event triggers"
(√)	7)	"Assistants" (already programmed "event triggers") for user level
*7	8)	Automatic generation of next step in a campaign
(√)	9)	Budgeting tool to calculate viability of planned campaigns
*5	10)	Graphic tools to show results
*7	11)	Possibility of seeing a list of all active campaigns incl. time-horizon
(√)	12)	Estimation and measuring of campaigns earnings efficiency
(√)	13)	Distribution of leads to campaign teams

Leads

√	1)	Management and creation of leads
√	2)	Calculation of success-rates on leads
√	3)	Status for leads' placing in a sales process
√	4)	Graphic tool that shows how many leads there are on each step of a sales funnel
√	5)	Possibility of attaching one or more competitors to a lead
√	6)	Status for leads' purchasing potential and the probability of the sale coming through
√	7)	Manual salesman assignment to leads
√	8)	Automatic salesman assignment to leads

Customer Data	√	1) Customer data table with the firms' own defined fields
	√	2) Possibility of more than one address per customer
	√	3) Possibility of attachments to customer database of previous e-mails, letters, documents (a so-called customer log)
	√	4) Registration of all previous meetings/contacts with customers including outcome
	√	5) Registration of own sales strategy and tactics towards each customer
	√	6) Registration of customers' goals, visions and key success factors
	√	7) Search possibilities on data on several dimensions simultaneously (for example area and age)
	√	8) Word/text search tool
	√	9) Registration and measurement of the customers' product interests over time
	√	10) Hyperlink to relations
Product Configuration and Contract Management	-	1) Product configuration from offline PC (being frequently replicated)
	-	2) Configuration of product by use of a hierarchic (one-way) system
	-	3) Configuration of product by use of a full dialogue (dynamic) system
	-	4) Configuration with circumstances, e.g. max price
	-	5) Calculation of delivery date of configured product/availability check
	√	6) Possible from offer to create order including data needed for invoicing
	-	7) Visualisation for customer of the product configuration online/via Internet
	-	8) Visualisation for the customer of the product configuration via print
	√	9) Verification of price offer from internal organisation
	√	10) Contract management tool
	-	11) Possibility of more than one price list for one product based on customer seniority, area, season, etc.
	-	12) Service level agreements integrated with contract processing
	√	13) Discounting tools supporting contract creation
	-	14) Possibility of maintaining configurations without the use of programming
Marketing Tools	*8	1) Library for storing marketing material (folders, brochures, etc.)
	*8	2) Historical product/price information library
	√	3) Competitor Information System
	(√)	4) Tool for customer satisfaction analysis
	-	5) Management and registration of materials (e.g. banners, stickers, etc.) from current and previous campaigns
	√	6) Possibility of mass-generated direct mail/mail-merging

Sales Force Automation	√	1)	Online data transfer from workstation to databases
	√	2)	Batch data transfer from workstation to databases
	√	3)	Possibility of quick synchronisation of offline laptops
	√	4)	Possibility of integration with PDA or the like via MS Outlook
	-	5)	Possibility of taking orders/making sales online via PDA to the CRM application
	√	6)	Graphs for salesman comparing actual sales to budget
Resource Management	√	1)	Planning calendar for each salesman
	√	2)	Possibility of booking a meeting on a calendar without the salesman's acceptance
	√	3)	Shared calendars (across several users)
	√	4)	Graphical calendar
	*2	5)	Possibility of setting alarms for meetings
	√	6)	Management of activities per user/customer/company/contact person
	√	7)	Possible for a customer to be member of numerous territories
	√	8)	Possibility of geographic, product type, and industry "territories"
	-	9)	Geographic route planning
	-	10)	Salesman resource planner
	√	11)	Registration of CRM related costs for each customer (e.g. travel costs for sales visits and marketing contribution costs etc.)
	√	12)	Front office logistics (storage repair, spares holding etc.)
Analysis Tools	*9	1)	Flexible report-generator for sales
	*9	2)	Flexible report-generator for marketing
	*9	3)	Flexible report-generator for service and support
	*9	4)	Standard Executive Information System incl. graphics
	-	5)	Advanced budgeting tools (includes e.g. fixed and variable calculation methods based on data from previous seasons, salesmen efficiency rates, etc.)
Forecasts	√	1)	Product forecasts (sales per month/year)
	√	2)	Revenue forecasts (revenue per month/year)
	t	3)	Roll-ups of forecasts across numerous organisations
	√	4)	Support for user-defined forecast dates
	√	5)	Roll-ups and forecasts on several levels in a firm

Other functionalities	-	1) Push technology for information-gathering on the Internet (active search on words)
	√	2) Active Briefing
	√	3) Multiple currencies
	√	4) Euro compliant
	-	5) Supports electronic scrollbar
	√	6) Security system that defines user-clearance
	√	7) Quick-print of document without having to open the application supporting the document
	√	8) Personal correspondence templates
	(√)	9) Full integration to word-processing and spreadsheet applications (automatic merging into these from the CRM-system), e.g. OLE technology (Object Link Enabling)
	(√)	10) Guide functions for using the application ("Wizards")
	√	11) Integrated fax tool that works seamless, as part of the application
Internet	t	1) Automatic assignment of leads from the Internet
	*8	2) Tool for creating web-sites with predefined links to CRM database fields and interactive fields to CRM application
	-	3) Tool for creating web-sites with "drop-down-box" or equivalent with "drag-and-drop" graphics
	*8	4) Possibility for web-site differentiation dependant on customer logging in
	√	5) Integrated e-mail tool that works seamless, as part of the application
	√	6) Support for electronic payment
Telemarketing, Call Centre and Help-Desk	√	1) Automatic dialling facilities (Predictive Dialling)
	√	2) Computer-Telephony Integration (CTI) enabled/supportive
	√	3) Application (through integration of CTI) enables routing possibilities of customer calling in, e.g. customer to specific operator, "A" customer first in queue, etc.
	√	4) Use of electronic scripts for telemarketing or response for Call Centre/guided dialogue management
	√	5) Dialogue management with a neural network/adaptive learning
	√	6) Cross-sales functions
	√	7) "Neural" inbound e-mail answering tool
	√	8) Calculation/prognosis of inbound call frequency during the day
	*10	9) Scheduling device for Call Centre operators (Schedule Planner)
	√	10) Technical problem resolution system
	√	11) "Trouble-Ticketing" – a system for requesting service
	√	12) Blending of Telemarketing and Call Centre function. That is the possibility of the system assigning telemarketing tasks to vacant operators during less busy periods

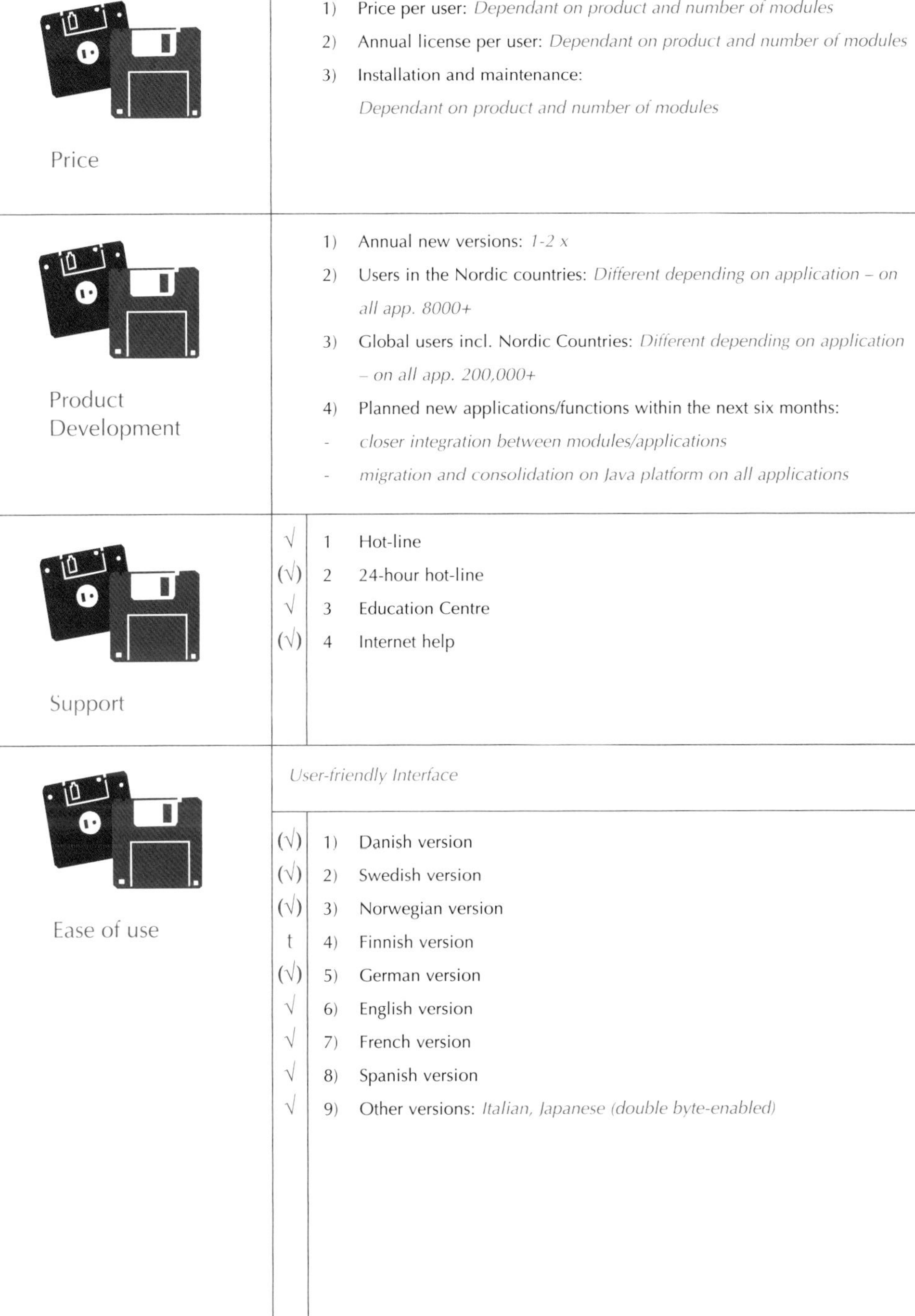

Price	1) Price per user: *Dependant on product and number of modules* 2) Annual license per user: *Dependant on product and number of modules* 3) Installation and maintenance: *Dependant on product and number of modules*
Product Development	1) Annual new versions: *1-2 x* 2) Users in the Nordic countries: *Different depending on application – on all app. 8000+* 3) Global users incl. Nordic Countries: *Different depending on application – on all app. 200,000+* 4) Planned new applications/functions within the next six months: - *closer integration between modules/applications* - *migration and consolidation on Java platform on all applications*
Support	√ 1 Hot-line (√) 2 24-hour hot-line √ 3 Education Centre (√) 4 Internet help
Ease of use	*User-friendly Interface* (√) 1) Danish version (√) 2) Swedish version (√) 3) Norwegian version t 4) Finnish version (√) 5) German version √ 6) English version √ 7) French version √ 8) Spanish version √ 9) Other versions: *Italian, Japanese (double byte-enabled)*

Industry Solutions

The following Industry Solutions are offered:

- *Banking*

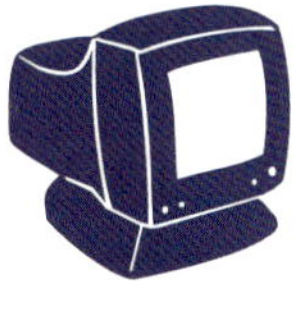

Platforms and Architecture

√	1)	Unix
√	2)	Win NT
(√)	3)	Win 95/98
(√)	4)	OS/2
√	5)	Mainframe, e.g. MVS
-	6)	MAC
√	7)	Netscape
√	8)	Internet explorer
(√)	9)	Full Web-based Architecture (Total 0 MB Thin Clients)
-	10)	Partial Web-based Architecture
√	11)	Client/Server based Architecture
√	12)	Runs Client/Server over WAN
√	13)	Runs Client/Server over Dialup

Configuration of CRM-System

	1)	Programming language: *Java, C++, Cobol, etc.*
	2)	Possibility for the firm to develop its own display: *High/(Java – Medium)*
	3)	Scalability from no. of users: *10* to no. of users: *10,000+*

√	4)	Automatic generation of connections between data fields
√	5)	When upgrading software customer-specific configurations are not lost
√	6)	The systems IT structure supports global operations with several servers

---

Databases

(√)	1)	Oracle
(√)	2)	Sybase
t	3)	Informix
-	4)	Scalable SQL
(√)	5)	MS SQL
√	6)	IBM DB2
-	7)	Access
-	8)	Ctree

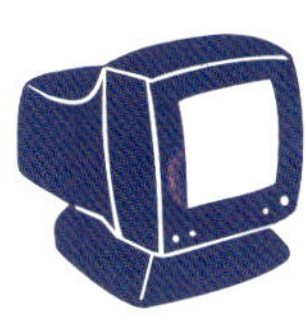

Integration

√	1)	Pre-built SAP Interface
-	2)	Pre-built Oracle Interface
-	3)	Pre-built Peoplesoft Interface
-	4)	Pre-built Baan Interface
-	5)	Pre-built JD Edwards Interface
-	6)	Other pre-built Interfaces
√	7)	Supports Application Program Interfaces or equivalent
√	8)	Supports Object Link Enabling technology or equivalent
√	9)	Tool for creation of Interfaces without the use of programming
√	10)	Integration to 3rd party data providers, incl. D&B

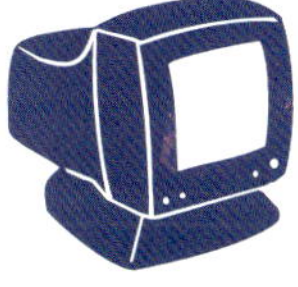

Hardware

Minimum requirements for workstation

Processor:	*Pentium 133*
RAM:	*32 MB RAM*
Free harddisk space:	*from 0 MB – dependant on applications chosen*

DM Software

Company Overview

DM Software has expanded by approximately 60% every accounting year since its foundation.

The bank of knowledge and the technical development which form the basis of DM Software's product deliveries and services are based on hand picked specialists within the IT and marketing industry. The know-how that has been established in connection with Direct Marketing – database marketing – dialogue marketing at DM Software is accordingly very large.

All employees with DM Software work with development and system services.

Vision

The recognition of the importance of maintaining good customers is spreading rapidly these years and will be setting the agenda for many business leaders in the future. On the concrete level this has caused an increasingly strong interest in CRM (Customer Relationship Management).

DM Software wishes to be part of this trend – primarily by developing and marketing the CRM application, which collects and integrates customer data across the organisation and the IT systems.

Through a strong engagement in the global development within marketing trends, DM Software is able to deliver an effective edp-based tool supporting all aspects of sales and marketing, including Call Centre solutions which in combination with administrative and other edp-tools create the CRM-universe.

Management Summary

DM Software's CRM-tool, the Dialog Manager is presently (according to own and leading DM bureaus' observations) completely unique in its dynamic ability to adjust to the demands and needs that a 'biological' development in a certain organisation goes through. This may be competition, altered market conditions, demands from authorities or a change in conditions for the preservation of a CRM universe.

The Dialog Manager has a very special facility incorporated in its user interface: The editor that is applied by the user for adjustment of screen pictures, fields and functions has an underlying function which automatically 'programs' the edge and function contact to the database employed.

Accordingly, the Dialog Manager adjusts itself to new and required demands and needs at the very moment these needs arise, and this happens completely without programmer assistance.

This entails quite naturally that the Dialog Manager lives up to total management at all levels within the CRM universe, e.g.:

- Management information
- Sales management
- Marketing activities
- IT (data integration)
- Call Centre – CTI/CT
- Personal communication
- PRM (Partner Relationship Management)
- IRM (Internet Relationship Management) and (Information Resources Management)
- ERM (Employee Relationship Management)

But even though "the right tool is half the work", the other half – CRM Brainware – is of course just as important. Accordingly, DM Software has on the one hand direct CRM expertise employed; on the other hand we are engaged in close co-operation with specialists in consultancy companies who can help secure optimum use of modern information technology.

References
PBS, Coloplast, Telia, Tobaksskaderådet and others.

Ownership and Equity
Today, FK Holding and SJ Holding own DM Software. DM Software is self-financed and has through the past two years shown a working profit on ordinary activities. The system development costs are part of the ordinary activities.

Address
www.dmsoftware.dk

DM Software ApS

Slotsmarken 11

DK-2970 Hørsholm

Denmark

Phone +45 76 69 00

Fax +45 76 69 10

Supplier analysis – DM Software

Segmentation	t	1) Automatic electronic ABC categorisation based on criteria defined by the company
	√	2) Possibility of manual categorisation (override of automatic categorisation)
	t	3) Segmentation can be based on different criteria based on the specific "territory". Furthermore, the possibility of a customer being A customer in one "territory" and B customer in another is also an issue
	√	4) Automatic warnings at low levels of activity on dimensions defined by the company
	√	5) Basic profiling tools (AND, OR, LIKE, NOT LIKE, *, -, +, /)
	√	6) Reuse of earlier group profiles in new profile definitions
	√	7) "Drop-down-box" or equivalent with predefined database field information for and creation of group profiles
Campaigns	√	1) Campaign can consist of a number of different tasks in a pre-defined order
	√	2) Costing on campaigns on more than one dimension
	√	3) Display campaigns and activities using graphic tools like flowcharts
	√	4) Management of several parallel campaigns
	√	5) Campaign surveillance tools
	√	6) "Event triggers"
	√	7) "Assistants" (already programmed "event triggers") for user level
	√	8) Automatic generation of next step in a campaign
	*1	9) Budgeting tool to calculate viability of planned campaigns
	√	10) Graphic tools to show results
	-	11) Possibility of seeing a list of all active campaigns incl. time-horizon
	√	12) Estimation and measuring of campaigns earnings efficiency
	√	13) Distribution of leads to campaign teams
Leads	√	1) Management and creation of leads
	t	2) Calculation of success-rates on leads
	√	3) Status for leads' placing in a sales process
	√	4) Graphic tool that shows how many leads there are on each step of a sales funnel
	√	5) Possibility of attaching one or more competitors to a lead
	√	6) Status for leads' purchasing potential and the probability of the sale coming through
	√	7) Manual salesman assignment to leads
	√	8) Automatic salesman assignment to leads

	√	1) Customer data table with the firms' own defined fields
	√	2) Possibility of more than one address per customer
	√	3) Possibility of attachments to customer database of previous e-mails, letters, documents (a so-called customer log)
	√	4) Registration of all previous meetings/contacts with customers including outcome
Customer Data	√	5) Registration of own sales strategy and tactics towards each customer
	√	6) Registration of customers' goals, visions and key success factors
	√	7) Search possibilities on data on several dimensions simultaneously (for example area and age)
	√	8) Word/text search tool
	√	9) Registration and measurement of the customers' product interests over time
	√	10) Hyperlink to relations
	√	1) Product configuration from offline PC (being frequently replicated)
	-	2) Configuration of product by use of a hierarchic (one-way) system
	t	3) Configuration of product by use of a full dialogue (dynamic) system
	√	4) Configuration with circumstances, e.g. max price
	-	5) Calculation of delivery date of configured product/availability check
	t	6) Possible from offer to create order including data needed for invoicing
	-	7) Visualisation for customer of the product configuration online/via Internet
Product Configuration and Contract Management	-	8) Visualisation for the customer of the product configuration via print
	-	9) Verification of price offer from internal organisation
	t	10) Contract management tool
	t	11) Possibility of more than one price list for one product based on customer seniority, area, season, etc.
	-	12) Service level agreements integrated with contract processing
	t	13) Discounting tools supporting contract creation
	√	14) Possibility of maintaining configurations without the use of programming
	-	1) Library for storing marketing material (folders, brochures, etc.)
	√	2) Historical product/price information library
	√	3) Competitor Information System
Marketing Tools	√	4) Tool for customer satisfaction analysis
	-	5) Management and registration of materials (e.g. banners, stickers, etc.) from current and previous campaigns
	√	6) Possibility of mass-generated direct mail/mail-merging

Sales Force Automation	√	1) Online data transfer from workstation to databases
	√	2) Batch data transfer from workstation to databases
	-	3) Possibility of quick synchronisation of offline laptops
	√	4) Possibility of integration with PDA or the like via MS Outlook
	-	5) Possibility of taking orders/making sales online via PDA to the CRM application
	t	6) Graphs for salesman comparing actual sales to budget
Resource Management	*2	1) Planning calendar for each salesman
	*2	2) Possibility of booking a meeting on a calendar without the salesman's acceptance
	*2	3) Shared calendars (across several users)
	*2	4) Graphical calendar
	*2	5) Possibility of setting alarms for meetings
	√	6) Management of activities per user/customer/company/contact person
	√	7) Possible for a customer to be member of numerous territories
	√	8) Possibility of geographic, product type, and industry "territories"
	-	9) Geographic route planning
	-	10) Salesman resource planner
	√	11) Registration of CRM related costs for each customer (e.g. travel costs for sales visits and marketing contribution costs etc.)
	-	12) Front office logistics (storage repair, spares holding etc.)
Analysis Tools	√	1) Flexible report-generator for sales
	√	2) Flexible report-generator for marketing
	√	3) Flexible report-generator for service and support
	t	4) Standard Executive Information System incl. graphics
	*1	5) Advanced budgeting tools (includes e.g. fixed and variable calculation methods based on data from previous seasons, salesmen efficiency rates, etc.)
Forecasts	√	1) Product forecasts (sales per month/year)
	√	2) Revenue forecasts (revenue per month/year)
	√	3) Roll-ups of forecasts across numerous organisations
	√	4) Support for user-defined forecast dates
	√	5) Roll-ups and forecasts on several levels in a firm

Other functionalities	√	1) Push technology for information-gathering on the Internet (active search on words)
	t	2) Active Briefing
	t	3) Multiple currencies
	-	4) Euro compliant
	√	5) Supports electronic scrollbar
	-	6) Security system that defines user-clearance
	√	7) Quick-print of document without having to open the application supporting the document
	√	8) Personal correspondence templates
		9) Full integration to word-processing and spreadsheet applications (automatic merging into these from the CRM-system), e.g. OLE technology (Object Link Enabling)
	√	10) Guide functions for using the application ("Wizards")
	-	11) Integrated fax tool that works seamless, as part of the application
Internet	√	1) Automatic assignment of leads from the Internet
	-	2) Tool for creating web-sites with predefined links to CRM database fields and interactive fields to CRM application
	-	3) Tool for creating web-sites with "drop-down-box" or equivalent with "drag-and-drop" graphics
	t	4) Possibility for web-site differentiation dependant on customer logging in
	√	5) Integrated e-mail tool that works seamless, as part of the application
	√	6) Support for electronic payment
Telemarketing, Call Centre and Help-Desk	√	1) Automatic dialling facilities (Predictive Dialling)
	√	2) Computer-Telephony Integration (CTI) enabled/supportive
	√	3) Application (through integration of CTI) enables routing possibilities of customer calling in, e.g. customer to specific operator, "A" customer first in queue, etc.
	-	4) Use of electronic scripts for telemarketing or response for Call Centre/guided dialogue management
	-	5) Dialogue management with a neural network/adaptive learning
	√	6) Cross-sales functions
	-	7) "Neural" inbound e-mail answering tool
	-	8) Calculation/prognosis of inbound call frequency during the day
	-	9) Scheduling device for Call Centre operators (Schedule Planner)
	-	10) Technical problem resolution system
	-	11) "Trouble-Ticketing" – a system for requesting service
	√	12) Blending of Telemarketing and Call Centre function. That is the possibility of the system assigning telemarketing tasks to vacant operators during less busy periods

Price	1) Price per user: *DKK 6,000 incl. investments in modules* 2) Annual license per user: *DKK 0* 3) Installation and maintenance: *Installation, consulting assistance at fixed price or ad hoc on hourly price. Upgrades are 15% per year of investments in licenses*
Product Development	1) Annual new versions: *2-4x* 2) Users in the Nordic countries: *520* 3) Global users incl. Nordic Countries: 5*40* 4) Planned new applications/functions within the next year:
Support	√ 1) Hot-line - 2) 24-hour hot-line √ 3) Education Centre - 4) Internet help
Ease of use	*Intuitive user Interface in Windows style* √ 1) Danish version √ 2) Swedish version t 3) Norwegian version t 4) Finnish version t 5) German version √ 6) English version t 7) French version t 8) Spanish version t 9) Other versions:

<table>
<tr>
<td>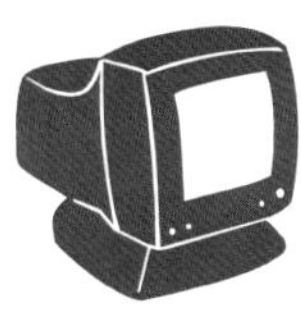
Industry Solutions</td>
<td colspan="2">The following Industry Solutions are offered: NA</td>
</tr>
<tr>
<td rowspan="13">Platforms and Architecture</td>
<td>√</td>
<td>1) Unix</td>
</tr>
<tr><td>√</td><td>2) Win NT</td></tr>
<tr><td>√</td><td>3) Win 95/98</td></tr>
<tr><td>√</td><td>4) OS/2</td></tr>
<tr><td>-</td><td>5) Mainframe, e.g. MVS</td></tr>
<tr><td>√</td><td>6) MAC</td></tr>
<tr><td>√</td><td>7) Netscape</td></tr>
<tr><td>√</td><td>8) Internet explorer</td></tr>
<tr><td>√</td><td>9) Full Web-based Architecture (Total O MB Thin Clients)</td></tr>
<tr><td>-</td><td>10) Partial Web-based Architecture</td></tr>
<tr><td>√</td><td>11) Client/Server-based Architecture</td></tr>
<tr><td>√</td><td>12) Runs Client/Server over WAN</td></tr>
<tr><td>√</td><td>13) Runs Client/Server over Dialup</td></tr>
<tr>
<td rowspan="6">Configuration of CRM-System</td>
<td></td>
<td>1) Programming language: powerbuilder</td>
</tr>
<tr><td></td><td>2) Possibility for the firm to develop its own display: High</td></tr>
<tr><td></td><td>3) Scalability from no. of users: 1
to no. of users: 999,999+</td></tr>
<tr><td>√</td><td>4) Automatic generation of connections between data fields</td></tr>
<tr><td>√</td><td>5) When upgrading software customer-specific configurations are not lost</td></tr>
<tr><td>√</td><td>6) The systems IT structure supports global operations with several servers</td></tr>
<tr>
<td rowspan="8">Databases</td>
<td>√</td>
<td>1) Oracle</td>
</tr>
<tr><td>√</td><td>2) Sybase</td></tr>
<tr><td>√</td><td>3) Informix</td></tr>
<tr><td>-</td><td>4) Scalable SQL</td></tr>
<tr><td>√</td><td>5) MS SQL</td></tr>
<tr><td>√</td><td>6) IBM DB2</td></tr>
<tr><td>-</td><td>7) Access</td></tr>
<tr><td>-</td><td>8) Ctree</td></tr>
</table>

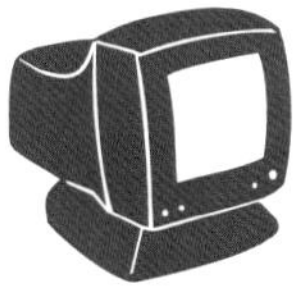

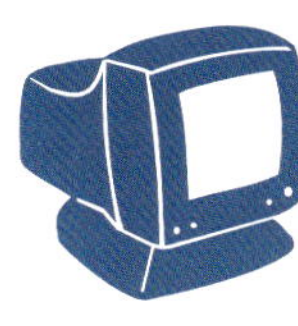

Integration

-	1) Pre-built SAP Interface
√	2) Pre-built Oracle Interface
-	3) Pre-built Peoplesoft Interface
-	4) Pre-built Baan Interface
-	5) Pre-built JD Edwards Interface
-	6) Other pre-built Interfaces
√	7) Supports Application Program Interfaces or equivalent
√	8) Supports Object Link Enabling technology or equivalent
√	9) Tool for creation of Interfaces without the use of programming
√	10) Integration to 3rd party data providers, incl. D&B

Hardware

Minimum requirements for workstation

Processor:	*Pentium 166*
RAM:	*32 MB RAM*
Free harddisk space:	*250 MB*

MultiMark AS

Company Overview
MultiMark is one of the leading Scandinavian software companies dealing with systems for Customer Relationship Management. The solutions are built on a framework of components based on the latest Microsoft COM standards. Since 1990 MultiMark has built up a sound and expansive company that has delivered full-service solutions to more than 600 Scandinavian and international server installations with several thousand users.

Vision
MultiMark creates measurable results for the customers by way of increased sales productivity, improved earnings, high customer satisfaction and loyalty combined with goal-oriented managerial information and a model for implementation of Customer Management strategies. MultiMark delivers a unique business model for development and implementation of CRM systems, building on nine years of experience, partnership with innovative customers and use of thoroughly tested technology as well as cooperation with leading partners on the market.

The success of our customers is mainly due to our "Time-to-Result" implementation model, which makes it possible for them quickly and easily to evaluate, implement and benefit from the MultiMark System series. MultiMark offers its customers a thoroughly tested solution, scalable, user-friendly and market leading technology, reliable implementation and flexible software, fast upgrading and support – and a very attractive "Return-on-Investment".

MultiMark's System Series primarily stands out with its wide functionality, its thoroughly tested mobile solutions, attractive price/performance relationship, flexible design and architecture plus its administrative tools and open database platform.

Management Summary
Software products – MultiMark offers a unique base of standard software components for design and implementation of customer oriented solutions. The MultiMark System Series is an integrated CRM system which supports sales, marketing and customer related employees in their cooperation to build an efficient One-to-One dialogue with customers and partners.

The MultiMark System Series guarantees a software functionality which systematically controls relations, transactions, information and knowledge and thus covers the entire "life cycle" of the company plus exchange of customer information between the users.

The facilities include contact control, sales force automation, order management, One-to-One marketing, service modules, management information and special modules for selected trades such as media, retail, pharmaceutical companies and banks.

Open and scalable technology – MultiMark's solutions are state-of-the-art Microsoft COM/DNA component-based applications. They match the customers' choice of database – MS SQL, Oracle or Sybase – and are easily integrated with Back Office systems and Microsoft Office. They are based on modern 32-bit client/server architecture; they support all important Microsoft standards and are scalable – and thus suitable for growth according to the companies' demands.

Professional service – MultiMark offers professional service. This means fast and problem-free implementation of software solutions. We offer a number of different performances that support every step in the implementation process – from the introductory planning to the continuing support and upgrading. Our "Time-to-Result" implementation model is a well-tested implementation method which builds bridges between the company's individual needs and a successful CRM project. Besides, we offer courses – either open or tailor-made – suited to the single customer's needs and specific business processes. We secure continuing support through hotline-service and necessary help immediately following implementation. Maintenance and upgrading of the software are adjusted to the single customer's business processes and are based on standard solutions. With large projects, project teams are used for project management.

MultiMark's consulting section consists of implementation consultants and project managers as well as database, system design and integration specialists. Management, system administrators and end users can use the section's expertise, which includes all aspects of system design and maintenance.

MultiMark co-operates with a number of partners who can also be in charge of implementation and system integration.

References

ABB, Boehringer Ingelheim, Bording Purup, Carlson Wagonlit, Cederroth, Danisco, F. L. Smith, In-vesteringsforeningen Danske Invest, Nilfisk Advance, Novo Nordisk, Software AG, Sybase, Unibank, Van den Bergh Foods, VækstFonden, etc.

Ownership and Equity

MultiMark is a privately owned company with a professional board of directors. On July 1, 1999 the MultiMark group had 70 employees in offices in Copenhagen, Kokkedal and Århus. The company has had a yearly growth rate of about 50% with constantly positive earnings during the last 9 years. The equity of the group is DKK 20 mill.

Address

www.multimark.dk

MultiMark AS
Avderødvej 20
DK-2980 Kokkedal
Denmark
Phone +45 4828 3838
Fax +45 4828 3800
E-mail: mail@multimark.dk

Supplier analysis – MultiMark

Segmentation

√	1)	Automatic electronic ABC categorisation based on criteria defined by the company
√	2)	Possibility of manual categorisation (override of automatic categorisation)
√	3)	Segmentation can be based on different criteria based on the specific "territory". Furthermore, the possibility of a customer being A customer in one "territory" and B customer in another is also an issue
√	4)	Automatic warnings at low levels of activity on dimensions defined by the company
√	5)	Basic profiling tools (AND, OR, LIKE, NOT LIKE, *, -, +, /)
√	6)	Reuse of earlier group profiles in new profile definitions
√	7)	"Drop-down-box" or equivalent with predefined database field information for and creation of group profiles

Campaigns

√	1)	Campaign can consist of a number of different tasks in a pre-defined order
√	2)	Costing on campaigns on more than one dimension
(√)	3)	Display campaigns and activities using graphic tools like flowcharts
√	4)	Management of several parallel campaigns
√	5)	Campaign surveillance tools
√	6)	"Event triggers"
√	7)	"Assistants" (already programmed "event triggers") for user level
√	8)	Automatic generation of next step in a campaign
√	9)	Budgeting tool to calculate viability of planned campaigns
*5	10)	Graphic tools to show results
t	11)	Possibility of seeing a list of all active campaigns incl. time-horizon
√	12)	Estimation and measuring of campaigns earnings efficiency
√	13)	Distribution of leads to campaign teams

Leads

√	1)	Management and creation of leads
√	2)	Calculation of success-rates on leads
√	3)	Status for leads' placing in a sales process
*5	4)	Graphic tool that shows how many leads there are on each step of a sales funnel
√	5)	Possibility of attaching one or more competitors to a lead
√	6)	Status for leads' purchasing potential and the probability of the sale coming through
√	7)	Manual salesman assignment to leads
√	8)	Automatic salesman assignment to leads

Customer Data	√	1) Customer data table with the firms' own defined fields
	√	2) Possibility of more than one address per customer
	√	3) Possibility of attachments to customer database of previous e-mails, letters, documents (a so-called customer log)
	√	4) Registration of all previous meetings/contacts with customers including outcome
	√	5) Registration of own sales strategy and tactics towards each customer
	√	6) Registration of customers' goals, visions and key success factors
	√	7) Search possibilities on data on several dimensions simultaneously (for example area and age)
	√	8) Word/text search tool
	√	9) Registration and measurement of the customers' product interests over time
	√	10) Hyperlink to relations
Product Configuration and Contract Management	-	1) Product configuration from offline PC (being frequently replicated)
	-	2) Configuration of product by use of a hierarchic (one-way) system
	-	3) Configuration of product by use of a full dialogue (dynamic) system
	-	4) Configuration with circumstances, e.g. max price
	-	5) Calculation of delivery date of configured product/availability check
	-	6) Possible from offer to create order including data needed for invoicing
	-	7) Visualisation for customer of the product configuration online/via Internet
	-	8) Visualisation for the customer of the product configuration via print
	-	9) Verification of price offer from internal organisation
	√	10) Contract management tool
	√	11) Possibility of more than one price list for one product based on customer seniority, area, season, etc.
	-	12) Service level agreements integrated with contract processing
	√	13) Discounting tools supporting contract creation
	-	14) Possibility of maintaining configurations without the use of programming
Marketing Tools	√	1) Library for storing marketing material (folders, brochures, etc.)
	√	2) Historical product/price information library
	√	3) Competitor Information System
	-	4) Tool for customer satisfaction analysis
	-	5) Management and registration of materials (e.g. banners, stickers, etc.) from current and previous campaigns
	√	6) Possibility of mass-generated direct mail/mail-merging

Sales Force Automation	√	1)	Online data transfer from workstation to databases
	√	2)	Batch data transfer from workstation to databases
	√	3)	Possibility of quick synchronisation of offline laptops
	√	4)	Possibility of integration with PDA or the like via MS Outlook
	-	5)	Possibility of taking orders/making sales online via PDA to the CRM application
	√	6)	Graphs for salesman comparing actual sales to budget
Resource Management	√	1)	Planning calendar for each salesman
	√	2)	Possibility of booking a meeting on a calendar without the salesman's acceptance
	√	3)	Shared calendars (across several users)
	√	4)	Graphical calendar
	*2	5)	Possibility of setting alarms for meetings
	√	6)	Management of activities per user/customer/company/contact person
	√	7)	Possible for a customer to be member of numerous territories
	√	8)	Possibility of geographic, product type, and industry "territories"
	-	9)	Geographic route planning
	√	10)	Salesman resource planner
	√	11)	Registration of CRM related costs for each customer (e.g. travel costs for sales visits and marketing contribution costs etc.)
	-	12)	Front office logistics (storage repair, spares holding etc.)
Analysis Tools	√	1)	Flexible report-generator for sales
	√	2)	Flexible report-generator for marketing
	√	3)	Flexible report-generator for service and support
	√	4)	Standard Executive Information System incl. graphics
	-	5)	Advanced budgeting tools (includes e.g. fixed and variable calculation methods based on data from previous seasons, salesmen efficiency rates, etc.)
Forecasts	√	1)	Product forecasts (sales per month/year)
	√	2)	Revenue forecasts (revenue per month/year)
	√	3)	Roll-ups of forecasts across numerous organisations
	√	4)	Support for user-defined forecast dates
	√	5)	Roll-ups and forecasts on several levels in a firm

		Other functionalities
-	1)	Push technology for information-gathering on the Internet (active search on words)
-	2)	Active Briefing
√	3)	Multiple currencies
√	4)	Euro compliant
-	5)	Supports electronic scrollbar
√	6)	Security system that defines user-clearance
√	7)	Quick-print of document without having to open the application supporting the document
√	8)	Personal correspondence templates
√	9)	Full integration to word-processing and spreadsheet applications (automatic merging into these from the CRM-system), e.g. OLE technology (Object Link Enabling)
√	10)	Guide functions for using the application ("Wizards")
√	11)	Integrated fax tool that works seamless, as part of the application

		Internet
√	1)	Automatic assignment of leads from the Internet
√	2)	Tool for creating web-sites with predefined links to CRM database fields and interactive fields to CRM application
√	3)	Tool for creating web-sites with "drop-down-box" or equivalent with "drag-and-drop" graphics
√	4)	Possibility for web-site differentiation dependant on customer logging in
√	5)	Integrated e-mail tool that works seamless, as part of the application
-	6)	Support for electronic payment

		Telemarketing, Call Centre and Help-Desk
-	1)	Automatic dialling facilities (Predictive Dialling)
-	2)	Computer-Telephony Integration (CTI) enabled/supportive
-	3)	Application (through integration of CTI) enables routing possibilities of customer calling in, e.g. customer to specific operator, "A" customer first in queue, etc.
√	4)	Use of electronic scripts for telemarketing or response for Call Centre/guided dialogue management
-	5)	Dialogue management with a neural network/adaptive learning
-	6)	Cross-sales functions
-	7)	"Neural" inbound e-mail answering tool
-	8)	Calculation/prognosis of inbound call frequency during the day
-	9)	Scheduling device for Call Centre operators (Schedule Planner)
√	10)	Technical problem resolution system
-	11)	"Trouble-Ticketing" – a system for requesting service
-	12)	Blending of Telemarketing and Call Centre function. That is the possibility of the system assigning telemarketing tasks to vacant operators during less busy periods

		Price
	1) Price per user: *DKK 7,950*	
	2) Annual license per user: *DKK 0*	
	3) Installation and maintenance: *Dependant on number of users*	

Product Development

	1)	Annual new versions: *1x*
	2)	Users in the Nordic countries: *9000*
	3)	Global users incl. Nordic Countries: *9,250*
	4)	Planned new applications/functions within the next six months:
	-	*Multimark 2000*
	-	*Multimark Weblink*

Support

√	1)	Hot-line
-	2)	24-hour hot-line
√	3)	Education Centre
√	4)	Internet help

Ease of use

MultiMark is built around user-friendly standard worksheets in a Windows environment with intuitive screen settings. MultiMark pictures the users' everyday processes in every way.

√	1)	Danish version
t	2)	Swedish version
t	3)	Norwegian version
t	4)	Finnish version
t	5)	German version
√	6)	English version
t	7)	French version
t	8)	Spanish version
t	9)	Other versions:

Industry Solutions

The following Industry Solutions are offered:

- *Construction*
- *Furniture*
- *Retail*
- *Financial Sector*
- *Media*
- *Medical Industry*

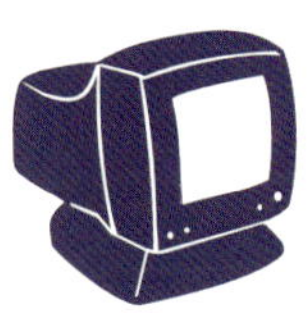

Platforms and Architecture

√	1)	Unix
√	2)	Win NT
√	3)	Win 95/98
√	4)	OS/2
-	5)	Mainframe, e.g. MVS
-	6)	MAC
√	7)	Netscape
√	8)	Internet explorer
√	9)	Full Web-based Architecture (Total O MB Thin Clients)
-	10)	Partial Web-based Architecture
√	11)	Client/Server-based Architecture
√	12)	Runs Client/Server over WAN
√	13)	Runs Client/Server over Dialup

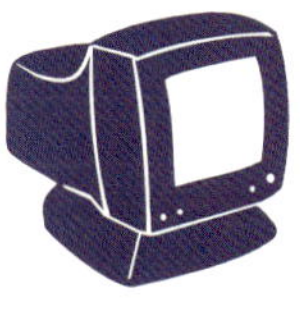

Configuration of CRM-System

1) Programming language: *Visual basic, Clarion, Interdev, Visual C++, Java, og Java Scripting*
2) Possibility for the firm to develop its own display: *High*
3) Scalability from no. of users: *1*
        to no. of users: *10,000+*

√	4)	Automatic generation of connections between data fields
√	5)	When upgrading software customer-specific configurations are not lost
√	6)	The systems IT structure supports global operations with several servers

Databases

√	1)	Oracle
√	2)	Sybase
-	3)	Informix
√	4)	Scalable SQL
√	5)	MS SQL
-	6)	IBM DB2
-	7)	Access
-	8)	Ctree

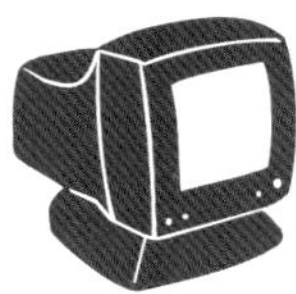

Integration

-	1)	Pre-built SAP Interface
-	2)	Pre-built Oracle Interface
-	3)	Pre-built Peoplesoft Interface
-	4)	Pre-built Baan Interface
-	5)	Pre-built JD Edwards Interface
-	6)	Other pre-built Interfaces
√	7)	Supports Application Program Interfaces or equivalent
√	8)	Supports Object Link Enabling technology or equivalent
√	9)	Tool for creation of Interfaces without the use of programming
√	10)	Integration to 3rd party data providers, incl. D&B

Hardware

Minimum requirements for workstation

Processor:	*Pentium 100*
RAM:	*32 MB RAM*
Free harddisk space:	*0 MB*

Oracle

Company Description

Oracle Corp. is the world's leading supplier of software for information management, and the world's second largest software company. With annual revenues of $7.5 billion, the company offers its database server, application server, tools and application products, along with related consulting, education and support services in more than 140 countries around the world. Headquartered in Redwood Shores, California, Oracle is one of the first software companies to implement network computing capable databases and products, and the first major software company to make full-featured products available electronically on the Internet.

Vision

Commercial organisations today are increasingly realising that the key to achieving revenue growth and customer retention in today's internet-centric business environments is enterprise wide customer intelligence. Leading organisations are differentiating themselves from their competition by supplying business information across all delivery channels for an integrated complete customer view, improving customer intimacy, responsiveness and satisfaction. Share our vision, empowering companies to ensure the fastest return on their investments by employing the 3i's: Intelligence, the Internet and Integration.

By treating customers individually, we believe that customers are willing to buy more products, and also to stay loyal to your company instead of buying from a competitor next time. Oracle's Solutions of Marketing, Sales and Service applications give you the complete overview of the customers' needs and behavior, making it possible to offer the customer exactly the product he wants, and the way he wants it.

Our vision is to grow our customers businesses and to make their customers happy and loyal through our suite of CRM products.

Management Summary

These days, managing customer relationships is about more than simply automating a sales force. It is about putting the strength and skills of an entire organisation behind every interaction with the customer from the time you first begin to market your products and services, to flexibly tailoring a service contract, to having the latest and most complete customer history at the fingertips of the person answering your phone.

Oracle Customer Relationship Management helps companies understand, antici-
pate and respond to their customers' needs, profitably. Oracle CRM distinguishes
itself in the CRM arena by offering:

Customer Intelligence – Increase customer satisfaction and reduce customer
defections by collecting and analysing information across Marketing, Sales,
Service and the entire corporation for a true 360 degree customer view and a
corresponding alignment of organisational resources with customer needs.

Unified Channels – Improve market reach and customer loyalty by implementing the most appropriate customer interaction strategy, whether it is through
the Web, telebusiness, field agents or partners.

100% Internet – Evolve to an Internet-centric business model using electronic
storefronts and self-service to expand your global reach, shorten your time to
market, improve efficiencies and reduce your costs for the fastest ROI.

Development of new technology happens at a constantly increasing pace which
often makes it difficult for the companies to absorb the new technology. Oracle
is convinced that we will be not only the technological leader but also be leading in transferring knowledge on solutions and new technologies to our customers. Therefore more than half of the Oracle employees are involved in
Consulting Services, Education and Support Services. Oracle provides implementation, education and service support through:
-   Oracle's Consulting Services
-   Oracle's Education Center
-   Oracle Support Services
-   Oracle's sales organisation

References
In EMEA (Europe, Middle East, Africa) around 200 CRM Customers.

Ownership and Equity
Oracle Corp is listed on the NASDAQ Stock Exchange (ORCL).
Stockholders Equity (31. May 1998) US $ 2,957,558,000.

Address
www.oracle.com

Oracle Corporation
World Headquarters
500 Oracle Parkway
Redwood Shores, CA 94065
USA

Supplier analysis – Oracle CRM

Segmentation

√	1)	Automatic electronic ABC categorisation based on criteria defined by the company
√	2)	Possibility of manual categorisation (override of automatic categorisation)
√	3)	Segmentation can be based on different criteria based on the specific "territory". Furthermore, the possibility of a customer being A customer in one "territory" and B customer in another is also an issue
√	4)	Automatic warnings at low levels of activity on dimensions defined by the company
√	5)	Basic profiling tools (AND, OR, LIKE, NOT LIKE, *, -, +, /)
√	6)	Reuse of earlier group profiles in new profile definitions
√	7)	"Drop-down-box" or equivalent with predefined database field information for and creation of group profiles

Campaigns

√	1)	Campaign can consist of a number of different tasks in a pre-defined order
√	2)	Costing on campaigns on more than one dimension
-	3)	Display campaigns and activities using graphic tools like flowcharts
√	4)	Management of several parallel campaigns
√	5)	Campaign surveillance tools
√	6)	"Event triggers"
√	7)	"Assistants" (already programmed "event triggers") for user level
√	8)	Automatic generation of next step in a campaign
√	9)	Budgeting tool to calculate viability of planned campaigns
√	10)	Graphic tools to show results
√	11)	Possibility of seeing a list of all active campaigns incl. time-horizon
√	12)	Estimation and measuring of campaigns earnings efficiency
√	13)	Distribution of leads to campaign teams

Leads

√	1)	Management and creation of leads
√	2)	Calculation of success-rates on leads
√	3)	Status for leads' placing in a sales process
-	4)	Graphic tool that shows how many leads there are on each step of a sales funnel
√	5)	Possibility of attaching one or more competitors to a lead
√	6)	Status for leads' purchasing potential and the probability of the sale coming through
√	7)	Manual salesman assignment to leads
√	8)	Automatic salesman assignment to leads

Customer Data	√	1) Customer data table with the firms' own defined fields
	√	2) Possibility of more than one address per customer
	√	3) Possibility of attachments to customer database of previous e-mails, letters, documents (a so-called customer log)
	√	4) Registration of all previous meetings/contacts with customers including outcome
	-	5) Registration of own sales strategy and tactics towards each customer
	√	6) Registration of customers' goals, visions and key success factors
	√	7) Search possibilities on data on several dimensions simultaneously (for example area and age)
	√	8) Word/text search tool
	√	9) Registration and measurement of the customers' product interests over time
	√	10) Hyperlink to relations
Product Configuration and Contract Management	√	1) Product configuration from offline PC (being frequently replicated)
	√	2) Configuration of product by use of a hierarchic (one-way) system
	√	3) Configuration of product by use of a full dialogue (dynamic) system
	√	4) Configuration with circumstances, e.g. max price
	√	5) Calculation of delivery date of configured product/availability check
	√	6) Possible from offer to create order including data needed for invoicing
	√	7) Visualisation for customer of the product configuration online/via Internet
	√	8) Visualisation for the customer of the product configuration via print
	√	9) Verification of price offer from internal organisation
	√	10) Contract management tool
	√	11) Possibility of more than one price list for one product based on customer seniority, area, season, etc.
	√	12) Service level agreements integrated with contract processing
	√	13) Discounting tools supporting contract creation
	√	14) Possibility of maintaining configurations without the use of programming
Marketing Tools	-	1) Library for storing marketing material (folders, brochures, etc.)
	√	2) Historical product/price information library
	-	3) Competitor Information System
	(√)	4) Tool for customer satisfaction analysis
	√	5) Management and registration of materials (e.g. banners, stickers, etc.) from current and previous campaigns
	√	6) Possibility of mass-generated direct mail/mail-merging

Sales Force Automation	√	1)	Online data transfer from workstation to databases
	√	2)	Batch data transfer from workstation to databases
	√	3)	Possibility of quick synchronisation of offline laptops
	√	4)	Possibility of integration with PDA or the like via MS Outlook
	√	5)	Possibility of taking orders/making sales online via PDA to the CRM application
	√	6)	Graphs for salesman comparing actual sales to budget
Resource Management	√	1)	Planning calendar for each salesman
	√	2)	Possibility of booking a meeting on a calendar without the salesman's acceptance
	-	3)	Shared calendars (across several users)
	-	4)	Graphical calendar
	√	5)	Possibility of setting alarms for meetings
	√	6)	Management of activities per user/customer/company/contact person
	√	7)	Possible for a customer to be member of numerous territories
	√	8)	Possibility of geographic, product type, and industry "territories"
	-	9)	Geographic route planning
	-	10)	Salesman resource planner
	-	11)	Registration of CRM related costs for each customer (e.g. travel costs for sales visits and marketing contribution costs etc.)
	-	12)	Front office logistics (storage repair, spares holding etc.)
Analysis Tools	√	1)	Flexible report-generator for sales
	√	2)	Flexible report-generator for marketing
	√	3)	Flexible report-generator for service and support
	√	4)	Standard Executive Information System incl. graphics
	OR	5)	Advanced budgeting tools (includes e.g. fixed and variable calculation methods based on data from previous seasons, salesmen efficiency rates, etc.)
Forecasts	√	1)	Product forecasts (sales per month/year)
	√	2)	Revenue forecasts (revenue per month/year)
	√	3)	Roll-ups of forecasts across numerous organisations
	√	4)	Support for user-defined forecast dates
	√	5)	Roll-ups and forecasts on several levels in a firm

Other functionalities	-	1) Push technology for information-gathering on the Internet (active search on words)
	√	2) Active Briefing
	√	3) Multiple currencies
	√	4) Euro compliant
	√	5) Supports electronic scrollbar
	√	6) Security system that defines user-clearance
	-	7) Quick-print of document without having to open the application supporting the document
	√	8) Personal correspondence templates
	√	9) Full integration to word-processing and spreadsheet applications (automatic merging into these from the CRM-system), e.g. OLE technology (Object Link Enabling)
	√	10) Guide functions for using the application ("Wizards")
	-	11) Integrated fax tool that works seamless, as part of the application
Internet	√	1) Automatic assignment of leads from the Internet
	*13	2) Tool for creating web-sites with predefined links to CRM database fields and interactive fields to CRM application
	*13	3) Tool for creating web-sites with "drop-down-box" or equivalent with "drag-and-drop" graphics
	√	4) Possibility for web-site differentiation dependant on customer logging in
	-	5) Integrated e-mail tool that works seamless, as part of the application
	√	6) Support for electronic payment
Telemarketing, Call Centre and Help-Desk	√	1) Automatic dialling facilities (Predictive Dialling)
	√	2) Computer-Telephony Integration (CTI) enabled/supportive
	√	3) Application (through integration of CTI) enables routing possibilities of customer calling in, e.g. customer to specific operator, "A" customer first in queue, etc.
	√	4) Use of electronic scripts for telemarketing or response for Call Centre/guided dialogue management
	-	5) Dialogue management with a neural network/adaptive learning
	-	6) Cross-sales functions
	√	7) "Neural" inbound e-mail answering tool
	√	8) Calculation/prognosis of inbound call frequency during the day
	√	9) Scheduling device for Call Centre operators (Schedule Planner)
	√	10) Technical problem resolution system
	√	11) "Trouble-Ticketing" – a system for requesting service
	√	12) Blending of Telemarketing and Call Centre function. That is the possibility of the system assigning telemarketing tasks to vacant operators during less busy periods

Price

1) Price per user:

   Depends on which parts of the CRM applications being used.

2) Annual license per user: *Varying*

3) Installation and maintenance: *Varying*

Product Development

1) Annual new versions: *App. 1 per 18 month*

2) Users in the Nordic countries: *NA*

3) Global users incl. Nordic Countries: *Approx. 200 companies in EMEA*

4) Planned new applications/functions within the next six months:

- *marketing: budget allocation, approval, task management, marketing knowledge base, multi-stage campaigns*

- *vertical datamarts*

- *Sales: Sales administration + more mobile products*

- *Service: new product called Oracle support*

- *Sparepart management, Customer care improvements,,contracts improvement*

- *Broader Callcenter: Product coverage*

Support

√ 1) Hot-line

√ 2) 24-hour hot-line

√ 3) Education Centre

√ 4) Internet help

Ease of use

User-friendly Interface

√ 1) Danish version

√ 2) Swedish version

√ 3) Norwegian version

√ 4) Finnish version

√ 5) German version

√ 6) English version

√ 7) French version

√ 8) Spanish version

√ 9) Other versions: *Global product with 26 different languages*

Industry Solutions

The following Industry Solutions are offered:

- *Telecom and utilities*
- *Financial services*

Platforms and Architecture

√	1)	Unix
√	2)	Win NT
√	3)	Win 95/98
-	4)	OS/2
√	5)	Mainframe, e.g. MVS
-	6)	MAC
√	7)	Netscape
√	8)	Internet explorer
(√)	9)	Full Web-based Architecture (Total O MB Thin Clients)
-	10)	Partial Web-based Architecture
√	11)	Client/Server-based Architecture
√	12)	Runs Client/Server over WAN
√	13)	Runs Client/Server over Dialup

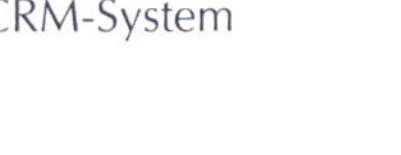

Configuration of CRM-System

	1)	Programming language: *C++, PL/SQL,Anything *) (Oracle supplies programmatic interfaces for most programming languages)*
	2)	Possibility for the firm to develop its own display: *High*
	3)	Scalability from no. of users: *25* to no. of users: *20,000+*

√	4)	Automatic generation of connections between data fields
√	5)	When upgrading software customer-specific configurations are not lost
√	6)	The systems IT structure supports global operations with several servers

---

Databases

√	1)	Oracle
-	2)	Sybase
-	3)	Informix
-	4)	Scalable SQL
-	5)	MS SQL
-	6)	IBM DB2
-	7)	Access
-	8)	Ctree

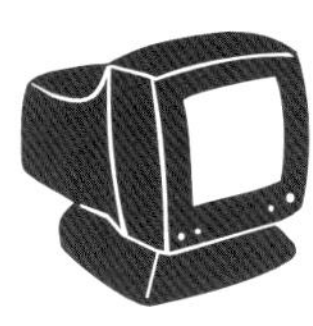

Integration

√	1)	Pre-built SAP Interface
√	2)	Pre-built Oracle Interface
-	3)	Pre-built Peoplesoft Interface
-	4)	Pre-built Baan Interface
-	5)	Pre-built JD Edwards Interface
(√)	6)	Other pre-built Interfaces
√	7)	Supports Application Program Interfaces or equivalent
√	8)	Supports Object Link Enabling technology or equivalent
√	9)	Tool for creation of Interfaces without the use of programming
(√)	10)	Integration to 3rd party data providers, incl. D&B

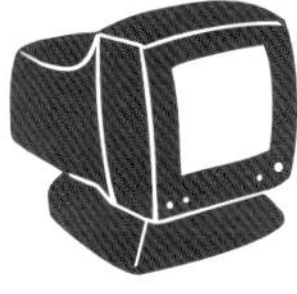

Hardware

Minimum requirements for workstation

Processor:	*Pentium 133*
RAM:	*32 MB RAM*
Free harddisk space:	*20 MB*

Prime Response

Company Overview

Prime Response was established in 1987 to offer traditional marketing service bureau functions including merge, purge and de-duplication of data and management of client databases. The company's initial success was mainly due to commitment to the new generation of technology that offered huge benefits in processing power and flexibility and to the development of an innovative multi-level de-duplication process. Prime Response continued to develop its Customer Relationship Marketing systems, providing software and services for organisations with large customer information challenges, particularly within the financial services, insurance, automotive, retail, communications, utilities and leisure sectors. The culmination of this marketing service experience activity is the award-winning software, Prime Vantage™ launched in December 1994.

The company operates in Boston (corporate headquarters) with offices in London (International headquarters), Paris and Dublin. The Prime Vantage™ software is sold to companies throughout Europe, Africa and the Middle East.

Vision

Responding to Market Demands – Organisations are now applying technology to help boost customer loyalty and profitability. Web-based marketing automation solutions from Prime Response manage continuous, highly segmented, multi-channel marketing activities. Drawing on complex, customer-specific behavioral data dynamically and continuously compiled from various data sources (e.g., Web site activity, point-of-sale analytics, direct mail response rates, etc.), Prime Response's software helps companies target 1:1 communications to the right people, at the right time, using the right Internet and traditional marketing channels. As a result, organisations are able to optimise marketing efficiency, reduce marketing waste, increase customer loyalty and experience substantial profitability gains.

Management Summary

Business Benefits: Prime Response's customers report several benefits related to increased profitability and customer loyalty, including:

- Response rates increased to 25 percent
- Churn reduced by 11 percent
- Revenue increase of 50 percent
- Six-fold increase in marketing efficiency

Industry Firsts: Among the numerous qualities and technologies that Prime Response can claim as firsts, the most notable include:

- 1st to support multiple media channels as part of a marketing campaign
- 1st to prove scalability to 100 million customers in a single marketing database
- 1st to integrate Web and e-mail channels into campaign management with contents management functionality

The Technology Solution: Prime@Vantage.com empowers e-businesses to analyse, plan, execute and measure multi-channel marketing initiatives, executed on an enterprise-scale via the Web; e-mail; direct mail; call centres; direct sales systems; points-of-sale (including ATM machines and check-out registers); and mass advertising (print and broadcast). Prime@Vantage.com is further differentiated by its ability to automate customer communications across these numerous channels in multi-stage, personalised campaigns: pre-defined events such as noticeable increases/drops in sales trigger new marketing communication methods tailor-made to address each customer's unique needs, preferences and business conditions

References

AirTouch, Advance Bank, Allianz, The Associates, Bank West, British Airways, Credit Suisse, CVS, Fiat, Honda, The Learning Company/Mattel, NatWest, Provident, Safeway, Standard Life, UPS, Royal Bank of Scotland, UBS, TeleDanmark and Telenor Mobil.

Addresses

www.prime-response.com

Goat Wharf

Brentford TW8 OBA

United Kingdom

Phone + 44 181 -400 -3000

Supplier analysis – Prime Response

Segmentation

√	1)	Automatic electronic ABC categorisation based on criteria defined by the company
√	2)	Possibility of manual categorisation (override of automatic categorisation)
√	3)	Segmentation can be based on different criteria based on the specific "territory". Furthermore, the possibility of a customer being A customer in one "territory" and B customer in another is also an issue
√	4)	Automatic warnings at low levels of activity on dimensions defined by the company
√	5)	Basic profiling tools (AND, OR, LIKE, NOT LIKE, *, -, +, /)
√	6)	Reuse of earlier group profiles in new profile definitions
√	7)	"Drop-down-box" or equivalent with predefined database field information for and creation of group profiles

Campaigns

√	1)	Campaign can consist of a number of different tasks in a pre-defined order
√	2)	Costing on campaigns on more than one dimension
√	3)	Display campaigns and activities using graphic tools like flowcharts
√	4)	Management of several parallel campaigns
√	5)	Campaign surveillance tools
√	6)	"Event triggers"
√	7)	"Assistants" (already programmed "event triggers") for user level
√	8)	Automatic generation of next step in a campaign
√	9)	Budgeting tool to calculate viability of planned campaigns
√	10)	Graphic tools to show results
√	11)	Possibility of seeing a list of all active campaigns incl. time-horizon
√	12)	Estimation and measuring of campaigns earnings efficiency
√	13)	Distribution of leads to campaign teams

Leads

√	1)	Management and creation of leads
√	2)	Calculation of success-rates on leads
-	3)	Status for leads' placing in a sales process
-	4)	Graphic tool that shows how many leads there are on each step of a sales funnel
-	5)	Possibility of attaching one or more competitors to a lead
-	6)	Status for leads' purchasing potential and the probability of the sale coming through
√	7)	Manual salesman assignment to leads
√	8)	Automatic salesman assignment to leads

Customer Data	√	1)	Customer data table with the firms' own defined fields
	√	2)	Possibility of more than one address per customer
	√	3)	Possibility of attachments to customer database of previous e-mails, letters, documents (a so-called customer log)
	-	4)	Registration of all previous meetings/contacts with customers including outcome
	√	5)	Registration of own sales strategy and tactics towards each customer
	√	6)	Registration of customers' goals, visions and key success factors
	√	7)	Search possibilities on data on several dimensions simultaneously (for example area and age)
	-	8)	Word/text search tool
	√	9)	Registration and measurement of the customers' product interests over time
	√	10)	Hyperlink to relations
Product Configuration and Contract Management	-	1)	Product configuration from offline PC (being frequently replicated)
	-	2)	Configuration of product by use of a hierarchic (one-way) system
	-	3)	Configuration of product by use of a full dialogue (dynamic) system
	-	4)	Configuration with circumstances, e.g. max price
	-	5)	Calculation of delivery date of configured product/availability check
	-	6)	Possible from offer to create order including data needed for invoicing
	-	7)	Visualisation for customer of the product configuration online/via Internet
	-	8)	Visualisation for the customer of the product configuration via print
	-	9)	Verification of price offer from internal organisation
	-	10)	Contract management tool
	-	11)	Possibility of more than one price list for one product based on customer seniority, area, season, etc.
	-	12)	Service level agreements integrated with contract processing
	-	13)	Discounting tools supporting contract creation
	-	14)	Possibility of maintaining configurations without the use of programming
Marketing Tools	√	1)	Library for storing marketing material (folders, brochures, etc.)
	-	2)	Historical product/price information library
	-	3)	Competitor Information System
	-	4)	Tool for customer satisfaction analysis
	-	5)	Management and registration of materials (e.g. banners, stickers, etc.) from current and previous campaigns
	√	6)	Possibility of mass-generated direct mail/mail-merging

Sales Force Automation	-	1) Online data transfer from workstation to databases
	-	2) Batch data transfer from workstation to databases
	-	3) Possibility of quick synchronisation of offline laptops
	-	4) Possibility of integration with PDA or the like via MS Outlook
	-	5) Possibility of taking orders/making sales online via PDA to the CRM application
	-	6) Graphs for salesman comparing actual sales to budget
Resource Management	-	1) Planning calendar for each salesman
	-	2) Possibility of booking a meeting on a calendar without the salesman's acceptance
	-	3) Shared calendars (across several users)
	-	4) Graphical calendar
	-	5) Possibility of setting alarms for meetings
	-	6) Management of activities per user/customer/company/contact person
	-	7) Possible for a customer to be member of numerous territories
	-	8) Possibility of geographic, product type, and industry "territories"
	-	9) Geographic route planning
	-	10) Salesman resource planner
	(√)	11) Registration of CRM related costs for each customer (e.g. travel costs for sales visits and marketing contribution costs etc.)
	-	12) Front office logistics (storage repair, spares holding etc.)
Analysis Tools	-	1) Flexible report-generator for sales
	√	2) Flexible report-generator for marketing
	-	3) Flexible report-generator for service and support
	√	4) Standard Executive Information System incl. graphics
	-	5) Advanced budgeting tools (includes e.g. fixed and variable calculation methods based on data from previous seasons, salesmen efficiency rates, etc.)
Forecasts	-	1) Product forecasts (sales per month/year)
	-	2) Revenue forecasts (revenue per month/year)
	-	3) Roll-ups of forecasts across numerous organisations
	-	4) Support for user-defined forecast dates
	-	5) Roll-ups and forecasts on several levels in a firm

Other functionalities	√	1)	Push technology for information-gathering on the Internet (active search on words)
	√	2)	Active Briefing
	C	3)	Multiple currencies
	-	4)	Euro compliant
	√	5)	Supports electronic scrollbar
	√	6)	Security system that defines user-clearance
	-	7)	Quick-print of document without having to open the application supporting the document
	-	8)	Personal correspondence templates
	√	9)	Full integration to word-processing and spreadsheet applications (automatic merging into these from the CRM-system), e.g. OLE technology (Object Link Enabling)
	√	10)	Guide functions for using the application ("Wizards")
	√	11)	Integrated fax tool that works seamless, as part of the application
Internet	√	1)	Automatic assignment of leads from the Internet
	√	2)	Tool for creating web-sites with predefined links to CRM database fields and interactive fields to CRM application
	√	3)	Tool for creating web-sites with "drop-down-box" or equivalent with "drag-and-drop" graphics
	√	4)	Possibility for web-site differentiation dependant on customer logging in
	√	5)	Integrated e-mail tool that works seamless, as part of the application
	√	6)	Support for electronic payment
Telemarketing, Call Centre and Help-Desk	-	1)	Automatic dialling facilities (Predictive Dialling)
	-	2)	Computer-Telephony Integration (CTI) enabled/supportive
	-	3)	Application (through integration of CTI) enables routing possibilities of customer calling in, e.g. customer to specific operator, "A" customer first in queue, etc.
	-	4)	Use of electronic scripts for telemarketing or response for Call Centre/guided dialogue management
	-	5)	Dialogue management with a neural network/adaptive learning
	-	6)	Cross-sales functions
	√	7)	"Neural" inbound e-mail answering tool
	-	8)	Calculation/prognosis of inbound call frequency during the day
	-	9)	Scheduling device for Call Centre operators (Schedule Planner)
	-	10)	Technical problem resolution system
	-	11)	"Trouble-Ticketing" – a system for requesting service
	-	12)	Blending of Telemarketing and Call Centre function. That is the possibility of the system assigning telemarketing tasks to vacant operators during less busy periods

Price		1)	Price per user: *The price is varying depending on the number of users etc.*
		2)	Annual license per user: *The price is varying depending on the number of users etc.*
		3)	Installation and maintenance: -
Product Development		1)	Annual new versions: *1*
		2)	Users in the Nordic countries: *3 organisations*
		3)	Global users incl. Nordic Countries: *60 organisations*
		4)	Planned new applications/functions within the next six months: -
Support	√	1)	Hot-line
	-	2)	24-hour hot-line
	√	3)	Education Centre
	√	4)	Internet help

Ease of use

End user resistance to attempts to automate what is viewed as one of the most dynamic and creative aspects of the organisation may limit the success of many marketing solutions. Prime Response provides tools and interfaces that properly support the way marketing users work and think.

t	1)	Danish version
t	2)	Swedish version
√	3)	Norwegian version
t	4)	Finnish version
√	5)	German version
√	6)	English version
√	7)	French version
√	8)	Spanish version
√	9)	Other versions: *Italian*

Industry Solutions

The following Industry Solutions are offered:

		Platforms and Architecture
√	1)	Unix
√	2)	Win NT
√	3)	Win 95/98
-	4)	OS/2
√	5)	Mainframe, e.g. MVS
-	6)	MAC
-	7)	Netscape
-	8)	Internet explorer
-	9)	Full Web-based Architecture (Total O MB Thin Clients)
-	10)	Partial Web-based Architecture
√	11)	Client/Server-based Architecture
-	12)	Runs Client/Server over WAN
-	13)	Runs Client/Server over Dialup

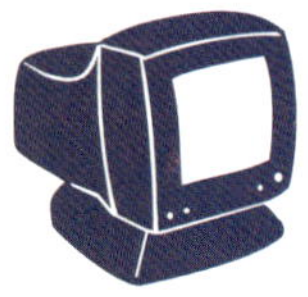

Platforms and Architecture

Configuration of CRM-System

	1)	Programming language: *C++*
	2)	Possibility for the firm to develop its own display: *Low*
	3)	Scalability from no. of users: *NA*
		to no. of users: *NA*
-	4)	Automatic generation of connections between data fields
-	5)	When upgrading software customer-specific configurations are not lost
√	6)	The systems IT structure supports global operations with several server

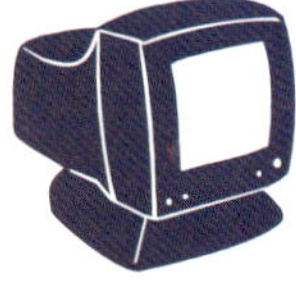

Databases

√	1)	Oracle
-	2)	Sybase
√	3)	Informix
-	4)	Scalable SQL
-	5)	MS SQL
√	6)	IBM DB2
-	7)	Access
-	8)	Ctree

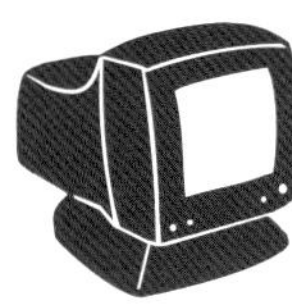

Integration

-	1)	Pre-built SAP Interface
-	2)	Pre-built Oracle Interface
-	3)	Pre-built Peoplesoft Interface
-	4)	Pre-built Baan Interface
-	5)	Pre-built JD Edwards Interface
-	6)	Other pre-built Interfaces
√	7)	Supports Application Program Interfaces or equivalent
√	8)	Supports Object Link Enabling technology or equivalent
-	9)	Tool for creation of Interfaces without the use of programming
√	10)	Integration to 3rd party data providers, incl. D&B

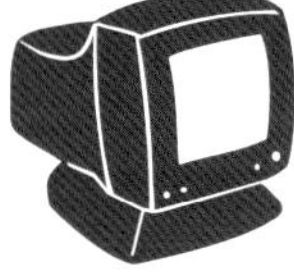

Hardware

Minimum requirements for workstation

Processor: *NA*

RAM: *NA*

Free harddisk space: *NA*

SAP

Company Overview

SAP, the world's largest enterprise software company, provides companies of all sizes with business solutions that deliver a better return information. SAP products and services integrate an organisation from financials and human resources to manufacturing and sales and distribution. This integration enables companies to optimise supply chains, strengthen customer relationships, and make more accurate management decisions. Founded in 1972, SAP today leverages a global network of people, processes and products to assure customer success.

Vision

An integrated view of the customer is essential for a successful enterprise to enable integrated customer interaction teams, to support the integration of customer-centric processes, and for the smooth functioning of customer relationship management applications. SAP's goal is to have an integrated set of applications to support processes between customers, the enterprise and also other business partners such as dealers, distributors, service providers and suppliers. Only a thorough integration of a company's mainly internal functions with its customer-centric functions allows it to get the maximum benefit from both its CRM and ERP systems.

Management Summary

Coupling customer-centric business areas (for example marketing, sales and service) with mainly internal ones (for example logistics, financials and HR) takes CRM into a new dimension and enables leading edge customer-centric solutions. Only the all-embracing view of customer related business processes enables companies to develop and manage customer relationships better than their competitors.

SAP strongly believes that the combination of a thorough understanding of CRM processes and the SAP experience of being the Enterprise Resource Planning (ERP) market leader will lead to a new and, so far, unprecedented dimension of enhanced customer processes, customer relationships and customer management.

SAP will deliver Marketing, Sales and Service applications based on customer-centric scenarios. This new suite of Customer Relationship Management applications builds upon existing best-of-class functionality and supplements it with new components such as Mobile Sales, Mobile Service, Telesales and Call Management.

SAP Marketing improves the efficiency and targeting of marketing efforts. This puts companies in a better position to attract and retain the most profitable customers and identify appropriate products and pricing strategies for targeted customer segments.

SAP Sales enables a company to cover the full sales cycle of its sales organisation, from lead qualification through opportunity management, quotation management, order entry, and tracking of the order fulfilment process to after-sales activities that lead to new opportunities. The application focuses in particular on key customer satisfaction and factors that influence sales success; for example on-time and complete delivery, which the SAP Sales' extensive delivery and order-status tracking functions provide.

SAP Service provides all the customer support tools a service organisation needs to meet the demands of the market-place of today and tomorrow. It transforms customer service into a cost-effective organisation that generates revenues, strengthens customer relationships and contributes directly to future sales.

Ownership and Equity

SAP is listed on several exchanges, including the Frankfurt stock exchange and NYSE under the symbol SAP.

References

As the biggest provider of ERP systems SAP has delivered applications to firms all over the world in the following industries: Aerospace & Defence, Automotive, Banking, Chemicals, Consumer Products, Engineering & Construction, Healthcare, Higher Education & Research, High Tech, Insurance, Media, Mill Products, Oil & Gas, Pharmaceuticals, Public Sector, Retail, Service Provider, Telecommunications, Utilities.

Addresses

www.sap.com

SAP Danmark	*SAP Norge*	*SAP Svenska AB*
Ringager 4B	Vollsveine 6	Gustavslundsvägen 151D, Alvik
DK-2605 Brøndby	Postboks 42	Box 12297
Denmark	N-1324 Lysaker	SE-102 27 Stockholm
Phone + 45 43 26 39 00	Norway	Sweden
	Phone + 47 67 52 94 00	Phone + 46 8 5 87 70 00

Supplier analysis – SAP

Segmentation

-	1)	Automatic electronic ABC categorisation based on criteria defined by the company
√	2)	Possibility of manual categorisation (override of automatic categorisation)
√	3)	Segmentation can be based on different criteria based on the specific "territory". Furthermore, the possibility of a customer being A customer in one "territory" and B customer in another is also an issue
√	4)	Automatic warnings at low levels of activity on dimensions defined by the company
*15	5)	Basic profiling tools (AND, OR, LIKE, NOT LIKE, *, -, +, /)
*15	6)	Reuse of earlier group profiles in new profile definitions
*15	7)	"Drop-down-box" or equivalent with predefined database field information for and creation of group profiles

Campaigns

R3	1)	Campaign can consist of a number of different tasks in a pre-defined order
R3	2)	Costing on campaigns on more than one dimension
-	3)	Display campaigns and activities using graphic tools like flowcharts
R3	4)	Management of several parallel campaigns
R3	5)	Campaign surveillance tools
-	6)	"Event triggers"
R3	7)	"Assistants" (already programmed "event triggers") for user level
R3	8)	Automatic generation of next step in a campaign
R3	9)	Budgeting tool to calculate viability of planned campaigns
R3	10)	Graphic tools to show results
R3	11)	Possibility of seeing a list of all active campaigns incl. time-horizon
R3	12)	Estimation and measuring of campaigns earnings efficiency
R3	13)	Distribution of leads to campaign teams

Leads

√	1)	Management and creation of leads
*15	2)	Calculation of success-rates on leads
√	3)	Status for leads' placing in a sales process
-	4)	Graphic tool that shows how many leads there are on each step of a sales funnel
√	5)	Possibility of attaching one or more competitors to a lead
√	6)	Status for leads' purchasing potential and the probability of the sale coming through
-	7)	Manual salesman assignment to leads
-	8)	Automatic salesman assignment to leads

Customer Data	√	1) Customer data table with the firms' own defined fields
	√	2) Possibility of more than one address per customer
	(√)	3) Possibility of attachments to customer database of previous e-mails, letters, documents (a so-called customer log)
	√	4) Registration of all previous meetings/contacts with customers including outcome
	√	5) Registration of own sales strategy and tactics towards each customer
	√	6) Registration of customers' goals, visions and key success factors
	*5	7) Search possibilities on data on several dimensions simultaneously (for example area and age)
	√	8) Word/text search tool
	√	9) Registration and measurement of the customers' product interests over time
	√	10) Hyperlink to relations
Product Configuration and Contract Management	√	1) Product configuration from offline PC (being frequently replicated)
	√	2) Configuration of product by use of a hierarchic (one-way) system
	-	3) Configuration of product by use of a full dialogue (dynamic) system
	-	4) Configuration with circumstances, e.g. max price
	√	5) Calculation of delivery date of configured product/availability check
	√	6) Possible from offer to create order including data needed for invoicing
	-	7) Visualisation for customer of the product configuration online/via Internet
	-	8) Visualisation for the customer of the product configuration via print
	t	9) Verification of price offer from internal organisation
	√	10) Contract management tool
	√	11) Possibility of more than one price list for one product based on customer seniority, area, season, etc.
	(√)	12) Service level agreements integrated with contract processing
	√	13) Discounting tools supporting contract creation
	-	14) Possibility of maintaining configurations without the use of programming
Marketing Tools	√	1) Library for storing marketing material (folders, brochures, etc.)
	*15	2) Historical product/price information library
	t	3) Competitor Information System
	-	4) Tool for customer satisfaction analysis
	R3	5) Management and registration of materials (e.g. banners, stickers, etc.) from current and previous campaigns
	R3	6) Possibility of mass-generated direct mail/mail-merging

Sales Force Automation	√	1) Online data transfer from workstation to databases
	√	2) Batch data transfer from workstation to databases
	√	3) Possibility of quick synchronisation of offline laptops
	√	4) Possibility of integration with PDA or the like via MS Outlook
	-	5) Possibility of taking orders/making sales online via PDA to the CRM application
	*5	6) Graphs for salesman comparing actual sales to budget
Resource Management	√	1) Planning calendar for each salesman
	R3	2) Possibility of booking a meeting on a calendar without the salesman's acceptance
	R3	3) Shared calendars (across several users)
	√	4) Graphical calendar
	-	5) Possibility of setting alarms for meetings
	√	6) Management of activities per user/customer/company/contact person
	√	7) Possible for a customer to be member of numerous territories
	√	8) Possibility of geographic, product type, and industry "territories"
	-	9) Geographic route planning
	-	10) Salesman resource planner
	R3	11) Registration of CRM related costs for each customer (e.g. travel costs for sales visits and marketing contribution costs etc.)
	R3	12) Front office logistics (storage repair, spares holding etc.)
Analysis Tools	*15	1) Flexible report-generator for sales
	*15	2) Flexible report-generator for marketing
	*15	3) Flexible report-generator for service and support
	R3	4) Standard Executive Information System incl. graphics
	R3	5) Advanced budgeting tools (includes e.g. fixed and variable calculation methods based on data from previous seasons, salesmen efficiency rates, etc.)
Forecasts	R3	1) Product forecasts (sales per month/year)
	R3	2) Revenue forecasts (revenue per month/year)
	R3	3) Roll-ups of forecasts across numerous organisations
	R3	4) Support for user-defined forecast dates
	R3	5) Roll-ups and forecasts on several levels in a firm

Other functionalities	-	1) Push technology for information-gathering on the Internet (active search on words)
	√	2) Active Briefing
	R3	3) Multiple currencies
	R3	4) Euro compliant
	√	5) Supports electronic scrollbar
	√	6) Security system that defines user-clearance
	√	7) Quick-print of document without having to open the application supporting the document
	-	8) Personal correspondence templates
	√	9) Full integration to word-processing and spreadsheet applications (automatic merging into these from the CRM-system), e.g. OLE technology (Object Link Enabling)
	-	10) Guide functions for using the application ("Wizards")
	√	11) Integrated fax tool that works seamless, as part of the application
Internet	R3	1) Automatic assignment of leads from the Internet
	R3	2) Tool for creating web-sites with predefined links to CRM database fields and interactive fields to CRM application
	-	3) Tool for creating web-sites with "drop-down-box" or equivalent with "drag-and-drop" graphics
	R3	4) Possibility for web-site differentiation dependant on customer logging in
	R3	5) Integrated e-mail tool that works seamless, as part of the application
	R3	6) Support for electronic payment
Telemarketing, Call Centre and Help-Desk	R3	1) Automatic dialling facilities (Predictive Dialling)
	R3	2) Computer-Telephony Integration (CTI) enabled/supportive
	R3	3) Application (through integration of CTI) enables routing possibilities of customer calling in, e.g. customer to specific operator, "A" customer first in queue, etc.
	R3	4) Use of electronic scripts for telemarketing or response for Call Centre/guided dialogue management
	-	5) Dialogue management with a neural network/adaptive learning
	R3	6) Cross-sales functions
	-	7) "Neural" inbound e-mail answering tool
	R3	8) Calculation/prognosis of inbound call frequency during the day
	R3	9) Scheduling device for Call Centre operators (Schedule Planner)
	R3	10) Technical problem resolution system
	R3	11) "Trouble-Ticketing" – a system for requesting service
	R3	12) Blending of Telemarketing and Call Centre function. That is the possibility of the system assigning telemarketing tasks to vacant operators during less busy periods

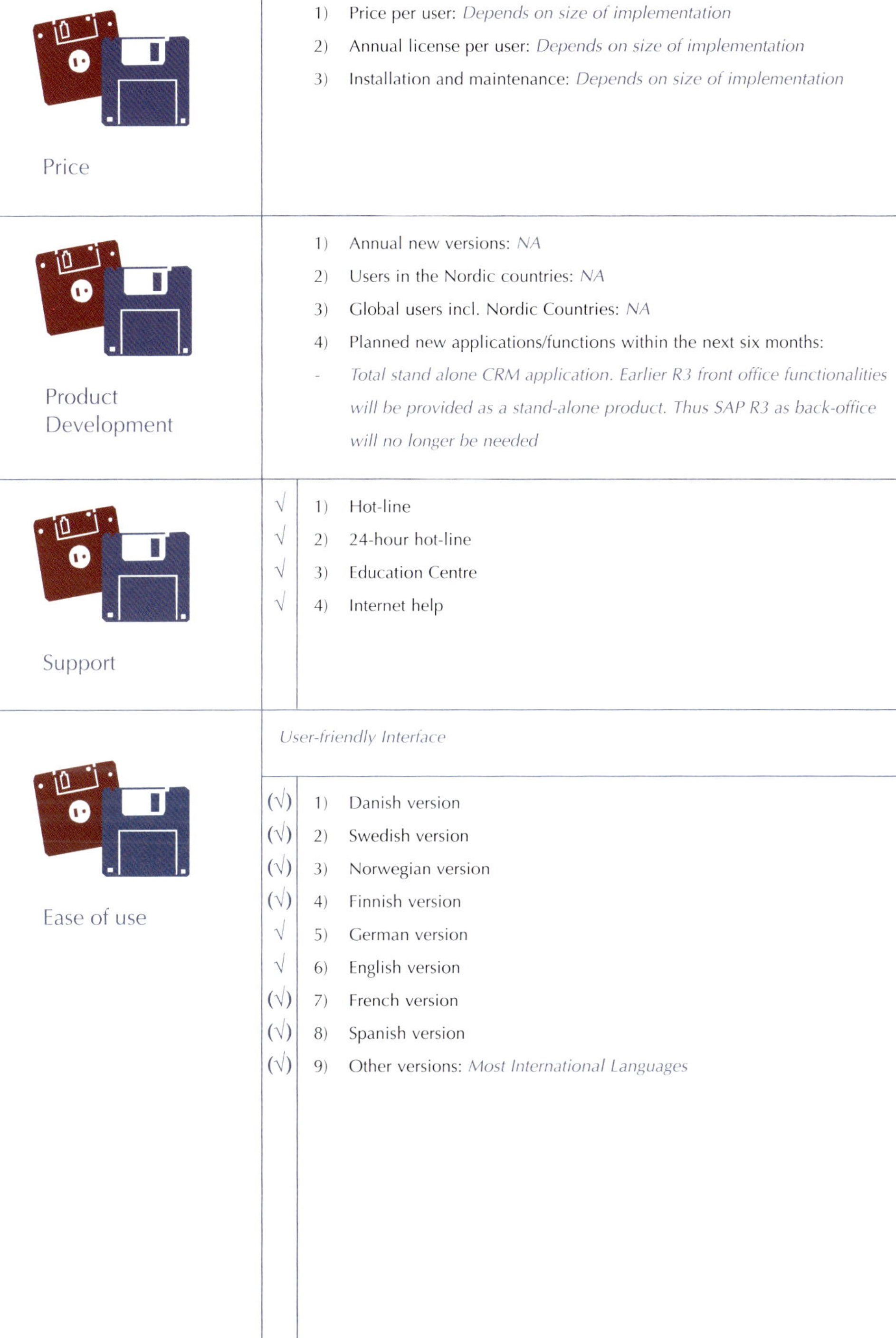

Price	1)	Price per user: *Depends on size of implementation*
	2)	Annual license per user: *Depends on size of implementation*
	3)	Installation and maintenance: *Depends on size of implementation*

Product Development	1)	Annual new versions: *NA*
	2)	Users in the Nordic countries: *NA*
	3)	Global users incl. Nordic Countries: *NA*
	4)	Planned new applications/functions within the next six months:
	-	*Total stand alone CRM application. Earlier R3 front office functionalities will be provided as a stand-alone product. Thus SAP R3 as back-office will no longer be needed*

Support	√	1)	Hot-line
	√	2)	24-hour hot-line
	√	3)	Education Centre
	√	4)	Internet help

User-friendly Interface

Ease of use	(√)	1)	Danish version
	(√)	2)	Swedish version
	(√)	3)	Norwegian version
	(√)	4)	Finnish version
	√	5)	German version
	√	6)	English version
	(√)	7)	French version
	(√)	8)	Spanish version
	(√)	9)	Other versions: *Most International Languages*

Industry Solutions

The following Industry Solutions are offered:

- *Consumer Packaged Goods*
- *High Tech*
- *Pharmaceutical*

Platforms and Architecture

R3	1)	Unix
R3	2)	Win NT
R3	3)	Win 95/98
R3	4)	OS/2
R3	5)	Mainframe, e.g. MVS
R3	6)	MAC
-	7)	Netscape
-	8)	Internet explorer
-	9)	Full Web-based Architecture (Total 0 MB Thin Clients)
√	10)	Partial Web-based Architecture
√	11)	Client/Server-based Architecture
√	12)	Runs Client/Server over WAN
√	13)	Runs Client/Server over Dialup

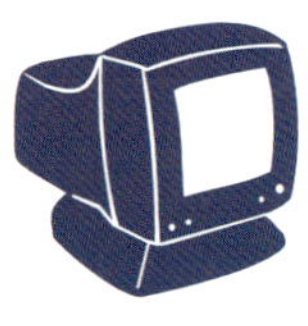

Configuration of CRM-System

	1)	Programming language: *ABAP, Visual Basic, Java*
	2)	Possibility for the firm to develop its own display: *Mobile Sales (High), R3 (Medium)*
	3)	Scalability from no. of users: *NA* to no. of users: *NA*

√	4)	Automatic generation of connections between data fields
√	5)	When upgrading software customer-specific configurations are not lost
√	6)	The systems IT structure supports global operations with several servers perationer med flere servere

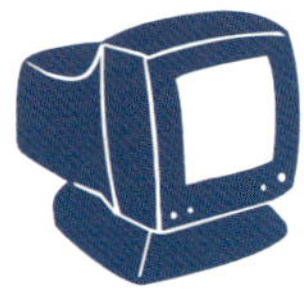

Databases

√	1)	Oracle
√	2)	Sybase
√	3)	Informix
-	4)	Scalable SQL
√	5)	MS SQL
√	6)	IBM DB2
-	7)	Access
-	8)	Ctree

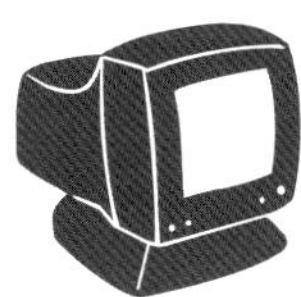

Integration

√	1)	Pre-built SAP Interface
-	2)	Pre-built Oracle Interface
-	3)	Pre-built Peoplesoft Interface
-	4)	Pre-built Baan Interface
-	5)	Pre-built JD Edwards Interface
-	6)	Other pre-built Interfaces
√	7)	Supports Application Program Interfaces or equivalent
√	8)	Supports Object Link Enabling technology or equivalent
-	9)	Tool for creation of Interfaces without the use of programming
*15	10)	Integration to 3rd party data providers, incl. D&B

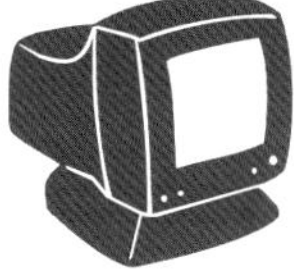

Hardware

Minimum requirements for workstation

Processor:	NA
RAM:	NA
Free harddisk space:	NA

Siebel

Company Overview

With over 800 customers worldwide, Siebel Systems has become the fastest growing enterprise application software company in history and is the world's largest provider of sales, marketing and customer service applications. Siebel's breakthrough Web-based architecture supports the needs of small, medium and large global organisations with a fully integrated sales, marketing and customer service solution that meets the needs of the entire enterprise.

Vision

At Siebel Systems, we do whatever it takes to make our customers successful. Our customers measure success by what they can offer their customers: shorter sales cycles, quicker resolution of service issues and more value delivered over time at each stage of sales and service.

We make success possible in a number of ways: with the most functionally complete closed-loop sales, marketing and customer service solutions available; through alliances with world-class partners that provide unrivaled business systems integration, hardware and software solutions; and through a systematic and responsive service and support infrastructure that is highly visible in each customer relationship at every business level – from the front line to the executive ranks.

At Siebel, the customer really does come first. If there is a technical problem, we immediately deploy the resources necessary to resolve it – whenever and wherever required. And if a tradeoff must be made between servicing an existing customer or a new prospect, the customer wins every single time.

Management Summary

Siebel Systems' e-commerce applications deliver the first entirely Web-based, enterprise class family of sales, marketing and customer service applications. Siebel Enterprise Applications are the global market leaders in the Front Office market, delivering acknowledged, best-of-class functionality in every category of sales, marketing and customer service, including:

Siebel Sales Enterprise, a comprehensive sales information system for sales professionals.

Siebel Service Enterprise, a complete customer service information system for Call centre service agents.

Siebel Call Centre, an integrated sales and service information system for universal agents in call centres.

Siebel Field Service, a complete customer service information system for field service professionals.

Siebel Marketing Enterprise, a comprehensive customer datamart and marketing process automation system for marketing professionals.

Siebel Product Configurator, a complete product configuration system for sales and marketing professionals.

Siebel InterActive dynamic, online briefings for sales, marketing and customer service applications.

Siebel also provides the first industry-specific sales, marketing and customer service applications for the Finance, Insurance, Consumer Goods, Pharmaceutical, Communications, High Technology and Utilities industries as well as for the public sector.

References

ABN AMRO Bank NV, Alcatel Business Systems Division, Bank of America, British-American Tobacco, Bayer, Bell Canada, Bell South, BBC, Boeing, CitiBank, Chase Manhattan, Compaq, Cigna, Daimler-Benz, Deutsche Telekom, DHL, Digital, Dow Chemical Company, Dow Corning, Dresdner Bank, Ford, Glaxo Wellcome, Genesys, Guiness, Hewlett Packard, Honeywell, JD Edwards, Johnson & Johnson, Kellogg Company, Lucent Technologies, MCI Worldcom, Microsoft Corporation, Nationwide Insurance Enterprise, Novell, Packard Bell NEC, Peoplesoft, Pioneer, Prudential Assurance Company Ltd, Reynolds Metals Company, Sequent Computer Systems, Siemens AG, Singapore Telecom, Sun Microsystems, Telenor Mobil, Telecom Italia Mobile SpA, United Distillers & Vintners, Unisys Corporation, US Robotics Access Corporation, Visa International, Volvo, WorldCom, Warner Home Video.

Ownership and Equity

The Company's current officers, directors and affiliated entities together beneficially owned approximately 31.1% of the outstanding shares of Common Stock as of December 31, 1998. In particular, Thomas M. Siebel, the Company's Chairman and Chief Executive Officer, owned approximately 18.6% of the outstanding shares of Common Stock as of December 31, 1998.

Addresse

www.siebel.com

US Headquarters	*United Kingdom*	*Germany*
Siebel Systems, Inc.	Siebel Systems UK Ltd	Siebel Systems Deutschland GmbH
1855 South Grant Street	Siebel Court	Lyoner Strasse 15
San Mateo, CA 94402	20-22 The Avenue	D-60528 Frankfurt-Niderrad
Phone 800-647-4300	Egham, Surrey	Germany
Direct: 650-295-5000	TW20 9AU	Phone +49 69 66577 286
	Phone +44 1784 494900	

Supplier analysis – Siebel

Segmentation

√ 1) Automatic electronic ABC categorisation based on criteria defined by the company

√ 2) Possibility of manual categorisation (override of automatic categorisation)

√ 3) Segmentation can be based on different criteria based on the specific "territory". Furthermore, the possibility of a customer being A customer in one "territory" and B customer in another is also an issue

√ 4) Automatic warnings at low levels of activity on dimensions defined by the company

√ 5) Basic profiling tools (AND, OR, LIKE, NOT LIKE, *, -, +, /)

√ 6) Reuse of earlier group profiles in new profile definitions

√ 7) "Drop-down-box" or equivalent with predefined database field information for and creation of group profiles

Campaigns

√ 1) Campaign can consist of a number of different tasks in a pre-defined order

√ 2) Costing on campaigns on more than one dimension

- 3) Display campaigns and activities using graphic tools like flowcharts

√ 4) Management of several parallel campaigns

√ 5) Campaign surveillance tools

√ 6) "Event triggers"

√ 7) "Assistants" (already programmed "event triggers") for user level

√ 8) Automatic generation of next step in a campaign

√ 9) Budgeting tool to calculate viability of planned campaigns

√ 10) Graphic tools to show results

- 11) Possibility of seeing a list of all active campaigns incl. time-horizon

√ 12) Estimation and measuring of campaigns earnings efficiency

√ 13) Distribution of leads to campaign teams

Leads

√ 1) Management and creation of leads

√ 2) Calculation of success-rates on leads

√ 3) Status for leads' placing in a sales process

√ 4) Graphic tool that shows how many leads there are on each step of a sales funnel

√ 5) Possibility of attaching one or more competitors to a lead

√ 6) Status for leads' purchasing potential and the probability of the sale coming through

√ 7) Manual salesman assignment to leads

√ 8) Automatic salesman assignment to leads

Customer Data	√	1) Customer data table with the firms' own defined fields
	√	2) Possibility of more than one address per customer
	√	3) Possibility of attachments to customer database of previous e-mails, letters, documents (a so-called customer log)
	√	4) Registration of all previous meetings/contacts with customers including outcome
	√	5) Registration of own sales strategy and tactics towards each customer
	√	6) Registration of customers' goals, visions and key success factors
	√	7) Search possibilities on data on several dimensions simultaneously (for example area and age)
	√	8) Word/text search tool
	√	9) Registration and measurement of the customers' product interests over time
	√	10) Hyperlink to relations
Product Configuration and Contract Management	√	1) Product configuration from offline PC (being frequently replicated)
	√	2) Configuration of product by use of a hierarchic (one-way) system
	√	3) Configuration of product by use of a full dialogue (dynamic) system
	√	4) Configuration with circumstances, e.g. max price
	√	5) Calculation of delivery date of configured product/availability check
	√	6) Possible from offer to create order including data needed for invoicing
	√	7) Visualisation for customer of the product configuration online/via Internet
	√	8) Visualisation for the customer of the product configuration via print
	√	9) Verification of price offer from internal organisation
	√	10) Contract management tool
	√	11) Possibility of more than one price list for one product based on customer seniority, area, season, etc.
	-	12) Service level agreements integrated with contract processing
	√	13) Discounting tools supporting contract creation
	√	14) Possibility of maintaining configurations without the use of programming
Marketing Tools	√	1) Library for storing marketing material (folders, brochures, etc.)
	-	2) Historical product/price information library
	√	3) Competitor Information System
	√	4) Tool for customer satisfaction analysis
	√	5) Management and registration of materials (e.g. banners, stickers, etc.) from current and previous campaigns
	√	6) Possibility of mass-generated direct mail/mail-merging

Sales Force Automation	√	1) Online data transfer from workstation to databases
	√	2) Batch data transfer from workstation to databases
	√	3) Possibility of quick synchronisation of offline laptops
	√	4) Possibility of integration with PDA or the like via MS Outlook
	√	5) Possibility of taking orders/making sales online via PDA to the CRM application
	√	6) Graphs for salesman comparing actual sales to budget
Resource Management	√	1) Planning calendar for each salesman
	√	2) Possibility of booking a meeting on a calendar without the salesman's acceptance
	√	3) Shared calendars (across several users)
	√	4) Graphical calendar
	√	5) Possibility of setting alarms for meetings
	√	6) Management of activities per user/customer/company/contact person
	√	7) Possible for a customer to be member of numerous territories
	√	8) Possibility of geographic, product type, and industry "territories"
	√	9) Geographic route planning
	-	10) Salesman resource planner
	√	11) Registration of CRM related costs for each customer (e.g. travel costs for sales visits and marketing contribution costs etc.)
	√	12) Front office logistics (storage repair, spares holding etc.)
Analysis Tools	√	1) Flexible report-generator for sales
	√	2) Flexible report-generator for marketing
	√	3) Flexible report-generator for service and support
	√	4) Standard Executive Information System incl. graphics
	-	5) Advanced budgeting tools (includes e.g. fixed and variable calculation methods based on data from previous seasons, salesmen efficiency rates, etc.)
Forecasts	√	1) Product forecasts (sales per month/year)
	√	2) Revenue forecasts (revenue per month/year)
	√	3) Roll-ups of forecasts across numerous organisations
	√	4) Support for user-defined forecast dates
	√	5) Roll-ups and forecasts on several levels in a firm

Other functionalities	√	1)	Push technology for information-gathering on the Internet (active search on words)
	√	2)	Active Briefing
	√	3)	Multiple currencies
	√	4)	Euro compliant
	√	5)	Supports electronic scrollbar
	√	6)	Security system that defines user-clearance
	√	7)	Quick-print of document without having to open the application supporting the document
	√	8)	Personal correspondence templates
	√	9)	Full integration to word-processing and spreadsheet applications (automatic merging into these from the CRM-system), e.g. OLE technology (Object Link Enabling)
	√	10)	Guide functions for using the application ("Wizards")
	√	11)	Integrated fax tool that works seamless,as part of the application
Internet	√	1)	Automatic assignment of leads from the Internet
	√	2)	Tool for creating web-sites with predefined links to CRM database fields and interactive fields to CRM application
	√	3)	Tool for creating web-sites with "drop-down-box" or equivalent with "drag-and-drop" graphics
	√	4)	Possibility for web-site differentiation dependant on customer logging in
	√	5)	Integrated e-mail tool that works seamless, as part of the application
	√	6)	Support for electronic payment
Telemarketing, Call Centre and Help-Desk	√	1)	Automatic dialling facilities (Predictive Dialling)
	√	2)	Computer-Telephony Integration (CTI) enabled/supportive
	√	3)	Application (through integration of CTI) enables routing possibilities of customer calling in, e.g. customer to specific operator, "A" customer first in queue, etc.
	√	4)	Use of electronic scripts for telemarketing or response for Call Centre/guided dialogue management
	(√)	5)	Dialogue management with a neural network/adaptive learning
	√	6)	Cross-sales functions
	√	7)	"Neural" inbound e-mail answering tool
	-	8)	Calculation/prognosis of inbound call frequency during the day
	-	9)	Scheduling device for Call Centre operators (Schedule Planner)
	√	10)	Technical problem resolution system
	√	11)	"Trouble-Ticketing" – a system for requesting service
	√	12)	Blending of Telemarketing and Call Centre function. That is the possibility of the system assigning telemarketing tasks to vacant operators during less busy periods

Price

1) Price per user: *depends on number of modules*
2) Annual license per user: *depends on number of modules*
3) Installation and maintenance: *depends on number of modules*

Product Development

1) Annual new versions: *NA*
2) Users in the Nordic countries: *NA*
3) Global users incl. Nordic Countries: *NA*
4) Planned new applications/functions within the next six months: *NA*

Support

√ 1) Hot-line
√ 2) 24-hour hot-line
√ 3) Education Centre
√ 4) Internet help

Ease of use

Follows Windows 98 design technics, with a browser look and feel. Uses Hyperlinking, back and forward buttons and history for navigating across screens according to the customers business processes. User profile-based menues can be put up by an administrator for each user group.

√ 1) Danish version
t 2) Swedish version
t 3) Norwegian version
√ 4) Finnish version
√ 5) German version
√ 6) English version
√ 7) French version
√ 8) Spanish version
√ 9) Other versions: *Japanese, Portuguese, etc.*

Industry Solutions

The following Industry Solutions are offered:

- *Insurance*
- *Finance*
- *Telco*
- *GPC*
- *Pharma*
- *(Utilities)*
- *(Automotive)*

Platforms and Architecture

√	1)	Unix
√	2)	Win NT
√	3)	Win 95/98
-	4)	OS/2
-	5)	Mainframe, e.g. MVS
-	6)	MAC
√	7)	Netscape
√	8)	Internet explorer
√	9)	Full Web-based Architecture (Total O MB Thin Clients)
-	10)	Partial Web-based Architecture
√	11)	Client/Server-based Architecture
√	12)	Runs Client/Server over WAN
√	13)	Runs Client/Server over Dialup

Configuration of CRM-System

	1)	Programming language: *C++*
	2)	Possibility for the firm to develop its own display: *High*
	3)	Scalability from no. of users: *1*
		to no. of users: *20,000+*
√	4)	Automatic generation of connections between data fields
√	5)	When upgrading software customer-specific configurations are not lost
√	6)	The systems IT structure supports global operations with several servers

Databases

√	1)	Oracle
√	2)	Sybase
√	3)	Informix
-	4)	Scalable SQL
√	5)	MS SQL
√	6)	IBM DB2
-	7)	Access
-	8)	Ctree

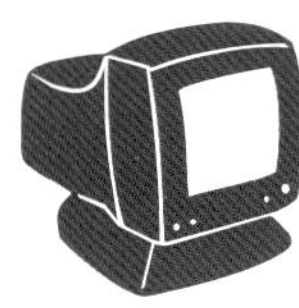

Integration

√	1)	Pre-built SAP Interface
-	2)	Pre-built Oracle Interface
√	3)	Pre-built Peoplesoft Interface
-	4)	Pre-built Baan Interface
-	5)	Pre-built JD Edwards Interface
-	6)	Other pre-built Interfaces
√	7)	Supports Application Program Interfaces or equivalent
√	8)	Supports Object Link Enabling technology or equivalent
√	9)	Tool for creation of Interfaces without the use of programming
√	10)	Integration to 3rd party data providers, incl. D&B

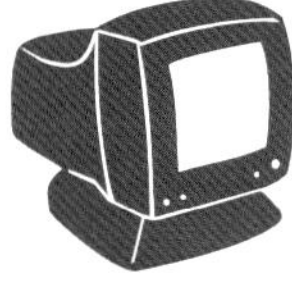

Hardware

Minimum requirements for workstation

Processor:	*Pentium 133*
RAM:	*32 MB RAM*
Free harddisk space:	*0 for thin clients to 300 MB for ordinary client*

Software Innovation

Company Overview

Software Innovation was established in 1984. Software Innovation is a leading Scandinavian vendor of IT solutions which enhance the efficiency of office-based companies. The company delivers both software and related consulting. Our goal is to become a leading professional player in this market segment, which internationally is designated Business Automation Systems. The company is divided into 10 self-supporting sections and has six active subsidiaries, each with its own clearly defined responsibility and business goal. The sections have their own budgets and accounts and are operated as profit centres. Today, Software Innovation has a strong line of business that is result oriented and holds a deep knowledge of leading technology. On this foundation, the company will win market shares through goal-oriented international commitment to specific vertical niches with an identified need for this type of software, such as offshore, banking and insurance.

Vision

The vision of Software Innovation is to develop its position as a leading vendor of business critical software with a combination of high technological competence, flexible standard products and adaptability. To reach the goal of becoming a central international player in our business area and secure efficient and successful market development we constantly strengthen our access to technology, to competencies and to the market. This is the basis for the industrial approach reflected in the strategy, a strategy with the following main elements:

- To offer the customers innovative solutions that incorporate knowledge of the customer's business as well as first-hand competence in technology development.
- To obtain a strong position on the home market.
- To achieve an industrial size and maturity.
- To build distribution channels for export.

Management Summary

Today, the Group delivers the following standard software in the area of business automation:

Salesmaker – Customer Relationship Management System (CRM) for medium-sized and large companies

ProArc – Document Management System (DMS) for medium-sized and large companies

Vega – CRM product for small and medium-sized companies

Genova – Development and method tool

VIS/Uniplan – Reporting and analysis tool for data collecting and processing

Miscellaneous – Various trade solutions for CRM

References

Vinmonopolet, DM-Huset, Navia ASA, Hjemmet Mortensen, Se og Hør Forlaget, Egmont Serieforlaget, Norsk Aller, Mandatum, Toll- og avgiftsdirektoratet, NRK, NSB, Postbanken, Telenor, Volvo, Alcatel, The Riksgälds office in Sweden and The New York Times.

Ownership and equity

Software Innovation is a limited company with the following major shareholders: Orkla ASA, SND, Den norske Stats Oljeselskap AS, Sundal Collier & Co. AS, Sanden A/S, Vesta Teknologi, Storebrand Livsforsikring AS, Fondspartner AS, Sundal Collier & Co. AS, Vesta Grønt Norden, and Vital Forsikring ASA. The rest of the shares are distributed among Software Innovation ASA and subsidiary employees and other external shareholders.

Addresses

www.softinn.no

Norway

Software Innovation

Drammensveien 175

Postboks 390 Skøyen

N-0212 Oslo

Norway

Phone +47 22 51 85 00

Fax +47 22 73 07 14

Sweden

Software Innovation AB

Karlstadvägen 9-11 3tr.

S-168 67 Bromma

Sweden

Phone +46 8 404 00 00

Fax +46 8 404 00 50

Supplier analysis – Software Innovation

Segmentation

√	1)	Automatic electronic ABC categorisation based on criteria defined by the company
√	2)	Possibility of manual categorisation (override of automatic categorisation)
√	3)	Segmentation can be based on different criteria based on the specific "territory". Furthermore, the possibility of a customer being A customer in one "territory" and B customer in another is also an issue
√	4)	Automatic warnings at low levels of activity on dimensions defined by the company
√	5)	Basic profiling tools (AND, OR, LIKE, NOT LIKE, *, -, +, /)
√	6)	Reuse of earlier group profiles in new profile definitions
√	7)	"Drop-down-box" or equivalent with predefined database field information for and creation of group profiles

Campaigns

√	1)	Campaign can consist of a number of different tasks in a pre-defined order
√	2)	Costing on campaigns on more than one dimension
-	3)	Display campaigns and activities using graphic tools like flowcharts
√	4)	Management of several parallel campaigns
√	5)	Campaign surveillance tools
(√)	6)	"Event triggers"
√	7)	"Assistants" (already programmed "event triggers") for user level
-	8)	Automatic generation of next step in a campaign
√	9)	Budgeting tool to calculate viability of planned campaigns
√	10)	Graphic tools to show results
-	11)	Possibility of seeing a list of all active campaigns incl. time-horizon
√	12)	Estimation and measuring of campaigns earnings efficiency
√	13)	Distribution of leads to campaign teams

Leads

√	1)	Management and creation of leads
*14	2)	Calculation of success-rates on leads
√	3)	Status for leads' placing in a sales process
*14	4)	Graphic tool that shows how many leads there are on each step of a sales funnel
√	5)	Possibility of attaching one or more competitors to a lead
√	6)	Status for leads' purchasing potential and the probability of the sale coming through
√	7)	Manual salesman assignment to leads
√	8)	Automatic salesman assignment to leads

Customer Data	√	1)	Customer data table with the firms' own defined fields
	√	2)	Possibility of more than one address per customer
	√	3)	Possibility of attachments to customer database of previous e-mails, letters, documents (a so-called customer log)
	√	4)	Registration of all previous meetings/contacts with customers including outcome
	√	5)	Registration of own sales strategy and tactics towards each customer
	√	6)	Registration of customers' goals, visions and key success factors
	√	7)	Search possibilities on data on several dimensions simultaneously (for example area and age)
	√	8)	Word/text search tool
	√	9)	Registration and measurement of the customers' product interests over time
	√	10)	Hyperlink to relations
Product Configuration and Contract Management	√	1)	Product configuration from offline PC (being frequently replicated)
	√	2)	Configuration of product by use of a hierarchic (one-way) system
	-	3)	Configuration of product by use of a full dialogue (dynamic) system
	-	4)	Configuration with circumstances, e.g. max price
	-	5)	Calculation of delivery date of configured product/availability check
	t	6)	Possible from offer to create order including data needed for invoicing
	-	7)	Visualisation for customer of the product configuration online/via Internet
	-	8)	Visualisation for the customer of the product configuration via print
	√	9)	Verification of price offer from internal organisation
	√	10)	Contract management tool
	√	11)	Possibility of more than one price list for one product based on customer seniority, area, season, etc.
	-	12)	Service level agreements integrated with contract processing
	√	13)	Discounting tools supporting contract creation
	-	14)	Possibility of maintaining configurations without the use of programming
Marketing Tools	√	1)	Library for storing marketing material (folders, brochures, etc.)
	√	2)	Historical product/price information library
	-	3)	Competitor Information System
	-	4)	Tool for customer satisfaction analysis
	-	5)	Management and registration of materials (e.g. banners, stickers, etc.) from current and previous campaigns
	√	6)	Possibility of mass-generated direct mail/mail-merging

Sales Force Automation	√	1) Online data transfer from workstation to databases
	√	2) Batch data transfer from workstation to databases
	√	3) Possibility of quick synchronisation of offline laptops
	√	4) Possibility of integration with PDA or the like via MS Outlook
	-	5) Possibility of taking orders/making sales online via PDA to the CRM application
	√	6) Graphs for salesman comparing actual sales to budget
Resource Management	√	1) Planning calendar for each salesman
	√	2) Possibility of booking a meeting on a calendar without the salesman's acceptance
	√	3) Shared calendars (across several users)
	√	4) Graphical calendar
	√	5) Possibility of setting alarms for meetings
	√	6) Management of activities per user/customer/company/contact person
	√	7) Possible for a customer to be member of numerous territories
	√	8) Possibility of geographic, product type, and industry "territories"
	-	9) Geographic route planning
	-	10) Salesman resource planner
	√	11) Registration of CRM related costs for each customer (e.g. travel costs for sales visits and marketing contribution costs etc.)
	-	12) Front office logistics (storage repair, spares holding etc.)
Analysis Tools	*5	1) Flexible report-generator for sales
	*5	2) Flexible report-generator for marketing
	*5	3) Flexible report-generator for service and support
	√	4) Standard Executive Information System incl. graphics
	√	5) Advanced budgeting tools (includes e.g. fixed and variable calculation methods based on data from previous seasons, salesmen efficiency rates, etc.)
Forecasts	√	1) Product forecasts (sales per month/year)
	√	2) Revenue forecasts (revenue per month/year)
	√	3) Roll-ups of forecasts across numerous organisations
	-	4) Support for user-defined forecast dates
	√	5) Roll-ups and forecasts on several levels in a firm

Other functionalities	-	1) Push technology for information-gathering on the Internet (active search on words)
	-	2) Active Briefing
	√	3) Multiple currencies
	√	4) Euro compliant
	-	5) Supports electronic scrollbar
	√	6) Security system that defines user-clearance
	-	7) Quick-print of document without having to open the application supporting the document
	-	8) Personal correspondence templates
	√	9) Full integration to word-processing and spreadsheet applications (automatic merging into these from the CRM-system), e.g. OLE technology (Object Link Enabling)
	-	10) Guide functions for using the application ("Wizards")
	√	11) Integrated fax tool that works seamless, as part of the application
Internet	-	1) Automatic assignment of leads from the Internet
	-	2) Tool for creating web-sites with predefined links to CRM database fields and interactive fields to CRM application
	-	3) Tool for creating web-sites with "drop-down-box" or equivalent with "drag-and-drop" graphics
	-	4) Possibility for web-site differentiation dependant on customer logging in
	√	5) Integrated e-mail tool that works seamless, as part of the application
	-	6) Support for electronic payment
Telemarketing, Call Centre and Help-Desk	-	1) Automatic dialling facilities (Predictive Dialling)
	-	2) Computer-Telephony Integration (CTI) enabled/supportive
	-	3) Application (through integration of CTI) enables routing possibilities of customer calling in, e.g. customer to specific operator, "A" customer first in queue, etc.
	√	4) Use of electronic scripts for telemarketing or response for Call Centre/guided dialogue management
	-	5) Dialogue management with a neural network/adaptive learning
	-	6) Cross-sales functions
	-	7) "Neural" inbound e-mail answering tool
	-	8) Calculation/prognosis of inbound call frequency during the day
	-	9) Scheduling device for Call Centre operators (Schedule Planner)
	-	10) Technical problem resolution system
	-	11) "Trouble-Ticketing" – a system for requesting service
	-	12) Blending of Telemarketing and Call Centre function. That is the possibility of the system assigning telemarketing tasks to vacant operators during less busy periods

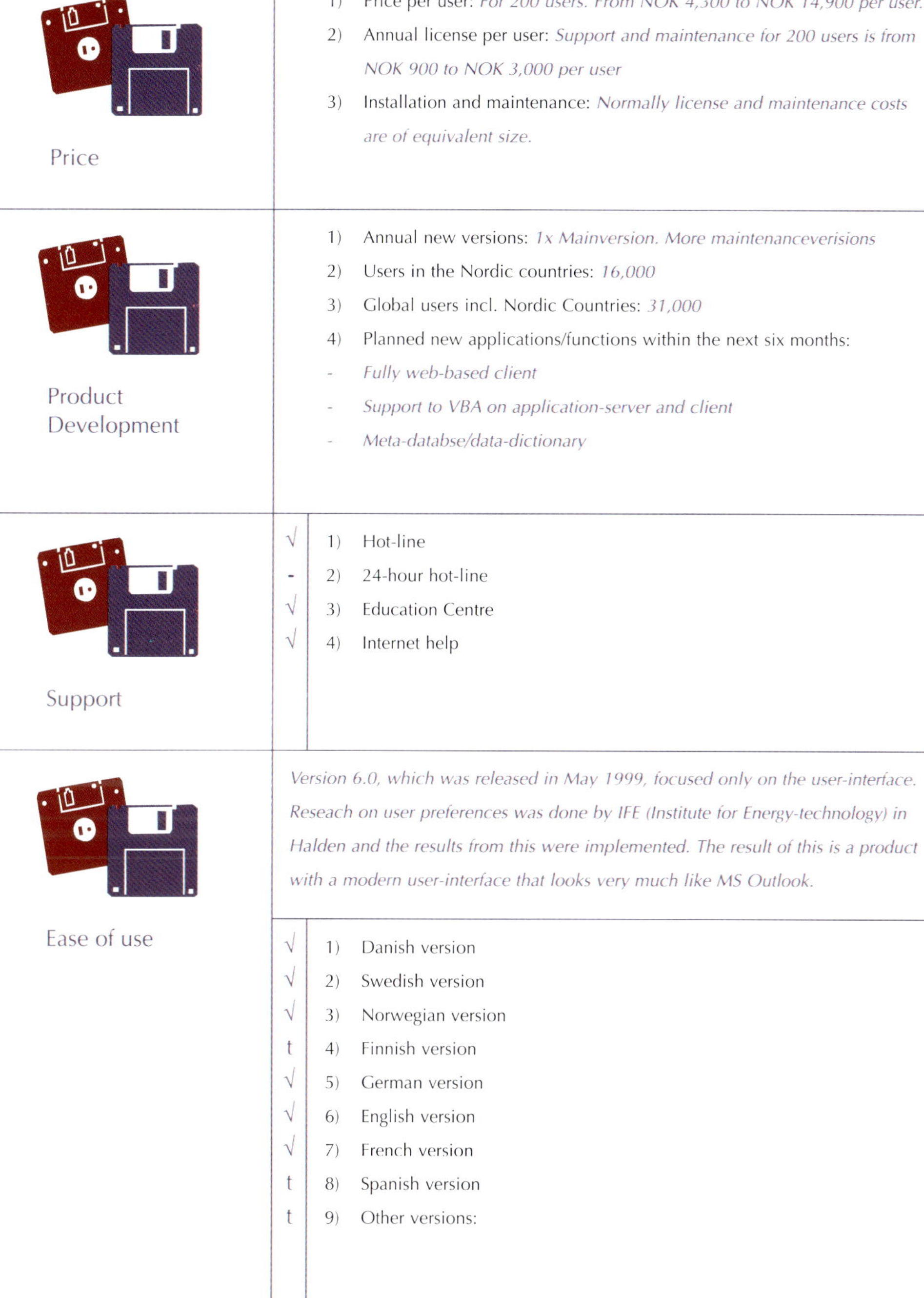

Price	1) Price per user: *For 200 users. From NOK 4,300 to NOK 14,900 per user.* 2) Annual license per user: *Support and maintenance for 200 users is from NOK 900 to NOK 3,000 per user* 3) Installation and maintenance: *Normally license and maintenance costs are of equivalent size.*
Product Development	1) Annual new versions: *1x Mainversion. More maintenanceverisions* 2) Users in the Nordic countries: *16,000* 3) Global users incl. Nordic Countries: *31,000* 4) Planned new applications/functions within the next six months: - *Fully web-based client* - *Support to VBA on application-server and client* - *Meta-databse/data-dictionary*
Support	√ 1) Hot-line - 2) 24-hour hot-line √ 3) Education Centre √ 4) Internet help
Ease of use	*Version 6.0, which was released in May 1999, focused only on the user-interface. Reseach on user preferences was done by IFE (Institute for Energy-technology) in Halden and the results from this were implemented. The result of this is a product with a modern user-interface that looks very much like MS Outlook.* √ 1) Danish version √ 2) Swedish version √ 3) Norwegian version t 4) Finnish version √ 5) German version √ 6) English version √ 7) French version t 8) Spanish version t 9) Other versions:

Industry Solutions

The following Industry Solutions are offered:

- *Banking*
- *Medical*
- *Oil Offshore*

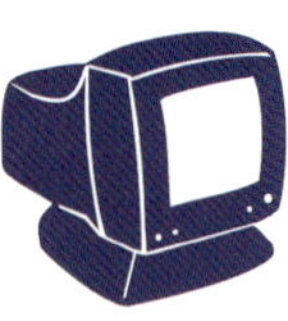

Platforms and Architecture

-	1)	Unix
√	2)	Win NT
√	3)	Win 95/98
-	4)	OS/2
-	5)	Mainframe, e.g. MVS
-	6)	MAC
-	7)	Netscape
-	8)	Internet explorer
-	9)	Full Web-based Architecture (Total 0 MB Thin Clients)
√	10)	Partial Web-based Architecture
√	11)	Client/Server-based Architecture
√	12)	Runs Client/Server over WAN
√	13)	Runs Client/Server over Dialup

Configuration of CRM-System

	1)	Programming language: *Visual Basic 6.0 and MS C++*
	2)	Possibility for the firm to develop its own display: *High*
	3)	Scalability from no. of users: *NA*
		to no. of users: *NA*
-	4)	Automatic generation of connections between data fields
√	5)	When upgrading software customer-specific configurations are not lost
√	6)	The systems IT structure supports global operations with several servers

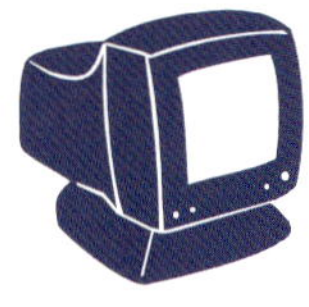

Databases

√	1)	Oracle
√	2)	Sybase
-	3)	Informix
-	4)	Scalable SQL
√	5)	MS SQL
√	6)	IBM DB2
-	7)	Access
-	8)	Ctree

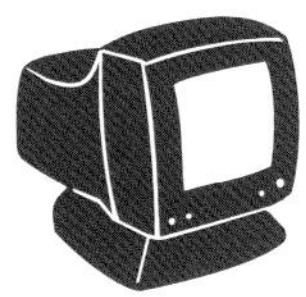

Integration

-	1)	Pre-built SAP Interface
-	2)	Pre-built Oracle Interface
-	3)	Pre-built Peoplesoft Interface
-	4)	Pre-built Baan Interface
-	5)	Pre-built JD Edwards Interface
√	6)	Other pre-built Interfaces: *Concorde, Agresso; Formula*
√	7)	Supports Application Program Interfaces or equivalent
√	8)	Supports Object Link Enabling technology or equivalent
√	9)	Tool for creation of Interfaces without the use of programming
√	10)	Integration to 3rd party data providers, incl. D&B

Hardware

Minimum requirements for workstation

Processor:	*Pentium 166*
RAM:	*32 MB RAM*
Free harddisk space:	*20 MB*

Vantive

Company Overview

Vantive is a worldwide leader in the front-office software market with more than 750 customers and $163 million in revenue in 1998. Vantive is supported by extensive software, consulting and service partner programs that integrate further technology and vertical expertise as well as integration support. Founded in 1990, Vantive is headquartered in Santa Clara, California, and distributes its products in more than 24 countries.

Vision

Vantive is the Provider of High-Powered e-customer Customer Relationship Management (CRM) Solutions for Enterprises Moving to The Web. Vantive brings technology solutions to the front office that create competitive advantage through strong and enduring customer relationships.

Management Summary

Single Customer Relationship Solution – One face to the customer, one customer knowledge base, one link to other systems, and one integrated, company-wide solution. That is Vantive's solution for turning your customer base into an annuity base. The power of Vantive's world-class product suite lies in its ability to put the customer at the center of your business and, by doing so, increase customer loyalty and partnership. The payoff is big. Not only do loyal customers generate lifelong revenues and referrals, but, because your sales and service costs drop significantly, they become increasingly profitable over time.

The Vantive Enterprise – Called The Vantive Enterprise, Vantive's customer relationship solution is a complete suite of web-enabled software products that integrate sales, marketing, call center, help desk, field service, inventory, procurement and quality assurance operations across your company.

The modules offered by Vantive are the following:
Vantive Sales, Vantive Support, Vantive FieldService, Vantive Inventory, Vantive Prochurement, Vantive Quality, Vantive HelpDesk.

The Vantive Enterprise collects the fragments of information about your customer that are spread across your organisation, unifies this information into one knowledge base, and makes it available to all the people within your company who talk to customers. Addressing customer interactions at both department and enterprise level, the Vantive Enterprise and a number of associated web-enabled products forge natural links across organisations via a shared database, common software and integration with back-office and legacy systems. The Enterprise is differentiated by its rich functionality; proven mobile solutions; component-based, high-performance architecture; and time and cost-effective implementations.

References

AT&T, France Telecom, SFR Swisscom, Viag Intercom, Belgacom, Telenor, Telekom Italia, Retevision, Dolphin, Telefonica, Franfinance, Charles Schwab, Chase Manhatten, Fidelity Investments, J.P. Morgan, Swift, Deutsche Bank, Scottish Widows, Bass Hotels & Resorts, Cathay Pacific Air, EDS, Federal Express, Waste Management, Caltex, Chevron, Shell, Union Energy, Utilicorp, EnBW, Lufthansa, Budget Rent-A-Car, Eastman Kodak, Home Depot, Office Depot, Sears, Rolls Royce, Alcoa, General Motors and Opel, Motorola, U.S. Surgical, Johnson Controls, Vorwerk, Compaq Computers, PeopleSoft, Hewlett-Packard, Lotus/IBM, Novell, Software AG, Schneider

Ownership and Equity

As of March 5, 1999, the shareholders who own more than 5% of outstanding Stock are:

Capital research and Management Company	11.9%
Amerindo Investment Advisors	9.8%
John Luongo	5.9%

The total stockholders equity as of March 3, 1999 equals 67,970,000 USD.

Addresses

www.vantive.com

USA

Vantive USA (Headquarters)
The Vantive Corporation
2455 Augustine Drive
Santa Clara, California 95054,USA
Phone/Fax 1-408-982-5700 /5738

England

EMEA North (UK)
Vantive (UK) Ltd.
Ashurst Manor, Church Lane
Sunninghill, Berkshire SL5 7DD
Phone/Fax: +44 1344 63 67-00 /63

Germany

EMEA Central (Germany, Austria)
Vantive GmbH Germany
Norsk-Data-Str. 3
D-61352 Bad Homburg
Phone/Fax: +49 6172 4018-0 /99

The Netherlands and other European countries

Vantive Holland
Wegalaan 26
2132 JC Hoofddorp
Phone/Fax: +31 23 554 2842 /30

Supplier analysis – Vantive

Segmentation

- 1) Automatic electronic ABC categorisation based on criteria defined by the company
- 2) Possibility of manual categorisation (override of automatic categorisation)
- 3) Segmentation can be based on different criteria based on the specific "territory". Furthermore, the possibility of a customer being A customer in one "territory" and B customer in another is also an issue
√ 4) Automatic warnings at low levels of activity on dimensions defined by the company
√ 5) Basic profiling tools (AND, OR, LIKE, NOT LIKE, *, -, +, /)
- 6) Reuse of earlier group profiles in new profile definitions
√ 7) "Drop-down-box" or equivalent with predefined database field information for and creation of group profiles

Campaigns

√ 1) Campaign can consist of a number of different tasks in a pre-defined order
√ 2) Costing on campaigns on more than one dimension
√ 3) Display campaigns and activities using graphic tools like flowcharts
√ 4) Management of several parallel campaigns
√ 5) Campaign surveillance tools
- 6) "Event triggers"
- 7) "Assistants" (already programmed "event triggers") for user level
√ 8) Automatic generation of next step in a campaign
- 9) Budgeting tool to calculate viability of planned campaigns
√ 10) Graphic tools to show results
- 11) Possibility of seeing a list of all active campaigns incl. time-horizon
√ 12) Estimation and measuring of campaigns earnings efficiency
√ 13) Distribution of leads to campaign teams

Leads

√ 1) Management and creation of leads
√ 2) Calculation of success-rates on leads
√ 3) Status for leads' placing in a sales process
√ 4) Graphic tool that shows how many leads there are on each step of a sales funnel
√ 5) Possibility of attaching one or more competitors to a lead
√ 6) Status for leads' purchasing potential and the probability of the sale coming through
√ 7) Manual salesman assignment to leads
√ 8) Automatic salesman assignment to leads

Customer Data	√	1) Customer data table with the firms' own defined fields
	√	2) Possibility of more than one address per customer
	√	3) Possibility of attachments to customer database of previous e-mails, letters, documents (a so-called customer log)
	√	4) Registration of all previous meetings/contacts with customers including outcome
	√	5) Registration of own sales strategy and tactics towards each customer
	√	6) Registration of customers' goals, visions and key success factors
	√	7) Search possibilities on data on several dimensions simultaneously (for example area and age)
	√	8) Word/text search tool
	√	9) Registration and measurement of the customers' product interests over time
	√	10) Hyperlink to relations
Product Configuration and Contract Management	√	1) Product configuration from offline PC (being frequently replicated)
	√	2) Configuration of product by use of a hierarchic (one-way) system
	-	3) Configuration of product by use of a full dialogue (dynamic) system
	-	4) Configuration with circumstances, e.g. max price
	√	5) Calculation of delivery date of configured product/availability check
	√	6) Possible from offer to create order including data needed for invoicing
	-	7) Visualisation for customer of the product configuration online/via Internet
	√	8) Visualisation for the customer of the product configuration via print
	√	9) Verification of price offer from internal organisation
	√	10) Contract management tool
	√	11) Possibility of more than one price list for one product based on customer seniority, area, season, etc.
	-	12) Service level agreements integrated with contract processing
	√	13) Discounting tools supporting contract creation
	-	14) Possibility of maintaining configurations without the use of programming
Marketing Tools	√	1) Library for storing marketing material (folders, brochures, etc.)
	√	2) Historical product/price information library
	√	3) Competitor Information System
	-	4) Tool for customer satisfaction analysis
	√	5) Management and registration of materials (e.g. banners, stickers, etc.) from current and previous campaigns
	√	6) Possibility of mass-generated direct mail/mail-merging

Sales Force Automation	√	1)	Online data transfer from workstation to databases
	√	2)	Batch data transfer from workstation to databases
	√	3)	Possibility of quick synchronisation of offline laptops
	√	4)	Possibility of integration with PDA or the like via MS Outlook
	-	5)	Possibility of taking orders/making sales online via PDA to the CRM application
	-	6)	Graphs for salesman comparing actual sales to budget.
Resource Management	*2	1)	Planning calendar for each salesman
	*2	2)	Possibility of booking a meeting on a calendar without the salesman's acceptance
	*2	3)	Shared calendars (across several users)
	2	4)	Graphical calendar
	2	5)	Possibility of setting alarms for meetings
	√	6)	Management of activities per user/customer/company/contact person
	√	7)	Possible for a customer to be member of numerous territories
	√	8)	Possibility of geographic, product type, and industry "territories"
	-	9)	Geographic route planning
	-	10)	Salesman resource planner
	√	11)	Registration of CRM related costs for each customer (e.g. travel costs for sales visits and marketing contribution costs etc.)
	√	12)	Front office logistics (storage repair, spares holding etc.)
Analysis Tools	*11	1)	Flexible report-generator for sales
	*11	2)	Flexible report-generator for marketing
	*11	3)	Flexible report-generator for service and support
	√	4)	Standard Executive Information System incl. graphics
	√	5)	Advanced budgeting tools (includes e.g. fixed and variable calculation methods based on data from previous seasons, salesmen efficiency rates, etc.)
Forecasts	√	1)	Product forecasts (sales per month/year)
	√	2)	Revenue forecasts (revenue per month/year)
	√	3)	Roll-ups of forecasts across numerous organisations
	-	4)	Support for user-defined forecast dates
	√	5)	Roll-ups and forecasts on several levels in a firm

Other functionalities	√	1)	Push technology for information-gathering on the Internet (active search on words)
	-	2)	Active Briefing
	√	3)	Multiple currencies
	√	4)	Euro compliant
	√	5)	Supports electronic scrollbar
	√	6)	Security system that defines user-clearance
	√	7)	Quick-print of document without having to open the application supporting the document
	√	8)	Personal correspondence templates
	√	9)	Full integration to word-processing and spreadsheet applications (automatic merging into these from the CRM-system), e.g. OLE technology (Object Link Enabling)
	-	10)	Guide functions for using the application ("Wizards")
	√	11)	Integrated fax tool that works seamless, as part of the application
Internet	√	1)	Automatic assignment of leads from the Internet
	-	2)	Tool for creating web-sites with predefined links to CRM database fields and interactive fields to CRM application
	-	3)	Tool for creating web-sites with "drop-down-box" or equivalent with "drag-and-drop" graphics
	-	4)	Possibility for web-site differentiation dependant on customer logging in
	√	5)	Integrated e-mail tool that works seamless, as part of the application
	-	6)	Support for electronic payment
Telemarketing, Call Centre and Help-Desk	√	1)	Automatic dialling facilities (Predictive Dialling)
	√	2)	Computer-Telephony Integration (CTI) enabled/supportive
	√	3)	Application (through integration of CTI) enables routing possibilities of customer calling in, e.g. customer to specific operator, "A" customer first in queue, etc.
	√	4)	Use of electronic scripts for telemarketing or response for Call Centre/guided dialogue management
	-	5)	Dialogue management with a neural network/adaptive learning
	√	6)	Cross-sales functions
	-	7)	"Neural" inbound e-mail answering tool
	-	8)	Calculation/prognosis of inbound call frequency during the day
	-	9)	Scheduling device for Call Centre operators (Schedule Planner)
	√	10)	Technical problem resolution system
	√	11)	"Trouble-Ticketing" – a system for requesting service
	√	12)	Blending of Telemarketing and Call Centre function. That is the possibility of the system assigning telemarketing tasks to vacant operators during less busy periods

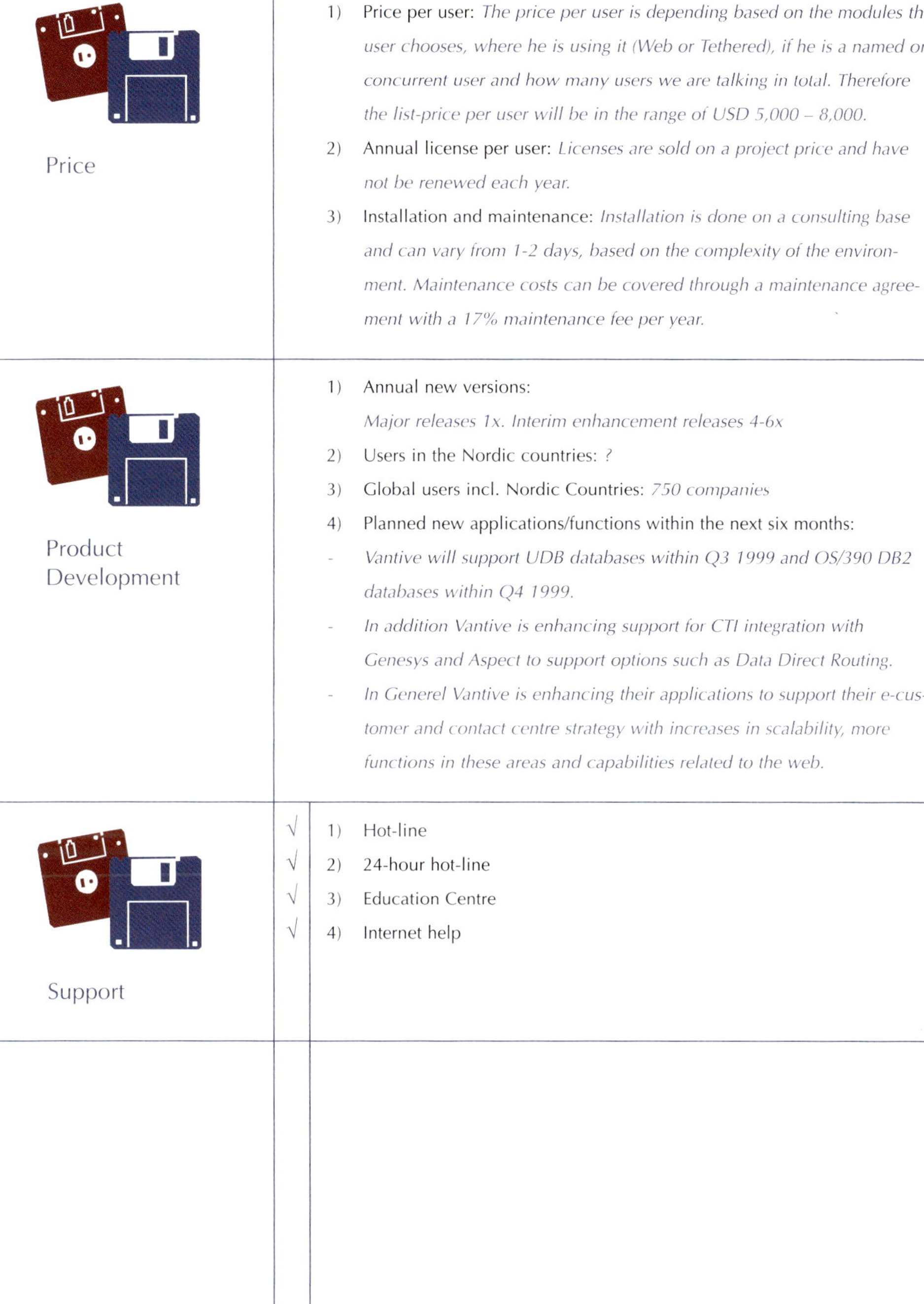

Price	1) **Price per user:** *The price per user is depending based on the modules the user chooses, where he is using it (Web or Tethered), if he is a named or concurrent user and how many users we are talking in total. Therefore the list-price per user will be in the range of USD 5,000 – 8,000.* 2) **Annual license per user:** *Licenses are sold on a project price and have not be renewed each year.* 3) **Installation and maintenance:** *Installation is done on a consulting base and can vary from 1-2 days, based on the complexity of the environment. Maintenance costs can be covered through a maintenance agreement with a 17% maintenance fee per year.*
Product Development	1) **Annual new versions:** *Major releases 1x. Interim enhancement releases 4-6x* 2) Users in the Nordic countries: *?* 3) Global users incl. Nordic Countries: *750 companies* 4) Planned new applications/functions within the next six months: - *Vantive will support UDB databases within Q3 1999 and OS/390 DB2 databases within Q4 1999.* - *In addition Vantive is enhancing support for CTI integration with Genesys and Aspect to support options such as Data Direct Routing.* - *In Generel Vantive is enhancing their applications to support their e-customer and contact centre strategy with increases in scalability, more functions in these areas and capabilities related to the web.*
Support	√ 1) Hot-line √ 2) 24-hour hot-line √ 3) Education Centre √ 4) Internet help

Ease of use

Same look and feel through one GUI. One tool for all customization. High sophisticated enterprise workflow. Bi-directional outlook integration. Integration with Office packages. Integrated systems, no interfaces and redundancy. Web-enabled products.

t	1)	Danish version
t	2)	Swedish version
t	3)	Norwegian version
t	4)	Finnish version
√	5)	German version
√	6)	English version
√	7)	French version
√	8)	Spanish version
√	9)	Other versions: *Dutch, Italian, Chinese, Japanese, Hebrew*

Industry Solutions

The following Industry Solutions are offered:

- *Vantive as an application has been implemented in virtually all vertical industries and has been configured due to the flexible nature of the Vantive architecture to support most of the critical business requirements in the CRM environment for these verticals.*

Platforms and Architecture

√	1)	Unix
√	2)	Win NT
√	3)	Win 95/98
-	4)	OS/2
-	5)	Mainframe, e.g. MVS
-	6)	MAC
√	7)	Netscape
√	8)	Internet explorer
√	9)	Full Web-based Architecture (Total O MB Thin Clients)
-	10)	Partial Web-based Architecture
√	11)	Client/Server-based Architecture
√	12)	Runs Client/Server over WAN
√	13)	Runs Client/Server over Dialup

Configuration of CRM-System		
	1)	Programming language: *VBA, SQL, Java*
	2)	Possibility for the firm to develop its own display: *High*
	3)	Scalability from no. of users: *1*
		to no. of users: *100,000+*
√	4)	Automatic generation of connections between data fields
√	5)	When upgrading software customer-specific configurations are not lost
√	6)	The systems IT structure supports global operations with several servers

Databases		
√	1)	Oracle
√	2)	Sybase
√	3)	Informix
-	4)	Scalable SQL
√	5)	MS SQL
√	6)	IBM DB2
-	7)	Access
-	8)	Ctree

Integration		
-	1)	Pre-built SAP Interface
√	2)	Pre-built Oracle Interface
√	3)	Pre-built Peoplesoft Interface
-	4)	Pre-built Baan Interface
-	5)	Pre-built JD Edwards Interface
√	6)	Other pre-built Interfaces: Kenan, LHS, Portal
√	7)	Supports Application Program Interfaces or equivalent
√	8)	Supports Object Link Enabling technology or equivalent
√	9)	Tool for creation of Interfaces without the use of programming
√	10)	Integration to 3rd party data providers, incl. D&B

Hardware	
Minimum requirements for workstation	
Processor:	*Pentium 100*
RAM:	*24 MB RAM*
Free harddisk space:	*0-500 MB*

Appendix

Higher demands, scenarios and specifications to the supplier analysis

Segmentation
1. The company can define the segmentation in which the customers can be divided into A, B, C and D (or a similar division) – whereas a division of the segmentation can depend on e.g.: [annual purchase in DKK], [number of sales visits and the costs thereof] and [number of goods returned from the company]. This functionality should be the basic part of the application and consequently you should not tick off "Yes" if it is implemented solely in a data warehouse.
2. The possibility of the automatic evaluation of the customer being overwritten if believed that the customer belongs to a higher or lower group than what the calculation immediately shows. This functionality has also been approved if the system does not allow automatic segmentation, however it is possible to categorise manually.
3. A territory refers to a specific division of the customer database. There might be numerous territories in which customers can be a part of the "Jutland territory" in one dimension and a member of "Production companies" in another dimension. Furthermore, a demand exists in this territory in which the segmentation of the customers is not based on the same calculation for everyone in a specific territory but rather on e.g. region, type of customer, type of product, etc.
4. The Possibility of putting up "warning signals" (e.g. an e-mail to "user x") when the level of activity is below a predefined limit for a certain month, for a certain group of customers (e.g. A customers).
5. A segmentation tool is used to define the group of customers who you will trace from the database. For example, you will be able to trace customers in Northern Jutland minus (–) customers who have bought the product within the past two years, plus (+) customers who have a purchasing behaviour on more than two products per year. The use of fixed concepts makes it easier for people without IT knowledge to use the system.
6. Demand for the supplier to be able to fulfil this functionality. He has an opportunity to choose if the previous group profile is dynamic or static. If it is static, it can be used in the new group profile for a further division of previous groups used previously with the same customers. If it is dynamic it is only a definition of a new type of group for a campaign. It was demanded that this group set-up be made on the same screen – in other words, that it is possible for a user to define a group immediately without having to program or use other applications.

7. The Possibility of defining a group profile without having to find specific
   terms in the database. You should only click them and they will then be
   placed in the logical sentence that you are about to set up.

Campaigns
1. The Possibility of a campaign consisting of printing a letter, a sales visit, a
   phone call etc. in an order predefined by the company.
2. Calculation costs of campaigns on several dimensions are available, e.g. on
   the basis of "How many customers bought products in area X in connection
   with campaign Y".
3. The Opportunity of controlling and setting up the campaign completion by
   graphic tools as e.g. process charts so that a user will be able to overview
   the consequences in an activity quickly and easily. The graphic presentation
   in a process chart is designed for people with minimum computer skills.
   The process chart must be an integrated part of the application with the
   opportunity to look further into sub-elements and to see specific information. Therefore, the functionality is not approved if it is made in an external
   report generator.
4. The Opportunity to have several campaigns running concurrently.
5. Campaign monitoring tools include success rates for the different progresses
   in a campaign.
6. The system vendor offers "Event triggers" which can be set up by users without the use of programming but through a built-in functionality in the program. For example, an "Event trigger" that starts a campaign when the purchase of a customer type "A" exceeds £1000 in February. The action in the
   campaign could be to send a letter of gratitude signed by the Key Account
   Manager of the Type "A" customer.
7. The system vendor offers "Assistants" (already programmed "event triggers").
   These give a more limited number of possibilities than real "Event triggers."
   For example, the "Campaign automatically starts on 1 May 2001."
8. Automatic generation of a next step in a Campaign - The system must be
   able to generate the next step in a campaign automatically. This means that
   the system can send e-mails to those customers who have not responded
   within a week from the day which they received a direct mail (without
   involving manual labour in the process). This functionality might improve
   the company's workflow. The system automatically generates the next step
   in the sales process when the previous step is completed. This functionality
   is not accepted if the user has to forward the activity to other members of
   the organisation.

9. The system can calculate whether the campaign has been successful. This is
    possible on the basis of: [expected number of potential customers] x
    [expected rate of success per customer] - [costs].
10. Column charts, line charts, pie charts, etc. for reporting campaigns.
11. The possibility to see a list of all active campaigns (graphically). It must be
    possible to see a list of active campaigns including time schedules graphi-
    cally in the application. This can be demonstrated in a Gantt chart or equiv-
    alent. It must be part of the application – and it should not be necessary to
    exit the CRM system into an external report generator to create it.
12. The possibility to check which campaign generates purchase. This is of
    course an advantage when you want to check which campaigns are effec-
    tive and efficient, what kind of sales the campaigns are catalysts for and
    which type of customer reacts on which type of campaigns.
13. The Possibility of connecting a particular team with a specific campaign.
    This can be a team that will gather when a certain stage in a campaign has
    been reached. This team then has to make sure that a sale is achieved. It
    can also be a team whose members function in conjunction with each other
    in a campaign.

Leads

1. Management and the creation of leads.
2. Calculation of the number of leads which actually become customers per
    campaign.
3. Give a status on where leads are placed in a campaign.
4. Graphic views of how many customers there are in parts of a sales-
    funnel/campaign. E.g. marking in a sales-funnel with percent-wise fill-outs.
    This provides an opportunity to see where "bottlenecks" occur and cause
    slow customer service. The view must be an integrated part of the applica-
    tion, with the possibility of drilling down to see who the leads are, and
    NOT generated in an external report-generator.
5. It is possible to attach one or more competitors to a lead.
6. Status for leads' purchasing potential and the probability of the sales coming
    through - It must be possible for the user to indicate the purchasing poten-
    tial and success probability of a lead in a text field in the application/data-
    base. This can be used for instance in the automatic ABC-categorisation and
    generation of a sales prognosis. Furthermore, there is a demand that these
    fields be used to forecast sales for each salesman and that these figures be
    rolled up into a sales forecast for the entire company.
7. The opportunity to link a specific salesman to a lead manually.
8. The opportunity for the system to link a specific salesman to a specific lead
    manually.

Customer Data

1. A table with the company's defined fields. It could be the state of health for the customers of an insurance company.
2. The possibility of more than one address per customer. This includes the opportunity to avoid sending out the same letter to the same person more than once – including duplicate checking on more than just one address if the address is used to look up the person in the customer database.
3. It is possible to attach e-mails, letters, documents to the customer database (a so-called customer log).
4. Registration of all previous meetings/contacts with customers including outcome.
5. Registration of the company's sales strategy and tactics towards each customer (only text-field).
6. Registration of customers' goals, visions, and key success factors (only text-field).
7. Search possibilities on data on several dimensions simultaneously, e.g. find all customers in area X in the age group 18-25.
8. Search on words in the customer database.
9. Measurement of the customer's product interest over time. Screen that gives a quick insight into the customer's product interest so that it is easier to define which campaigns to focus on. This may be of interest in cross-sales situations.
10. Link to relations (family or firm). Possibility to scroll directly between two customers' personal data templates. This may be of interest in cross-sales situations.

Product/Price configuration & Contract Management

1. Possibility of product /price calculation from an offline PC. This can be done if there is a replication function which quickly transfers new configuration opportunities to a laptop.
2. Configuration of product/price using a hierarchical (one-way) system.
3. Configuration of product/price using a full dialogue (dynamic) system.
4. Possibility of putting up limits on selections before configuring a product. This can, for example, be the maximum price of a product.
5. Possibility of calculating delivery date of a configured product.
6. The opportunity to create an order from an offer and include necessary data for invoicing.
7. Visualisation of the product configuration on-line/via Internet.
8. Visualisation of the product configuration on-line/via print.
9. Verification of a quotation from the internal organisation – e.g. if there has been a sale exceeding DKK 300,000 the sale has to be verified by a manger before effectuation.

10. Contract Management Tool (incl. integration to Call Centre)

11. Possibility of differentiation on the quotation based on e.g. seniority – e.g. that customer X can receive 10 per cent discount on all products exceeding DKK 100,000.

12. Service level agreement integrated with contract processing. It must be possible to create service level agreements on more complicated products. This can for example be on a configured product with many different parts each requesting its own specific service level agreement. The salesman does not necessarily need the managers to write this agreement; however they can just request the CRM application to create the agreement according to rules set up in the system. Thus, merely to be able to set-up a number of different Service Level Agreements in a word processing tool with names and dates merged into the documents it is not enough to put a "YES" on this functionality.

13. Discount tools for contract management and contract processing.

14. It must be possible to put in new logic in one line. If suddenly parts A and B no longer fit in the same product – the only thing the user has to do is to put in one new "logic": A + B = false. In other words, it is not necessary to enter a hierarchical structure and change all the IF-THEN associated with parts A and B. This IT structure is a configuration tool that can notably reduce the needed time for changing product and price configurations. Furthermore, it saves a lot of time when new configurations are set up.

Marketing Tools

1. Library for storing marketing material. Logic database tool for systematisation of all electronic marketing material e.g. PowerPoint slides, blue prints of product configurations, product fact sheets, newspaper articles and other marketing material. The material is stored in a logical order where it can be easily found and viewed from the CRM application. This reduces the time spent by sales and marketing personnel on preparing presentations and marketing events.

2. Product/price information library (history). The system must contain a history log on price and product developments, including when special discounts/bonuses were given, which areas received specific promotion offers, etc. To obtain a check in this box it must be possible for the users to see for example at which price a specific product was sold in a specific area several months ago.

3. Competitor Information System. The system must contain an overview of the competitive situation on the different markets on which the company operates such as viewing a list of competitors related to certain products. The sales personnel gather this information when they register which competitors were present for a lead at each stage of the salesfunnel. The business advan-

tage of this is facts about where the strengths and weaknesses of the company is in relation to its competitors and at which stage in reality sales are lost. Furthermore, there is a demand that this "module" save information on new competitor products, competitor promotions, etc.

4. Registration of customers' satisfaction with analysis, diagrams, etc. – It should be possible to tap a questionnaire into the application that is later distributed to a given number of customers. The customer will answer the questions on a quantified scale (e.g. 1 to 5) so that the system can generate a graphic customer satisfaction survey. It should further be possible to use the received answers and surveys in connection with a diagram on customer loyalty. An example could be the connection between satisfaction and loyalty. If the degree of satisfaction on the chosen questions is high enough it can be used as identification for future loyal behaviour. If the system can show a graphical illustration of customer satisfaction/loyalty it fulfils the above mentioned functionality.

5. Management and registration of materials (e.g. banners, stickers, etc.) from current and previous campaigns.

6. Possibility to merge personal data on each customer into letters in a marketing campaign directed towards a large number of customers.

Sales Force Automation

1. Online data transfer from work stations to databases.

2. Batch data transfers from work stations to databases.

3. The opportunity of fast daily synchronisation of offline PCs. In other words, replication of all basic databases onto a laptop through a one button system in the application

4. Possibility of integration with Personal Digital Assistent (PDA) or the like via MS Outlook. Basically, management of a calendar and a to-do list.

5. The possibility of integration with PDA or the like. It must be possible to have customer data and product/price information on the PDA and to integrate this information with the application. The PDA is easier to handle than a laptop and a large number of salesmen already use the PDA's calendar function. To say "YES" to this question the vendor must at least have made one installation where parts of the CRM application are running on a PDA.

6. Graphic display to the seller of actual sales in relation to the forecast. A screen showing the seller when he closes more or fewer sales than his forecast.

Resource Management

1. A planning calendar for each salesman – when fully integrated with MS Outlook a *2 reference is given.
2. The possibility of booking a meeting in a salesman's calendar from a call-centre without conferring with him in advance – when fully integrated with MS Outlook a *2 reference is given.
3. Sharable calendars (across several users) – possibility of booking only once and then set up a meeting on e.g. 20 users calendars– when fully integrated with MS Outlook a *2 reference is given.
4. Graphic calendar in application – when fully integrated with MS Outlook a *2 reference is given.
5. Possibility of setting up alarms for meetings – this could be an e-mail or on-line announcement for a salesman that he should remember a meeting – when fully integrated with MS Outlook a *2 reference is given.
6. Manage/view activities per user/customer/firm/contact person. A summary of which resources go where.
7. The opportunity for a customer to be a member of several territories. E.g. that the same customer is both in the "London" group and the "Tractor" group.
8. Support for "geographic territories", "product-type territories", and "industry territories".
9. Geographic route planning - possible to feed the system maps from external map providers and have the system calculate optimal routes.
10. Salesman resource planner – a tool that uses information on the time schedule of the salesman, meetings and sales visits that need to be carried out, area that the meetings are in and calculate an efficient time and meeting plan for the salesman.
11. Registration of CRM related costs for each customer, e.g. travel costs for sales visits and marketing contribution costs. These are also used in connection with calculating the cost/benefit of the customer. This has to be an integrated function in the application.
12. Front Office Logistics (Depot Repair, Spares holding etc.). Control of the logistics behind transport and storage of goods and spare parts in connection with service and support.

Analysis Tools

1. Flexible report generator for Sales.
2. Flexible report generator for Marketing.
3. Flexible report generator for Service and Support Marketing Administration Screens.
4. Standard Executive Information System including graphics – specifically defined analysis tool for management reporting.
5. Advanced budgeting tools – includes e.g. fixed and variable calculation methods based on data from previous seasons, salesmen efficiency rates, etc.

Forecasts

1. The opportunity to generate Product Forecasts (sale per month/year).
2. The opportunity to generate Forecasts on Earnings (earnings per month/year).
3. Rollups of forecasts on numerous organisations – the opportunity to generate company forecasts consisting of the figures from different organisations.
4. The opportunities to divide forecasts into the companies' own defined periods, e.g. 14-day forecasts.
5. Rollups and forecasts on numerous levels in the company – rollups within the company which make forecasts possible per seller, per department and for the entire company.

Other Functions

1. Push technology for information management on the Internet (active search on words). An advanced system where the application seeks on e.g. "Yahoo", daily or the newspapers' homepages to find new information related to subjects which are of interest to the company.
2. Active Briefing is a system where the employees are notified by internal or external sources on new developments in areas relevant to them.
3. Multiple currencies (The opportunity to run several currencies at the same time reporting both currencies and functional currencies).
4. Euro-compliance.
5. Support news streamer/other internal newspaper. An internal method to report where e.g. a "text line" is running at the bottom of the screen updating the user with new information.
6. The opportunity to specify exactly which user may see the specific screens and which specific information. It could be to prevent access for one seller to another seller's customer information.
7. You may order a word document (with specific customer information) and print it without opening the Word application.
8. Personal template for correspondence.

9. Full integration for Word and Spreadsheet applications (automatically merged into these from the system) so-called OLE technology (Object Link Enabling).
10. Guide Functions for using application ("Wizards"). It is possible to get help on the screen when using the application, e.g. through a "wizard" that guides your way step-by-step through a process
11. It must be possible for the user to include information from the company's database in faxes by merging the database fields with the content of the fax. It must be possible to send the fax automatically without manual involvement, i.e. the application sends the fax number to the fax – not to a human operator.

Web

1. Automatic assignment of leads from the Internet.
2. Tool for creating web-sites: w/ predefined links to CRM database fields and interactive fields to CRM application.
3. Tool for creating web-sites:w/ drop down box with drag and drop graphics.
4. Possibility for web-site differentiation depending on the specific customer logging in – the customer can for example have a password and user-name. Dependent on the profile of the customer specific screens that fit, his demands are created from rules set-up in the application.
5. Integrated e-mail tool that works seamless as part of the application. It must be possible for the user to include information from the company's database in e-mails by merging database fields information into the e-mail.
6. E-commerce enabled links (purchasing integrated with databases) - are created which enable payment by credit cards fed directly into the CRM application – possibly with links to back-office systems.

Telemarketing, Call Centre and Help-Desk

1. The automatic calls facilities (Predictive Dialling). The operator does not have to look up a phone number nor dial – this is done automatically by the system.
2. Computer-Telephony Integration (CTI) enabled/supportive.
3. Application (through Integration of CTI) enables routing possibilities of customer calling in, e.g. a customer to a specific campaign, "A" customer first in queue, etc.
4. On-line information system integrated with dialogue management system. Possibility to integrate dialogue and customer with on-line information from an information system (e.g. price and product information). In other words – you do not have to scroll to another picture to find this information.

5. Dialogue management through neural network - dialogue management with dynamic outcomes based on the customers' reply but not based on the order in which the answers turn up. In other words, dialogue can take place more freely than through normal hierarchical methods.

6. Cross-sales functions (possibility to sell other products to a customer in connection with a phone-call) integrated with dialogue management. For example: 1) lamps are offered when people buy a bicycle, 2) you can quickly change to the screen where the other product is described and the additional amount can be on the same invoice, 3) links to product and price information from the dialogue management system.

7. "Neural" inbound e-mail answering tool. The system can be fed a huge number of e-mails from customers who are manually categorised into e.g. ten categories. Afterwards the system is able to categorise and propose an answer to the inbound e-mail. This function reduces notably the amount of time spent on answering inbound e-mail.

8. Calculation/prognosis of inbound call frequency. In order to optimise the number of personnel in the call centre, it is important that you are able to forecast the number of inbound calls. This functionality must be an integrated part of the application.

9. Scheduling device for call-centre operators. A functionality that is able to create time and work schedules for operators in the call centre. This functionality can optimise the use of labour in the call centre. Usually CRM vendors choose to integrate with an external provider of this functionality.

10. This includes a number of predefined solutions to different problems. Furthermore, the system is able to generate procedures for handling new types of problems and re-use these if someone with the same problem turns up again (e.g. re-use of previously created solution models). The system also needs to be able to create an overview for an administrator of where the most common problems seem to be (could be a Pareto diagram or the like).

11. Service Request Management/"Trouble-Ticketing". A functionality where the service requester is given a time and date when a service operator comes for a visit to solve the problem. There is a demand that this functionality is integrated with the facts in the specific customers Service Level Agreements so that the right service level is provided.

12. Blending of Telemarketing and Call Centre function. A recent "buzz" word in Telemarketing and Call Centres is "blending". This is a method whereby the Tele-marketers and Call Centre Operators are the same people working on Call Centre operations at peak hours and on Telemarketing tasks when it is more quiet in the Call Centre. This creates the optimal use of labour. It is a demand to be able to have this functionality that the system itself can forward the task which the Tele-marketer/Operator needs.

Price

The price for the application and costs, in connection with implementation and maintenance, are important decision criteria concerning the choice of IT systems since the return on investment depends heavily on this.

Product Development

When purchasing an application you will also need to think ahead to evaluate how high the risk is of the supplier constantly developing new versions and new functionalities to upgrade the system.

The following areas could be indicators:

1. Number of new versions annually
2. Number of licensees in the Nordic Countries at the end of April 1999
3. Number of licensees globally at the end of April 1999
4. Actual new functionalities planned for introduction in the next 6 months.

Support

To get the complete benefit of an installed application it is of great importance that you have access to system support.

The following would be an advantage:

1. Whether the supplier has a hotline to which you can turn in case of problems with the application. For a "YES" in this field the hotline does not need to be open 24 hours a day.
2. 24-hour hotline.
3. When the supplier (or a representative of the supplier) has an actual educational centre/systematised educational program focused on the system implementers or members of the user organisation.
4. Possibilities of seeking help on the Internet.

Ease of Use

Whether the system is easy to use is of essential importance, but concerning large implementations focus need not be on the specific language that is available, because a translation is offered by the supplier.

Industry Solutions

When choosing a system it is important to investigate whether the supplier has worked out a specific industry solution for your industry. This reduces the need for adaptation of the application considerably and thus makes implementation quicker and cheaper. If a supplier has worked out an industry specific solution this indicates better knowledge of the problems surrounding the implementation in this industry. There is a demand that the supplier put up a minimum of three installations with industry specific solutions before he can be accepted as such in this analysis.

Platforms and Architecture

The decision to buy a CRM system is partly dependent on whether a given system can run on the firm's current operating system (server) or whether you will have to replace it, which could be expensive. The applications have to be able to run a full version of the CRM system on the platform on a server.

Configuration of CRM system

The costs of running an application and implementing depend not only on the initial product price but also on how easy it is to configure. The firm can save a lot of money by making configurations of displays themselves – should they have a need for this in the years following implementation. Furthermore, the programming language can be important for the kind of competencies needed by the system implementers for configurations and the creation of interfaces for other systems.

Database

This is important to a company's initial investment due to the fact that buying a new database is of course more expensive than using the one the firm has already. Furthermore, it eases information exchange between applications if the same database is used.

Integration

The CRM application will need to co-operate with the company's other IT applications and thus be integrated with these. The question is whether the supplier provides finished interfaces to the company's back office applications. It is enough for the companies to be able to get a checkmark in this category if they have the ability to design interfaces.

Hardware

The demand for hardware is important to the total price. If a lot of new portable laptops and servers are needed due to the fact that the application demands a lot of system resources – the final price for the application and the implementation may be a lot higher than planned.

Index